DATE		

NATHANIEL'S NUTMEG

ALSO BY GILES MILTON

The Riddle and the Knight:
In Search of John Mandeville

NATHANIEL'S NUTMEG

or,

The True and Incredible Adventures

of the Spice Trader Who

Changed the Course of History

GILES MILTON

FARRAR, STRAUS AND GIROUX

New York

Farrar, Straus and Giroux
19 Union Square West, New York 10003

Library of Congress Cataloging-in-Publication
Milton, Giles, 1966-
Nathaniel's Nutmeg / Giles Milton.
    p.   cm.
Includes index.
ISBN 0-374-21936-2 (alk. paper)
    1. Nutmeg industry—Indonesia—Maluku—History—17th century.
2. Spice trade—Indonesia—Maluku—History—17th century.
3. Nederlandsche Oost-Indische Compagnie—History. 4. Courthope,
Nathaniel. 5. Coen, Jan Pieterszoon, 1587-1629. 6. Indonesia—
History—1478-1798. 7. Maluku (Indonesia)—History. I. Title.
HD9211.N883155 1999
338.1'7383—dc21   98-41955

ACKNOWLEDGEMENTS

The hand-written journals of the gentlemen adventurers who form the *dramatis personae* of this book are almost unreadable to the untrained eye. I owe a debt of gratitude to the handful of Victorian scholars – long deceased – who transcribed these voluminous writings. George Birdwood, Sir William Foster and Henry Stevens made this book possible, as did W. Noel Sainsbury and his indefatigable daughter Ethel who together edited and indexed more than five thousand pages of Jacobean script – all done without the aid of computers.

Thank you to Des Alwi on Neira Island for his hospitality, enthusiasm and the use of his twin-engined power boat; to Monsignor Andreas Sol of St Francis Xavier Cathedral in Ambon (Amboyna) for allowing me free access to his extensive library; and to James Lapian at the BBC's Indonesian Service.

In London, I am grateful to Marjolein van der Valk for rendering obscure Dutch chronicles into fluent English; to the staff of the London Library and the British Library's Oriental and India Office Collections; and to Frank Barrett, Wendy Driver, Maggie Noach and Roland Philipps.

I am particularly indebted to Paul Whyles and Simon Heptinstall, both of whom read numerous versions of the manuscript and suggested much-needed changes.

Finally, I wish to thank my wife Alexandra whose patience, encouragement and cheerfulness will always prove an inspiration.

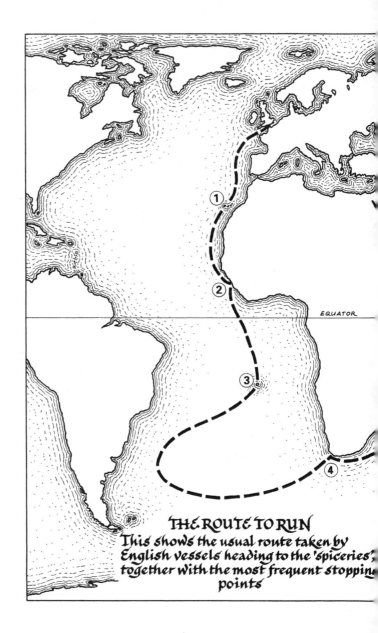

THE ROUTE TO RUN

This shows the usual route taken by English vessels heading to the 'spiceries', together with the most frequent stopping points

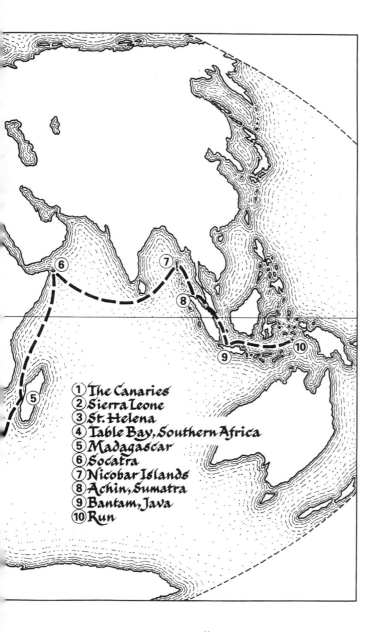

1. The Canaries
2. Sierra Leone
3. St. Helena
4. Table Bay, Southern Africa
5. Madagascar
6. Socatra
7. Nicobar Islands
8. Achin, Sumatra
9. Bantam, Java
10. Run

CONTENTS

LIST OF ILLUSTRATIONS

List of Illustrations

LIST OF MAPS

PROLOGUE

T HE ISLAND CAN BE SMELLED before it can be seen. From more than ten miles out to sea a fragrance hangs in the air, and long before the bowler-hat mountain hoves into view you know you are nearing land.

So it was on 23 December 1616. The *Swan*'s captain, Nathaniel Courthope, needed neither compass nor astrolabe to know that they had arrived. Reaching for his journal he made a note of the date and alongside scribbled the position of his vessel. He had at last reached Run, one of the smallest and richest of all the islands in the East Indies.

Courthope summoned his crew on deck for a briefing. The stalwart English mariners had been kept in the dark about their destination for it was a mission of the utmost secrecy. They were unaware that King James I himself had ordered this operation, one of such extraordinary importance that failure would bring dire and irrevocable consequences. Nor did they know of the notorious dangers of landing at Run, a volcanic atoll whose harbour was ringed by a sunken reef. Many a vessel had been dashed to splinters on the razor-sharp coral and the shoreline was littered with rusting cannon and broken timbers.

Courthope cared little for such dangers. He was far more worried about the reception he would receive from the native islanders, head-hunters and cannibals, who were feared and mistrusted throughout the East Indies. 'At your arrival at Run,' he had been told, 'show yourself courteous and affable, for they are a peevish, perverse, diffident and perfidious people and apt to take disgust upon small occasions.'

As his men rowed towards land, Courthope descended into his cabin and brushed down his finest doublet, little imagining the momentous events that were to follow. For his discussions with Run's native chieftains – conducted in sign language and broken English – would change the course of history on the other side of the globe.

The forgotten island of Run lies in the backwaters of the East Indies, a remote and fractured speck of rock that is separated from its nearest land mass, Australia, by more than six hundred miles of ocean. It is these days a place of such insignificance that it fails even to make it onto the map: *The Times Atlas of the World* neglects to record its existence and the cartographers of Macmillan's *Atlas of South East Asia* have reduced it to a mere footnote. For all they cared, Run could have slumped beneath the tropical waters of the Indies.

It was not always thus. Turn to the copper-plate maps of the seventeenth century and Run is writ large across the page, its size out of all proportion to its geography. In those days, Run was the most talked about island in the world, a place of such fabulous wealth that Eldorado's gilded riches seemed tawdry by comparison. But Run's bounty was not derived from gold – nature had bestowed a gift far more precious upon her cliffs. A forest of willowy trees fringed the island's mountainous backbone; trees of exquisite fragrance. Tall and foliaged like a laurel, they were adorned with bell-shaped flowers and bore a fleshy, lemon-yellow fruit. To the botanist, they were called *Myristica fragrans*. To the plain-speaking merchants of England they were known simply as nutmeg.

Nutmeg, the seed of the tree, was the most coveted luxury in seventeenth-century Europe, a spice held to have such powerful medicinal properties that men would risk their lives to acquire it. Always costly, it rocketed in price when the physicians of Elizabethan London began claiming that their nutmeg pomanders were the only certain cure for the plague, that 'pestiferous pestilance' that started with a sneeze and ended in death. Overnight, this withered little nut – until now used to cure flatulence and the common cold – became as sought after as gold.

There was one drawback to the sudden and urgent demand: no one could be sure from exactly where the elusive nutmeg originated. London's merchants had traditionally bought their spices in Venice, and Venice's merchants had in turn bought them in Constantinople. But nutmeg came from much further east, from the fabled Indies which lay far beyond Europe's myopic horizons. Ships had never before plied the tropical waters of the Indian Ocean and maps of the far side of the globe remained a blank. The East, as far as the spice dealers were concerned, could have been the moon.

Had they known in advance of the difficulties of reaching the source of nutmeg they might never have set sail. Even in the East Indies where spices grew like weeds, nutmeg was a rarity; a tree so fussy about climate and soil that it would grow only on a tiny cluster of islands, the Banda archipelago, which were of such impossible remoteness that no one in Europe could be sure if they existed at all. The spice merchants of Constantinople had scant information about these islands and what they did know was scarcely encouraging. There were rumours of a

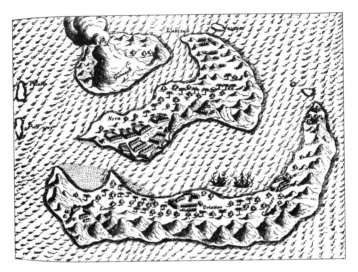

The Banda Islands at the turn of the sixteenth century were the goal of every Elizabethan adventurer. 'There is not a tree but the nutmeg,' wrote one early English visitor, 'so that the whole countrey seemes a contrived orchard.' Run Island, marked Pulorin, is on the extreme left.

monster that preyed on passing ships, a creature of 'devillish possession' that lurked in hidden reefs. There were stories of cannibals and head-hunters – bloodthirsty savages who lived in palm-tree shacks decorated with rotting human heads. There were crocodiles that lay concealed in rivers, hidden shoals to catch captains unawares, and 'such mightie stormes and extreme gusts of winde' that even the sturdiest of ships were placed in grave risk.

None of these dangers deterred Europe's profit-hungry merchants who would chance everything in their desperation to be the first to find nutmeg's source. Soon the shipyards of Portugal, Spain and England were alive to the clatter of shipbuilding, a flurry of activity that sparked what would later become known as the spice race, a desperate and protracted struggle for control of one of the smallest groups of islands in the world.

In 1511, the Portuguese became the first Europeans to set foot in the Banda Islands, a group of six lumps of rock boasting rich volcanic soil and a strange micro-climate. Distracted by hostilities elsewhere in the East Indies, they did not return until 1529 when a Portuguese trader named Captain Garcia landed troops on the Bandas. He was surprised to discover that the islands which had caused such commotion in Europe had a combined area that was not much larger than Lisbon. Five of the Bandas were within gunshot of each other, and it was immediately apparent to Garcia that by building a castle on the principal island, Neira, he would have virtual control over the entire archipelago.

But one island, Run, was different. It lay more than ten miles to the west of Neira and was surrounded by dangerous and hidden reefs. It was also buffeted by the twice-yearly monsoon, putting it beyond the reach of Garcia's carracks for much of the year. This was galling to the Portuguese, for Run was thickly forested in nutmeg and its annual yield was enough to fill a large flotilla of ships. But Captain Garcia soon found himself troubled less by the inaccessibility of this outlying island than by the hostility of the native Bandanese whose warlike antics proved both tiresome and costly. Scarcely had his sailors set to work on a massive castle than a flurry of arrows and the threat of head-hunting sent them scurrying back to their ship. Henceforth, the Portuguese rarely visited the islands, preferring instead to buy their nutmeg from the native traders who were frequent visitors at their fortress in Malacca.

The misfortunes suffered by the Portuguese did not

discourage England's merchants from launching themselves into the spice race and nor did it deter the captains chosen to lead these expeditions; bold and fearless men who steered their ships through such 'greevous stormes' that one in three was lost. The weather was not the only threat: scurvy, dysentery and the 'blody flux' killed hundreds of men, and countless vessels had to be scuppered when there was no longer a crew to sail them. When the ships finally limped back from the East the surviving crews found the wharves of London packed with people anxious to catch a glimpse of these heroic men. The crowds were fuelled by stories that the sailors on board were returning with untold wealth; that they wore doublets of silk, that their main sail was made of damask and their top sails trimmed with cloth of gold. Although the humble sailors had been strictly forbidden from indulging in 'private trade', the temptations proved too great for many. After all, nutmeg commanded fabulous prices in Courthope's day and brought spectacular profits to all who traded in it. In the Banda Islands, ten pounds of nutmeg cost less than one English penny. In London, that same spice sold for more than £2.10s. – a mark-up of a staggering 60,000 per cent. A small sackful was enough to set a man up for life, buying him a gabled dwelling in Holborn and a servant to attend to his needs. London's merchants were so concerned about the illegal trade in nutmeg when their first fleet arrived back in London that they ordered the dockyard workers to wear 'suits of canvas without pockets'. This did little to deter the sea-hardened mariners from filching their masters' spice and although punishments grew ever more severe over the decades, many still managed to amass private fortunes. As late as 1665, Samuel Pepys records a clandestine meeting with some sailors 'at a blind alehouse at the further end of town' where he exchanged a sackful of gold for a small quantity of nutmeg and cloves.

The men that survived the expeditions to the Spice Islands returned with such fabulous tales and scrapes, true Boy's Own adventures, that their audiences were left spellbound. David Middleton had a dramatic escape from the cannibals of Ceram; the dilettantish William Keeling performed Shakespeare in the mangrove swamps of West Africa, whilst William Hawkins paid a visit to the Indian Great Moghul and spent the next two years watching gladiator battles of a scale and brutality not seen since the days of imperial Rome. There was Sir Henry Middleton, David's brother, who dropped anchor off the coast of Arabia and distinguished himself by becoming the first Englishman to visit the interior of the country, albeit as a prisoner with 'a great paire of fetters clapt upon my legges'. And there was James Lancaster, commander of the pioneering first expedition to be organised by the East India Company, who spent a delightful evening listening to a scantily clad gamelan orchestra that belonged to the lusty Sultan of Achin.

After all the disasters and false starts it was appropriate that England's first contact with the nutmeg islands should be with Run, the smallest and least accessible of them all. It was also fitting that they should arrive in such an undignified fashion, washed up as shipwrecks after a ferocious tropical storm in 1603. But what was all the more remarkable was that these English mariners, unlike the Portuguese, struck up an instant and lasting friendship with the native chieftains. Long before the sea-salt had stiffened their hair they were toasting each other with the local palm toddy.

England had scarcely launched herself into the spice race when she learned there was a new power to contend with.

In 1595, the Dutch despatched their first fleet eastwards with a crew more menacing and warlike than had ever before been encountered in the tropics. Faced with competition from both the English and Portuguese, they changed their goal from trade to conquest – the conquest of the Banda Islands – and they pursued this with a brutality that shocked even their own countrymen. But on the island of Run they were to meet their match. What happened on that remote atoll, just two miles long and half a mile wide, was to have consequences that no one could ever have imagined.

The extraordinary story of Nathaniel's nutmeg has been largely forgotten for more than three centuries. It is not always a pleasant tale, for although the captains and leaders of expeditions liked to refer to themselves as 'men of qualitye', that did not stop them from indulging in torture, brutality and gratuitous warfare. Such were the grim realities of life in the East, a harsh and bloody existence that was lightened by the occasional flash of humanity and courage – true feats of heroism that were epitomised by the bravery of Nathaniel Courthope.

But more than a century of expeditions and mis-adventures were to pass before Courthope set sail in the *Swan*. His story begins not in the sultry climes of the nutmeg islands, but in a land of icebergs and snow.

CHAPTER ONE

ARCTIC
WHIRLWINDS

I T WAS THE LOOK-OUT who saw them first. Two crippled vessels, rotting and abandoned, lay at anchor close to the shoreline. Their hulls were splintered and twisted, their sails in tatters and their crew apparently long since dead. But it was not a tropical reef that had wrecked the ships and nor was it malaria that had killed the crew. England's maiden expedition to the Spice Islands had come to grief in the ice-bound waters of the Arctic.

The historic 1553 voyage was the brainchild of a newly founded organisation known as the Mystery, Company and Fellowship of Merchant Adventurers for the Discovery of Unknown Lands. So impatient were these merchants to enter the spice race – yet so unprepared for the risks and dangers – that they allowed enthusiasm to overrule practicalities and long before the ships had left port a catalogue of errors threatened to jeopardise their mission. The choice of expedition leader, or 'pilot-general', was sensible enough. Richard Chancellor was 'a man of great estimation' who had gained some experience of seafaring in his formative years. His adoptive father, Henry Sidney, so eulogised his young charge when presented to the Company that the merchant adventurers thought they had a new Magellan in their midst. Sidney explained that it was Chancellor's 'good parts of wit' that made him so invaluable and, never shy to blow his own trumpet, added, 'I rejoice in myself that I have nourished and maintained that wit.'

When a doubting merchant tackled Sidney on his enthusiasm for being separated from Chancellor the old man had a ready answer. 'I do now part with Chancellor not because I make little reckoning of the man, or because his maintenance is burdenous and chargeable unto me. You know the man by report, I by experience; you by words, I by deeds; you by speech and company, but I by the daily trial of his life.'

Sidney's rhetoric won the day and Chancellor was promptly given command of the *Edward Bonaventure*, the largest of the expedition's three ships. The governors then turned to choosing a captain for the expedition's other large ship, the *Bona Esperanza*. For reasons that remain obscure they plumped for Sir Hugh Willoughby, a 'goodly personage' according to the records, but one who had absolutely no knowledge of navigation. Such a man would have been a risk for the short hop across the English Channel; to despatch him to the uttermost ends of the earth was to court disaster.

When it came to deciding the passage to the Spice Islands the merchant adventurers were most insistent. Although they had watched the Spanish and Portuguese successfully sail both east and west to the East Indies, they plumped for an altogether more eccentric option. Their ships, it was decided, would head due north; a route that would shave more than two thousand miles off the long voyage to the Spice Islands. It would have the added benefit of avoiding conflict with the Portuguese who had been sailing the eastern route for almost a century and had established fortified bastions in every port. There was also the question of illness and climate to consider. English mariners had seen the Portuguese ships return home with their crews decimated by dysentery and typhoid, often contracted in the tropical climes of the Indian Ocean. At least one man in five could expect death on the long voyage to the East but that number was frequently much higher and often entire ships had to be abandoned due to a shortage of crew. Since the Portuguese were acclimatised by birth to a hot climate men questioned how English sailors, brought up on the frosty fringes of northern Europe, could hope to return in rude health.

The expedition ran into trouble before it even set sail. During delays at Harwich, it was discovered that a large part of the provisions was already rotten, while the wine casks had been so badly assembled that the wine was leaking freely though the joints in the wood. But with the wind in their favour the captains decided there was no time to restock the ships and the expedition set sail on 23 June 1553.

So long as the vessels stuck together under the capable direction of Richard Chancellor they were unlikely to run into trouble. But as they rounded the rocky shores of northern Norway, 'there came such flows of winde and terrible whirlewinds' that Willoughby's ship was blown off course. Chancellor had planned for such an eventuality, suggesting that the ships regroup at Vardohuus, a small island in the Barents Sea. He waited for seven days but, hearing nothing of either the *Bona Esperanza* or the *Confidentia*, the third ship of the fleet, he pushed on eastwards towards the White Sea.

The other two vessels had also survived the storm. After riding out the gale, Sir Hugh re-established contact with

Disaster strikes Dutch explorer William Barents, who believed there was a quick route to the 'spiceries' via the North Pole. The engravings (shown here and on pp. 17, 167 and 169) illustrate how his ship was wrecked on 'a great store of ice' and how his men survived the winter.

the *Confidentia* and both headed towards the coastline. Here Willoughby's inexperience began to tell. He sounded the sea floor, pored over charts and scratched his head before concluding that 'the land lay not as the globe made mention.' Failing to locate Vardohuus's or Chancellor's vessel, he decided to press on with the expedition without the flagship.

On 14 August 1553, he 'descried land', apparently un-inhabited, at 72 degrees latitude but failed to reach it due to the quantity of ice in the water. If this reading is correct, his ship must have reached the barren islands of Novaya Zemlya which lie, remote and isolated, in the Barents Sea. From here he appears to have sailed south-east, then north-west, then south-west, then north-east. The ignorance of Willoughby and his men is staggering, for their course, more than three hundred miles inside the Arctic Circle, must have taken them in a giant arc through a dangerous sea littered with melting pack-ice. On 14 September, they again sighted land and shortly afterwards 'sailed into a faire bay' somewhere close to the present border between Finland and Russia. Willoughby's men were cheered by the sight of 'very many seal fishes, and other great fishes; and upon the main we saw beares, great deere, foxes with divers strange beasts'. They planned at first to spend a week here but 'seeing the yeare far spent, and also very evill weather, as frost, snow, and haile', they decided to winter in the bay.

The expedition's directors in London must by now have hoped that their ships had found the North-East Passage, broken through it, and be well on their way to the Spice Islands. But instead of balmy evenings and gently swaying palm trees, Willoughby and his men had met with freezing fog, impenetrable ice, and the realisation that London's merchants had made a terrible mistake when they chose the route over the North Pole. Those merchants had vociferously defended their decision, presenting logical and compelling arguments to support their theories. As far back as the year 1527, Robert Thorne, an English trader living in Seville, had written to King Henry VIII with the exciting (and highly secret) news that the Spice Islands could be reached by way of the North Pole: 'I know it is my bounden duty to manifest this secret unto your Grace,' he wrote, 'which hitherto, as I suppose, hath beene hid.' The King was left in no doubt that 'by sailing northward and passing the Pole, descending to the Equinoctial line, we shall hit these islands [the Spice Islands], and it should be a much shorter way than either the Spaniards or Portingals have.'

The more the experts researched the north-eastern route to the Spice Islands the more plausible it proved to be. In an age when men still looked for perfect symmetry on their maps, the northern cape of Norway showed an exact topographical correspondence to the southern cape of Africa. Geographers agreed that this was indeed good news; the chilly northern land mass must surely be a second Cape of Good Hope. The writings of the ancients also lent credence to the idea of reaching the East Indies by a northerly route. Pliny the Elder had written of a circular sea at the top of the globe and a land called Tabis penetrating into the far north. To the east of Tabis there was said to be an opening which connected the Polar Sea to the warm waters of the Indian Ocean.

Such arguments were cold comfort to Willoughby and his men, stuck fast in an expanse of ice. The bay in which they had chosen to winter soon transformed itself into a desolate wilderness; fishing proved impossible due to the thickness of the ice and the wildlife disappeared with the first snows. Even the birds, aware of the onslaught of winter, migrated to warmer climes. Soon the ice floes had trapped, then crushed, the ships and there was no escape. With his crew growing hungrier by the day, Willoughby sent out search parties to look for food, for people, for help. 'We sent out three men south-south-west to search if they could find people,' wrote Sir Hugh, 'but [they] could find none.' Next he sent a party westwards, 'which also returned without finding any people'. A final team confirmed what Willoughby had feared – that they were imprisoned in an uninhabited wilderness.

More than five years was to pass before a search ship from England finally discovered what had happened to the *Bona Esperanza* and *Confidentia*. Sailing into the bay where

Willoughby had chosen to winter, the would-be rescuers stumbled across the ghostly and rotting hulks of the two ships – ships which had ended their days as charnel houses. The crew's final grim months remain a mystery, for Willoughby, racked by hunger, stopped recording daily entries in his ship's log. All that is certain is that he and his crew survived much of the winter, for the rescue party found wills dated January 1554, a full four months after the vessels had entered the bay.

The final, macabre twist in the tale was recorded by Giovanni Michiel, the Venetian ambassador to Moscow. The search party, he wrote, 'has returned safe, bringing with them the two vessels of the first voyage, having found them on the Muscovite coast with the men on board all frozen. And they [the rescuers] narrate strange things about the mode in which they were frozen, pen still in hand, and the paper before them, others at tables, platter in hand and spoon in mouth; others opening a locker, and others in various postures, like statues, as if they had been adjusted and placed in those attitudes.'

While Willoughby and his men froze to death, Richard Chancellor had fared rather better. Relying on the wit that had so enamoured him to his adoptive father, he quickly foresaw the danger of Arctic pack-ice. Dropping anchor in the White Sea close to present-day Archangel, he abandoned ship and trudged his way overland to Moscow. At first he was disappointed in what he found. The city, he thought, was 'very rude' and the houses 'all of timber'. Even the imperial palace was disappointing – 'rather low' and with 'small windows' it was 'much like the old buildings of England'. But Chancellor soon changed his tune when confronted with the barbaric splendour of Ivan the Terrible's court. Ivan greeted him in 'a long garment of beaten golde, with an imperial crowne upon his head and staffe of cristall and golde in his right hand'. The emperor's conduct was as majestic as it was awe-inspiring: at a courtly banquet he 'sent to every man a great sliver of bread, and the bearer called the party so sent to by his name aloud, and said, Ivan Vasilivich, Emperor of Russia and great Duke of Moscova doth reward thee with bread.' Even the wine goblets caught Chancellor's eye – weighing the golden beakers in his hand he declared they were 'very massie' and better than anything he had seen in England.

The time spent in Moscow was one of endless pleasure for Chancellor's crew. Many had expected their journey to end in disaster or death but instead they were living it up in the bejewelled pavilion of the Emperor of Russia. Chancellor was no less impressed: 'I have seen the King's majesties of England and the French King's pavilion,' he wrote, 'but none are like this.'

After lengthy negotiations, Ivan sent the English commander back to England with a letter conferring trading privileges upon a group of merchants in London. In doing so he had unwittingly laid the foundations of the Muscovy Company, a precursor to the East India Company.

Of the three ships that set sail for the Spice Islands not one achieved its goal of locating the elusive North-East Passage. The men who sailed north to escape the tropical diseases of the Indian Ocean little thought they would perish in the sub-zero waters of the Arctic. It would take another four hundred years, and a nuclear-powered submarine, before the northern route to the Pacific would finally be conquered.

While London's merchants anxiously awaited news of their historic first voyage to the Spice Islands, many people in

Barents' sailors faced continual danger from polar bears. 'We presently leaped forth to defend ourselves as well we could.'

the country were left wondering what all the fuss was about. Nutmeg, after all, made for an unpromising luxury. Dry, wrinkled and not much bigger than a garden pea it scarcely had the same appeal as a golden ducat or finely hewn sapphire.

The doubters were soon to learn that it was of potentially far greater value. London's leading doctors of physic made increasingly extravagant claims as to the efficacy of nutmeg, holding it to cure everything from the plague to the 'blody flux', both of which were regular visitors to the capital, sweeping through its insanitary back streets with devastating effect. One leading authority pronounced that his sweet-smelling pomander, which contained a large quantity of the spice, could even stave off the dreaded 'sweating syckness' that accompanied the 'pestiferous time of the pestilence'. Since this sickness – the plague – was said to kill in just two hours the pomander had to be made with all possible haste. After all, the old patter ran: 'mery at dinner, dead at supper.'

It was not just life-threatening illnesses that nutmeg was said to cure. A growing interest in the medicinal value of plants had led to an explosion in the number of dietary books and herbals, all of which claimed that nutmeg and other spices were beneficial in combating a host of minor ailments. For chesty coughs, doctors recommended mulled wine suffused with nutmeg. Cloves were said to cure earache, pepper stifled colds, while those embarrassed by trapped wind were recommended to take an extraordinary pot-pourri of fifteen spices including cardamom, cinnamon and nutmeg – a recipe that would have been out of reach of all but the flatulent rich. Spices were even held to revive those who had shuffled off this mortal coil. Ten grams of saffron taken with sweet wine was enough (it was claimed) to bring back the dead. There were not known to be any side-effects.

One of the more popular books was Andrew Borde's *Dyetary of Helth*, a guide to good living which earned the author even more fame than his seminal *Treatyse upon Beardes*. 'Nutmeges,' he wrote in his *Dyetary,* 'be good for them which have cold in their head and doth comforte the syght and the brain.' His home-produced nutmeg cocktail was said to be extremely efficacious; not only did it cleanse 'the mouthe of the stomacke and the spleen', it was also 'good against the blody flux', a virulent and dangerous strain of dysentery.

Borde's *Dyetary* is a curious mixture of herbal and lore. To any gentleman wishing to live a long life he suggests wearing a red petticoat and avoiding 'snaily rooms', while those able to 'rise with mirth' every morning were assured of good health. His suggestion that nutmeg dampens sexual desire had signally failed to work on him, for this celibate former monk died in disgrace. 'Under the colour of virginitie and of wearing a shirt of hair [he kept] three whores at once in his chamber … to serve not only himself but also help the virgin priests about in the country.' Borde of all people should have kept taking the nutmeg but as he wearily admitted, 'it is hard to get out of the flesh what is bred in the bone.'

Other authorities, turning Borde's misfortune to good effect, began to claim that far from dampening sexual desire, nutmeg was actually a powerful aphrodisiac. The licentious Charles Sackville, sixth Earl of Dorset, jested that Julius Caesar's libido was so low that even if Cleopatra had used 'nutmeg, mace and ginger' upon her 'Roman swinger' she would have failed to stir his loins. Such ingredients could scarcely have failed to work on his lordship, for he knew to his cost that a spoonful of nutmeg before bedtime could cause no end of sweet but troublesome dreams:

> Dreaming last night on Mrs Farley,
> My p – – – k was up this morning early,
> And I was fain without my gown
> To rise in th'cold to get him down
> Hard shift, alas, but yet a sure,
> Although it be no pleasing cure.

Sackville's love of nutmeg was to prove his downfall. His neighbour, Samuel Pepys, recorded how he was imprisoned for indecent exposure 'after running up and down all night almost naked through the street'.

Beneath all the quackery about nutmeg there lurked a grain of truth, particularly in the claims that it was a powerful preservative. Perishables had traditionally been conserved by salting, drying or smoking, none of which suppressed the foul taste of rank meat. A sprinkling of nutmeg over the viands not only disguised the stench, it also helped stay the natural process of rotting by dramatically slowing the rate of oxidation.

The use of spices as preservatives and flavourings was, in fact, nothing new. The ancient Egyptians had imported cumin, cinnamon and cassia to embalm the bodies of their pharaohs whilst the apothecaries of the Old Testament crushed spices into holy unguents for their temples. The Romans were more practical in their use of such luxuries, using nutmeg and aniseed to preserve meat and flavour wine, adding cumin to their pastries and using fennel as a flavouring for the city's famed vinegar sauces.

In Chaucer's day such spices had been a rare luxury. In the *Canterbury Tales* the doughty Sir Topaz speaks longingly of gingerbread, licorice and 'notemuge'-flavoured ale. By the time Shakespeare was writing, less than twenty years before Nathaniel Courthope arrived at Run, such luxuries were fast becoming commonplace. In *The Winter's Tale*, the clown has a lengthy list of ingredients needed for his dish of spiced pears, all of which were readily available in London: 'I must have saffron to colour the warden pies [pears]. Mace, dates, none; that's out of my note; nutmegs, seven, a race or two of ginger, but that I may beg; four pound of prunes, and as many raisins o'the sun.'

Throughout the Middle Ages, Venice had controlled the spice trade with an iron fist. Nutmeg, cloves, pepper and cinnamon all travelled across Asia to the great trading emporium of Constantinople where they were snapped up by Venetian merchants and shipped westward across the Mediterranean. From here they were sold, at vastly inflated prices, to traders from northern Europe. By the time Marco Polo made his 1271 voyage to China, Venice's monopoly on spices was complete, yet no one from the West had ever visited the countries from which these spices originated. Polo was the first European to describe the clove tree, 'a little tree with leaves like laurel', but his claim to have seen one in mainland China owes more to his imagination than to reality for, unbeknown to the Venetian, the tree could only be found on a handful of islands in the Indonesian archipelago.

In the two centuries that followed Polo's return, spices had become so popular that demand had long since outstripped supply. Venice's merchants were sufficiently adept at the art of money-making to know that a shortage of supply meant that prices could be kept high. So long as they controlled the trade routes and kept a monopoly over the souks of the Middle East they could retain their stranglehold on trade. But in the closing days of 1511 a startling and wholly unwelcome piece of news reached the Venetian merchants. A small flotilla of Portuguese ships, they learned, had just arrived in the Spice Islands and acquired a full lading of spices. After more than four centuries the Venetian monopoly had been broken.

The spice race could now begin.

The Portuguese had made spectacular progress in their quest to find a sea route to the East. Just forty years after their first tentative crossing of the equator in 1471, they had successfully sailed to the Spice Islands of the East Indies and returned with their ships crammed with pepper, nutmeg and cloves. These islands, known as the 'spiceries' or Moluccas, were scattered over an area of ocean more than half the size of Europe. Although these days they form

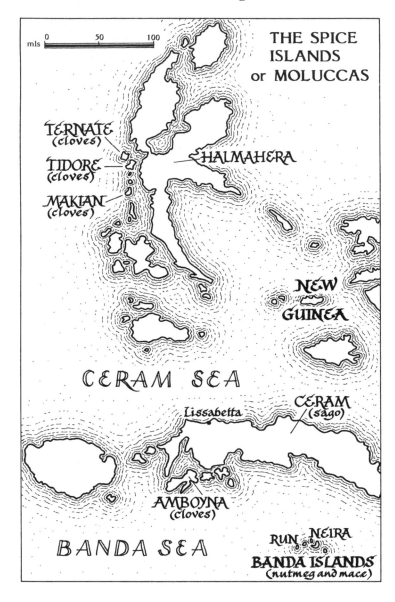

a single province of Indonesia, called Maluku, the hundred or so islands in fact fall into three distinct groups. To the north lie the volcanic islands of Tidore and Ternate, powerful sultanates which spent much of the sixteenth century fighting a desperate battle to retain their independence. Some four hundred miles to the south of here are the islands of Amboyna and Ceram, rugged places whose sweet-smelling cloves would eventually spark a terrible and infamous massacre. The southernmost group, the Banda Islands, were the richest and least accessible of them all, requiring bravado and a deft hand to steer a vessel safely through the archipelago's treacherous waters.

The Portuguese touched at all of these islands and, before long, were consolidating their position by force of arms. The important spice port of Malacca fell under their control in 1511 and, just months later, the remote Banda Islands were first visited by a Portuguese carrack. Next, they seized the spice ports on India's west coast, wresting control from the Muslim middlemen, before returning to the outlying and far-flung 'spiceries'. Here they built a series of heavily guarded forts and bastions and, within a few years, the islands of Ternate and Tidore, Amboyna and Ceram, had all fallen into their grasp.

The other countries of Europe had got off to a faltering start in the spice race. Columbus had sailed westwards across the Atlantic in 1492 convinced that he could detect the whiff of spice in the air. Although he went to great lengths to persuade the King and Queen of Spain that he had found the East Indies, he had of course discovered America. The Venetian explorer John Cabot also believed that the quickest way to the East Indies was to sail west and he visited Arabia at a very early age in order to quiz the local merchants about 'whither spices are brought by caravans from distant countries'. These merchants were understandably reticent to part with such priceless information and spoke vaguely of spices coming from the easternmost reaches of the world. It was exactly what Cabot had hoped to hear and he concluded that 'presupposing the rotundity of the earth' – not a foregone conclusion even in those days – the merchants must have bought the spices 'at the north towards the west'.

Cabot was unable to interest any Venetian sponsors in a westerly voyage across the Atlantic so he travelled to England and persuaded King Henry VII to commission his search for the 'spiceries'. Setting sail across the Atlantic in 1497 he landed at Cape Breton Island which he confidently declared to be an uninhabited part of China. Although spices were distinctly thin on the ground Cabot returned to an England fascinated by his supposed discovery. 'Great honour is paid him,' wrote a Venetian merchant living in London, 'and he dresses in silk; and these English run after him like mad people.' So, indeed, did the King who promptly provided the finances for a second expedition.

On this new voyage Cabot decided to follow the coast of 'China' until he reached Japan where 'all the spices of the world originate'. Certain he would return with his ships filled with nutmeg, his confidence only faltered when the mercury slumped below zero and the icebergs grew ever more threatening.

Despite his failure to bring home a single nutmeg, Cabot's voyages aroused considerable interest in the ports of Spain and Portugal. One man in particular was keen to know more about his discoveries: Ferdinand Magellan, a 'gentleman of great spirit', had long believed there was a far quicker route to the Spice Islands than the lengthy voyage around the Cape of Good Hope and was sure that Cabot had been right to sail westwards across the Atlantic.

Magellan had sailed to the East Indies in his youth and would certainly have returned had circumstances allowed. But after taking part in a military campaign in Morocco, he was accused of treachery and informed by the Portuguese king that his services were no longer required. King Manuel had made a grave error in dismissing Magellan for he was an expert navigator who had read widely the geographical theories of his day. He argued that the only reason that Columbus and Cabot had failed to find the Spice Islands was that they had not found a passage through the American continent.

Magellan travelled to the court of King Charles V of Spain in 1518 and 'acquainted the Emperour that the islands of Banda and of the Molucca's [were] the only one store-house of nature for nutmegs and mace'. The King immediately realised that Magellan offered him the best chance of challenging the seemingly indomitable position of the Portuguese, and placed him in charge of a fleet of ships which were to sail southwards down the coast of Brazil, find a passage through to the Pacific Ocean, then sail west until they reached the 'islands of Banda'. It is fortunate that Magellan took with him a scholar by the name of Antonio Pigafetta, for Pigafetta faithfully recorded everything that happened on that historic first Spanish voyage to the Spice Islands. His journal, in turn, found its way into the hands of the learned English vicar Samuel Purchas whose monumental anthology of exploration, *Purchas His Pilgrimes*, was to inspire London's merchant adventurers.

Magellan's voyage began well: he revictualled in the Canary Islands, crossed the equator, and reached the South

American coastline three months later. Here, simmering resentment between the Spanish crew and their Portuguese captain exploded into mutiny and Magellan was forced to hang the troublemakers from a hastily constructed gibbet. At that point the mutiny died down.

The remaining mutineers soon found their attentions diverted by the extraordinary behaviour of the natives; not least the giant-like menfolk of Patagonia who, noted Pigafetta, 'when they are sicke at the stomache they put an arrow half a yard downe the throate which makes them vomit greene choler and blood.' Their cure for headaches was no less dramatic; they gashed their heads open and purged the blood. And as soon as they detected the first chill of winter, 'they would truss up themselves so the genitall member is hidden in the body'.

A year after leaving Tenerife, Magellan's ship nudged through the straits that now bear his name and entered the warm waters of the Pacific. 'He was so glad thereof,' records his diarist, 'that for joy the teares fell from his eyes.' Magellan had been right all along: it was now simply a question of following the spice-filled breezes all the way to the East Indies.

Unfortunately it was not so simple. Magellan, like most explorers of his day, had no idea of the massive distances involved and after more than three months at sea with no sight of land his men began to starve. 'Having consumed all their biskits and other victuals, they fell into such necessitie that they were enforced to eate the powder that remained thereof, being now full of wormes and stinking like pisse by reason of the salt water. Their fresh water was also putrified and became yellow.' Soon even the worm-ridden powder ran out, forcing them 'to eate pieces of leather which were folded about certain great ropes of the shippes;

but these skinnes being very hard, by reason of the sunne, raine and winde, they hung them by a cord in the sea for the space of four or five days to mollifie them'. It was no diet for sick men and it soon took its toll: 'By reason of this famine, and unclean feeding, some of their gummes grew so over their teeth that they died miserably for hunger.'

Despite the terrible hardship, the ships limped on until they reached the Philippines where the men learned that they were nearing their goal. But Magellan was destined not to see the Spice Islands for he made the mistake of involving himself in a local power struggle and, during the fighting, was struck down and killed. It was a devastating blow to all those left alive and Pigafetta, shocked by the news, struggled to express their loss. 'There perished our guide, our light, and our support.'

So many men had died that a decision was taken to abandon one of the ships. The remaining vessels then sailed for the most northerly of the Spice Islands, sighting the clove-covered cone of Tidore's volcano in the first week of November 1521. Suddenly, the lurid descriptions that characterise Pigafetta's journal acquire a more practical tone. Magellan's men had sailed half-way around the world to make money and, for the next few pages, Pigafetta records every conceivable weight and measure in use on the island.

Laden with twenty-six tons of cloves, a cargo of nutmeg, and sackloads of cinnamon and mace, the expedition's remaining two ships finally left the Spice Islands in the winter of 1521. The *Trinidad* got no farther than the harbour: rotten, leaking and hopelessly overloaded, she needed extensive repairs before making the return journey. With a tearful farewell, the crew of the *Victoria* set sail alone. The men faced an appalling homeward journey and more than half of them died of dysentery. Pigafetta, diligent as ever, noted every sickness and death and even found significance in the way the corpses floated. 'The corpses of the Christians floated with the face towards heaven,' he wrote, 'but those of the Indians with the face downwards.'

Nine months after leaving the Spice Islands the *Victoria* at last reached Seville and, anchoring off the mole, 'discharged all her ordinance for joy'. Although her crew were half dead and Magellan was long-since buried, King Charles V was overjoyed and one of his first actions was to honour the captain, Sebastian del Cano, with a coat of arms. Its design included three nutmegs, two sticks of cinnamon and twelve cloves.

Portugal's merchants were livid at losing their short-lived monopoly and protested in the strongest terms to King Charles. They argued that the Spice Islands belonged to Portugal, not Spain, citing the infamous Treaty of Tordesillas. But their case was not as straightforward as they claimed. The Treaty of Tordesillas, signed some two decades previously, was based on a papal bull which had divided the world into two parts. Pope Alexander VI had drawn a line down the middle of the Atlantic which stretched 'from Pole Artike to the Pole Antartike' some hundred leagues west of the Cape Verde Islands. Any land discovered west of this line, declared the Pope, belonged to Spain. Everything east of the line belonged to Portugal. By the time the treaty had been signed, the Portuguese had successfully managed to shift the line westwards by several hundred miles allowing them to argue that Brazil, whose coastline was cut by the line, rightly belonged to them.

The treaty was easy enough to uphold with discoveries close to home but it was more complicated when dealing with distant and little-known islands. When continued on the far side of the world the Pontiff's line placed the Spice Islands unquestionably within the Portuguese sphere, but sixteenth-century maps were extremely inaccurate and the Spanish argued that these islands fell into their half of the globe and that their riches belonged to the king of Spain.

Unfortunately, no one could be sure who was right. In 1524, representatives from both sides submitted themselves to a board of inquiry but although they examined countless maps and charts no agreement was reached. It took a further five years of squabbling before King Charles of Spain sold his claims to the Spice Islands for the massive sum of 350,000 gold ducats.

This deal would have solved the problem had it been only the Spanish and Portuguese who were interested in the Spice Islands. But other powers were beginning to turn their attentions to the East: England, in particular, was developing an attachment to the sweet smell of spice. It could only be a matter of time before an English adventurer would once again attempt the journey.

Although the failure of Sir Hugh Willoughby's Arctic expedition brought to an abrupt end England's search for a North-East Passage, it did little to dampen the enthusiasm for sailing to the Spice Islands. Yet more than two decades were to pass before London's merchants contemplated financing a new expedition, and it was not until 1577 – some twenty-four years after Willoughby's voyage – that a flotilla of ships finally set sail under the command of Sir Francis Drake.

Drake's expedition was backed by Queen Elizabeth I and its ostensible object was to conclude trade treaties with the people of the South Pacific and to explore an unknown continent rumoured to exist in the southern hemisphere. But the Queen also gave Drake full licence to plunder Spanish ships and ports and to carry off as much treasure as his vessel could hold for, she told him, 'I would gladly be revenged on the King of Spain for divers injuries that I have received.' Since it was imperative that none of this information should fall into Spanish hands, the expedition was shrouded in secrecy from the very outset and the crew had no idea of their destination until the English coastline had receded into the distance.

The five ships under Drake's command, none of which exceeded the length of two London buses, used Magellan's route as their blueprint and revictualled in many of the same bays and harbours. These stops did not always go according to plan: dropping anchor in Patagonia the crew had fully expected to be entertained by giants vomiting 'green choler' and trussing up their genitals. Instead, they walked straight into an ambush and were only saved by swift intervention from Drake who picked up a musket, fired at a native, and, 'tore out his bellie and guts with greate torment, as it seemed by his crye, which was so hideous and horrible a roare, as if ten bulls had joined together in roaring'.

A few days later it was time to turn his fire on a fellow Englishman. One of Drake's subordinates, a 'gentelman' by the name of Thomas Doughty, was rumoured to be threatening mutiny. These rumours eventually reached the captain who promptly confronted Doughty with the allegations. What happened next is difficult to determine for Doughty had many enemies and each account tells a different story. But all follow a similar line: that Doughty admitted his guilt to an astonished Drake and was given three choices – to be executed, set on land, or return to

England to answer the charges before a full council. Doughty showed not a moment's hesitation: 'He professed that with all his heart he did embrace the first branch of the general's proffer … and without any dallying or delaying the time he came forth and kneeled downe, preparing at once his necke for the axe and his spirit for heaven.'

With this unpleasant episode over the ships continued on their way, successfully crossing from the Atlantic into the Pacific through the notoriously tempestuous straits. Drake's smaller vessels had already been abandoned. Now, sailing into a storm, he lost sight of the second ship in his fleet (it had, in fact, headed back towards England) leaving his flagship alone and in a perilous state. Tossed about 'like a ball in a racket' Drake raced up the South American coastline plundering wherever he could before steering his vessel westwards in the direction of the Spice Islands, a desolate journey for there was 'nothing in our view but aire and sea [for] the space of full sixty-eight dayes together'. At last – more than a generation after the Portuguese had first sailed to the East Indies – the English vessel sighted the luxuriant shores of the Spice Islands.

Drake had intended to drop anchor at the volcanic island of Tidore but as he edged his ship through the treacherous shallows a canoe drew alongside carrying a viceroy from the neighbouring island of Ternate. Arguing that Tidore was all but controlled by the hated Portuguese, he begged the English commander to change his course. Drake consented and, selecting a fine velvet cloak from his cabin, asked that it might be presented to the King with the message that he had come to buy spices. The messenger promptly returned with the news that the King 'would sequester the commodities and traffique of his whole island [and] reserve it to the intercourse of our nation'.

Drake and his men were treated to a fabulous display of Oriental politesse when the King at last visited their ship. His courtiers, all in white linen, rowed round and round the vessel and 'as they passed by us, did us a kind of homage with great solemnity, the greatest personages beginning first, with reverend countenance and behaviour, to bow their bodies right to the ground'. The King was not far behind. 'He also with six grave and ancient fathers in his canoe approaching, did at once, together with them, yield us a reverend kind of obeisance, in far more humble manner than was to be expected.' Drake found him 'of tall stature, very corpulent and well set together, of a very princely and gracious countenance; his respect amongst his own was such that neither his viceroy nor any other counsellors dared speak to him unless they were upon their knees'.

The English were at first unsure how to react to the affected manners of the East but they eventually commemorated the occasion in time-honoured fashion. They primed their cannon and listened with delight as 'our ordinance thundered, which we mixed with great store of small shot, among which sounding our trumpets and other instruments of music.' The King was dazzled by the fireworks and 'so much delighted that, requesting our music to come unto the boat, he joyned his canoe to the same, and was towed at least a whole hour together, with the boat at the stern of our ship'.

After a further blitz of cannon fire the King made his excuses and left, but not before he had sanctioned the English to buy whatever spices they needed from his island. By the time Drake was ready to leave Ternate his ship was so weighed down with goods – and so low in the water – that she was 'laid up fast upon a desperate shoal'. To lighten her, eight of the cannon were cast into the water, followed by much of the meal and pulse, and finally three tons of the precious cloves that he had bought. As the tide turned the ship was slowly lifted off the shoal and started on the long voyage back to England.

Drake arrived to a hero's welcome. Not only was his vessel, renamed the *Golden Hind*, laden with fragrant spices, she was also 'very richly fraught with gold, silver, pearls and precious stones', most of which had been pillaged from Spanish and Portuguese vessels. Men and women turned out in force to watch the arrival of the ship in Plymouth, and Queen Elizabeth herself came aboard the vessel at Deptford and conferred a knighthood on her gallant commander. Within days of his return, songs, sonnets, odes and poems were being composed in honour of his historic voyage.

Drake's astonishing feat of seamanship fired the imagination of Elizabethan England and fuelled the belief that the East was a land of fabulous potentates. But Drake had sailed as a freebooter, not a trader, and although he had successfully bought large quantities of spices in Ternate, their value was nothing compared to the gold and silver he had stolen from Spanish galleons. Worse still, he brought back little practical information about the market-places of the East. The records of his voyage include no details of prices, no mention of weights and measures, no clues as to the goods most sought after for barter. Yet his triumphant return caused great excitement among the merchants of London and they began to cast around for a suitable candidate to open trading links with the East Indies. Drake himself was the obvious choice but he had set his sights on some old-fashioned piracy and the merchants were forced to look elsewhere for a commander. Showing the singular lack of foresight that they had manifested when choosing Sir Hugh Willoughby for their Arctic adventure, they now entrusted command to a Nottinghamshire landowner called Edward Fenton, a headstrong man with little experience of seamanship.

Fenton came from a prosperous family and, had he so desired, could have lived a life of ignominious ease. Instead he chose a different path: eschewing the comforts of his stately home he sold his patrimony and embarked on a swashbuckling career as a soldier of fortune, allowing himself to be carried to wherever there was the chance for adventure. His first major expedition saw him travelling in the company of Martin Frobisher in search of the fabled North-West Passage and it was while on this expedition that Fenton first learned that orders given in London could be safely ignored once at sea. Landing on Baffin Island and finding what appeared to be large deposits of gold ore, Fenton abandoned his search for the North-West Passage and set up an impromptu mining venture with the aim of getting rich quick.

Fenton was a strange choice to lead a voyage to the East Indies: an incurable romantic, he had only a slim understanding of the responsibilities that befell a commander. His eccentricities had raised many an eyebrow before he even left England and there was considerable opposition to his appointment, but as the Earl of Leicester's preferred man he was duly entrusted with the post. When the merchants came to choose Fenton's second-in-command they plumped for a solidly dependable captain named William Hawkins, a relative of his more famous namesake, who had served in Drake's voyage to the South Seas. But they continued to harbour doubts about the whimsical Fenton and set down in great detail their plans for the voyage, including the exact route that he was to follow. 'You shall go on your course by the Cape of Good Hope,' they wrote, 'not passing the Strait of Magellan either going or returning ... you shall not pass to the north-eastward of the 40 degree of latitude at the most, but shall take your right course to the Isles of Moluccas.'

Such instructions fell on deaf ears for hardly had Fenton set sail than he cooled on the idea of sailing to the East Indies, a hazardous and tiresome voyage that would profit the merchants far more than him. As his ship plied its way southwards down the Atlantic, the 'gentelman' commander spent the long hours at the helm indulging his dream of a nobler and more glorious profession. It is unfortunate that the records of the expedition fall silent just at the point when it slides into farce. The most interesting account of the voyage – the journal belonging to William Hawkins – was partially destroyed by fire in the last century. But its disintegrating pages are sufficiently legible to allow for a reconstruction of the tumultuous events on board the *Bear*. Fenton, it seems, had long realised that the quickest way to riches was to plunder and ransack the Portuguese carracks that made their way up and down the African coastline. But as his ship drifted listlessly in the mid-Atlantic he was struck by an altogether more fantastic idea. On 25 September 1582, he summoned his lieutenants to a meeting in his cabin and told them of his plan to seize the island of St Helena 'and theire to be proclaimed kyng'.

They could scarcely believe their ears. They were only too aware of Fenton's propensity for disregarding orders but this was an entirely unforeseen turn of events. Attempting to talk him out of this lunatic scheme only fuelled his desire and when the practical Hawkins became too vociferous in his arguments against the plan Fenton promised him 10,000 pounds of silver if he would change his mind, as well as great riches to 'all the well willers.' When news reached the on-board preacher he was horrified and 'fell down upon his knees and besought [Hawkins] that for God's sake he would not give his consent to this determination'. The crew had a similar reaction; they had no wish to spend the rest of their lives on the remote Atlantic islet that, two centuries later, would prove such an effective prison for Napoleon. Several pointed out the impracticalities of Fenton's plan, arguing that it would be almost impossible for them to defend the island against foreign vessels. Without mastery of the sea, King Edward of St Helena would be deposed before the year was out.

Hawkins agreed and, deciding to 'tell [Fenton] my mind', stormed back to the commander's cabin. Unfortunately the next few lines of his journal are illegible but he must have eloquently argued his case for Fenton abandoned his mad scheme with as much haste as it had originally been conceived. Perhaps he realised that without Hawkins's help, he would not even have been able to locate the island. His romantic dream in tatters, Fenton locked himself in his cabin in a mood of black despair. 'He saide then he would go back agayne to the islands of Cape de Verde to fetch some wine,' which, noted Hawkins, 'was only a desire to pick and steale'.

As his ship headed back towards England, Fenton awoke to the fact that he had done little to endear himself to London's merchants. He tried to silence Hawkins by clapping him in irons and threatening to kill him if he breathed a word about the more ludicrous episodes of the voyage. In the event, Hawkins survived but this final act completed Fenton's fall from grace and his name was conspicuously absent from any future expedition to the East. The detailed plans and orders laid down by the expedition's financiers proved to be entirely in vain: the 1582 expedition to the Spice Islands never even left the Atlantic.

The merchants of London now realised that the best way forward was for one of their own – a sober and hard-nosed businessman – to travel east to investigate the practicalities of trade. The man they chose to conduct this research was Ralph Fitch, a practically minded merchant of the Levant Company who left London in 1583 accompanied by four partners. The journal he compiled while travelling was filled with facts and figures about the ports and cities of the Indies and although it is not the most exciting of reads, its importance lies in the fact that it marked England's entry as a serious player in the spice race.

Fitch tells how he set off with four companions-in-trade – Messrs Newberry, Eldred, Leedes and Story – in the winter of 1583. After travelling by ship to Tripolis in Syria the small party teamed up with a caravan as far as Aleppo, then continued to the Euphrates on camel-back. Here they pooled their resources, bought a boat, and floated downstream to the Persian Gulf. Newberry had travelled this way once before and returned with stories about huge-breasted ladies with 'great rings in their noses and about their legs, arms and necks iron hoops'. Suffering from the stinking heat of midday, he had watched in amazement as they unblushingly 'threw their dugs over their shoulders'. Such a colourful tale would never have found its way into Fitch's journal; as Newberry eyed up the local ladies, his colleague was busy noting how their boat was constructed, the exact cost of the journey, and the weights and measures in use.

No sooner had the party of Englishmen arrived in Hormuz than the town's Portuguese authorities grew suspicious. Arrested and clapped in jail, they were eventually shipped to Goa to be dealt with by the Portuguese viceroy. Here, the men had a stroke of luck. One of the Jesuit fathers in the town was an Oxfordshire man named Thomas Steven who had arrived in Goa four years previously, earning himself the distinction of being the first Englishman ever to visit India. Hearing that a group of his compatriots were incarcerated in the town's 'fair stronge prison', Steven immediately provided sureties for them and the men were allowed to go free.

Once out of prison they went their separate ways. Story promptly locked himself up in a monastery to pursue his new-found vocation as a monk. Newberry found Goa to his liking and settled in the town, Eldred discussed trade with the local merchants, while Leedes entered the service of the Emperor Akbar and was never heard of again. But Fitch was not to be swayed from his original plans. In transporting him to Goa the Portuguese had unwittingly aided his project by dropping him behind enemy lines. Before they had the chance to rearrest him he fled the town in disguise and, after years on the road, eventually arrived in Malacca. Fitch shows no triumphalism in having finally reached his goal; he records his arrival with the same methodical detachment that marks the rest of his journey, compiling a dossier of information about commodities and prices.

After no less than eight years of painstaking research into the spice trade, Fitch decided it was time to return home. When he finally reached London, he was surprised to discover that he had become something of a celebrity and that his journal was eagerly sought after by the bards and playwrights of London. One who was particularly interested in his story was a young writer called William Shakespeare who adapted the opening sentence of Fitch's account for his new play *Macbeth*. Fitch had written: 'I did ship myself in a ship of London, called the Tiger, wherein we went for Tripolis in Syria, and from thence we took the way for Aleppo.' In *Macbeth* this is echoed in the words: 'Her husband's to Aleppo gone, master o'th' *Tiger*.'

While Fitch laid the groundwork for the first serious trading venture Sir Francis Drake was taking more practical measures to ensure its success. As King Philip of Spain's massive Armada sailed up the English Channel, Drake attacked the fleet, wreaking chaos on the would-be invaders. Each day he picked off straggling ships until, at the end of July 1588, 'the winds of God blew.' Surveying the destruction he had caused, Drake declared that none of the Spanish commanders 'will greatly rejoice of this day's service'.

The psychological effects of victory were to change England forever. For decades the high seas had been the exclusive preserve of Spain and Portugal but now there was a new power to be reckoned with. Within months, news of England's naval prowess had reached the kings and princes of the East Indies, rulers who had never before heard of England. In a region where military strength counted for everything, the local potentates of Java and Sumatra awaited their first glimpse of this newly victorious power, and when the first English mariners finally pitched up at the court of Sultan Ala-uddin of Achin – the most powerful ruler in Sumatra – they found that the Sultan knew every detail of the historic victory. So anxious was he to make an impression on this new naval power, and so keen to strike up a trading alliance, that he sent a train of elephants magnificently decked with streamers to meet them.

In the congratulatory letter that he sent to Queen Elizabeth I he was most effusive in his greetings. Imagining her as victorious ruler of vast swathes of Europe, he addressed his letter to the Sultana of England, France, Ireland, Holland and Friseland. Even good Queen Bess must have blushed at that.

CHAPTER TWO

WONDERFULLY
UNWHOLESOME
CLIMES

TWO MONTHS AFTER Sir Francis Drake's spectacular success against the Armada, London merchants heard rumours that an English vessel was sailing up the Channel after an adventurous voyage to the East Indies. The captain of this ship was Thomas Cavendish, the second Englishman to circumnavigate the globe, who was returning from his expedition laden with rich merchandise. On his home-bound journey he had attacked the huge Spanish galleon, *Great St Anne*, along with a staggering nineteen other vessels, and he arrived back in England to a rapturous welcome, a welcome that was heightened by reports that his sailors wore silken doublets and that his top sails were trimmed with gold.

Scarcely had Cavendish set foot on land than he was writing to his old friend, the Lord Chamberlain, urging him to promote an English expedition to the Spice Islands without delay. 'I sailed along the islands of the Moluccas,' he wrote, 'where our countrymen may have trade as freely as the Portugals if they themselves will.'

There was by now a pressing need to send a successful trading mission to the East Indies for, ever since King Philip II had acceded to the throne of Portugal in 1580, the markets of Lisbon had been closed to English shipping. Not only had this dramatically reduced the quantity of spice arriving in England, it had also closed an important export market for English broadcloths and woollens. The old argument against an English expedition to the Spice Islands — that the Portuguese had exclusive rights over the eastern sea routes — was no longer valid. The papal bull that had divided the world between the Catholic powers of Spain and Portugal was openly scorned in England and Queen Elizabeth I personally challenged its legality, famously arguing that 'it is as lawful for my subjects to sail [around the Cape] as the Spanish, since the sea and air are common to all men.' The voyages of Drake and Cavendish had demonstrated to the sceptics that English ships, though small, could indeed go anywhere they chose and when Drake captured a massive carrack in the eastern Atlantic it proved once and for all that such ships 'were no such bugs that they might be taken'. This particular bug was a rich prize indeed: its hold was filled with more than £100,000 of treasure.

In 1591, after years of vacillating, the merchants of London acted upon Cavendish's advice. They petitioned Queen Elizabeth for a licence to trade in the East Indies and, on gaining her consent, began searching for a suitable commander. This time they paid heed to their mistakes of the past and plumped for James Lancaster, an experienced merchant seaman who had fought bravely against the Spanish Armada.

Little is known of Lancaster's early life. His will relates that he was born in Basingstoke in 1554 or 1555 and died when he was well into his sixties. Known to be 'by birth of gentillity' he was despatched to Portugal at a tender age in order to learn the language and business of trade. Lancaster himself recorded only the briefest outlines of his years in

*James Lancaster survived two long journeys to the East Indies braving
scurvy, storms and Portuguese carracks. One of his letters, written
during a hurricane, entered the legends of the East India Company.
'I cannot tell where you should look for me,' he wrote,
'because I live at the devotion of the
winds and seas.'*

the country. 'I have been brought up among these people,' he later wrote, 'and have lived among them as a gentleman, served with them as a soldier, and lived among them as a merchant.' What else he did in Portugal remains uncertain, but it seems likely that he, like many other English living there, espoused the cause of Don Antonio in the struggle for the Portuguese throne and fought on his behalf. With the victory of Spain his days were numbered and he fled back to England as a virtual refugee, losing all his property and money in the process. But his knowledge of Portuguese was to stand him in good stead for by 1587, the year before the Armada, he was once again trading, this time from London.

An oil painting of James Lancaster has survived to show the manner of the man. Magnificently attired in buttoned doublet and flamboyant ruff he looks the typical Elizabethan, stiff and rigid with one hand resting on sword and the other fingering a globe. His journals and writings add flesh to what remains an archetypal Elizabethan portrait, revealing that Lancaster was a mixture of gruff sea dog and stern moraliser. A strict disciplinarian, he was a keen advocate of daily prayers on board ship and forbade any sort of gaming. He particularly abhorred bad language and instituted severe penalties 'against the blaspheming of the name of God and all idle and filthy communication'. Yet his disciplinarian nature was always tempered by compassion. When his vessel was in danger of sinking, he was at first furious that the accompanying ship ignored his orders to leave them to their fate. 'These men regard no commission,' he growled darkly; yet no one was punished when he later learned that they had remained alongside because of their love for him. The respect he showed for his crew was also a new departure: Lancaster did everything in his power to save the weak and, unlike many other captains, was genuinely horrified to watch helplessly as dozens of his crew succumbed to illness and death.

The vessel that Lancaster had captained against the Armada, the *Edward Bonaventure*, was not a warship; rather, she was one of the many London merchant vessels that sailed down the English Channel to aid in the defence of the realm. She was also destined to become, under Lancaster's skilful command, one of three ships to set off on the long 1591 voyage to the East Indies.

The merchants who financed this expedition viewed it as a reconnaissance mission rather than a trading venture and little cargo was loaded on board the ships. Instead, all available space was converted into living space for the large number of men on board, a necessary feature of long voyages into the unknown. Many would die on the outward trip and for those that survived there was a cornucopia of tropical diseases awaiting them on their arrival in the East.

Decked with streamers and bunting, the *Edward Bonaventure*, *Penelope* and *Merchant Royal* sailed from Plymouth on a warm spring day in 1591. A large crowd had assembled to bid the ships farewell and many families wept openly as they pulled away from the shore. Lancaster himself took the helm of the flagship, leading the other vessels into the choppy waters of the English Channel. His bullish optimism was not mirrored by the crowd gathered to see him off. The chances of them seeing their loved ones again were slim, and many were already questioning the wisdom of putting to sea so late in the season.

At first all went well; the ships arrived safely at the Canary Islands before setting off with the wind in their sails for Cape Verde and the equator. Here, they had the good fortune to capture a Portuguese caravel laden with sixty tons of wine, a thousand jars of oil and numerous barrels of capers. Despite this unexpected revictualling men began to die. Two expired on the *Edward Bonaventure* before she had even crossed the equator whilst others soon 'tooke their sicknesse in those hote climates, for they be so wonderful unwholesome'. Worse, the weather was on the turn. No sooner had the ships entered the southern hemisphere than 'we had nothing but tornadoes, with such thunder, lightening and raine that we could not keep our men drie three houres together which was an occasion of the infection among them.' With provisions running low, the ships followed the trade winds to Brazil before turning in the direction of the Cape of Good Hope.

The crew had by now been at sea for more than three months without eating any fresh fruit. Stuck in the doldrums and with nothing but 'salt victuals' and biscuits on board, they began to fall sick. Failure of strength and persistent breathlessness were the first signs that the body was beginning to weaken and many could no longer climb the rigging. Next, their skin turned sallow, their gums tender and their breath rank and offensive. 'The disease that hath consumed our men hath bene the skurvie,' wrote Edmund Barker, one of the on-board chroniclers of the expedition. 'Our soldiers, which have not been used to the sea, have best held out, but our mariners dropt away; which (in my judgement) proceedeth of their evil way of living at home.'

Most of Lancaster's men were soon suffering from these early signs of the sickness and it was not long before the scurvy took on a more dramatic form. Their teeth dropped out and purple blotches sprouted all over their bodies. Eating salted meat did nothing to assuage their condition;

indeed, it only seemed to make matters worse. As their muscles swelled and their joints stiffened, thin streams of blood began to trickle from their eyes and noses. By the time the ships staggered towards the Cape of Good Hope many were also suffering from acute diarrhoea, as well as from lung and kidney troubles.

The usual port of call for ships rounding the Cape was Table Bay, a sheltered watering place first discovered by the Portuguese in 1503. Here the English ships dropped anchor and sent an advance party ashore where they were met by 'certaine blacke savages, very brutish, which would not stay'. This first meeting between Lancaster's Elizabethan hosed and doubleted seamen and the natives of southern Africa must have made for a strange sight. Never had the English crew seen such a primitive and barbarous people and they watched the savages with a mixture of awe and disgust. 'They wear only a short cloake of sheepe or seale skinnes to their middle, the hairie side inward, and a kind of rat's skinne about their privities.' So wrote Patrick Copland, the priest on a later voyage who was unamused by the titillating behaviour of their womenfolk. 'They would lift up their rat skinnes and shew their privities.' Mealtimes were an occasion for even greater disgust. One Englishman watched in horror as a band of natives ravenously munched through a pile of stinking fish entrails that had lain for more than two weeks in the tropical heat. As the 'savages' smacked their lips and sucked their fingers he concluded that 'the world doth not yield a more heathenish people and more beastly', adding that their meals smelt so foul 'that no Christian could abide to come within a myle of it'. The jewellery worn by the women was equally offensive: 'Their neckes were adorned with greasie tripes which sometimes they would pull off and eat raw.

When we threw away their beasts' entrails, they would eat them half raw, the blood lothsomely slavering.'

For three weeks Lancaster's crew were disappointed in their search for fresh fruit. They managed to shoot geese and cranes with their muskets, and gathered mussels on the foreshore, but found it difficult to acquire food in sufficient quantities to feed all their company. But eventually they had some luck. After capturing a native and explaining in sign language their need for meat and fruit, he set off up country and returned eight days later with forty bullocks and oxen, as well as several dozen sheep. The men could not believe how cheap these animals were. One knife bought a bullock, two secured an ox, and a broken blade was all that was needed to buy a sheep. While the crew bartered on the foreshore, a small party set off around the bay in a small pinnace and returned with a huge number of seals and penguins. Lancaster even managed to shoot an antelope.

Despite all the fresh meat many of the men remained desperately sick. A health check revealed that less than two hundred men were 'sound and whole' and fifty were too ill to work. A decision was taken: the *Penelope* and *Edward Bonaventure* would continue eastwards while the *Merchant Royal* 'was sent home for England with diverse weake men'. The expedition was now down to two ships, both of which were dangerously undermanned.

It was only a matter of days before the expedition met with disaster. No sooner had the two remaining vessels rounded the Cape of Good Hope than a tremendous storm sank the *Penelope* with the loss of all hands:

We encountered with a mighty storme and extreme gusts of wind, wherein we lost our General's companie [the *Penelope*] and could never heare of him nor his ship any more, though we did our best endeavour to seeke him ... Foure dayes after this uncomfortable separation, in the morning, toward ten of the clocke, we had a terrible clap of thunder, which slew foure of our men outright, their necks being wrung in sonder without speaking any word, and of 94 men there was not one untouched; whereof some were striken blind, others were bruised in their legs and arms, and others in their brests, so that they voided blood two dayes after; others were drawne out at length, as though they had been racked. But (God be thanked) they all recovered, saving only the foure which were slaine outright. Also with the same thunder our main mast was torn very greviously from the head to the deck, and some of the spikes, that were ten inches into the timber, were melted with the extreme heate thereof.

Lancaster's vessel, the *Edward Bonaventure*, was now alone, a dangerous situation for a ship about to enter uncharted waters. Worse still the ship's master, William Mace, was killed by natives while making a sortie for water on the shores of Mozambique. Luckily help was at hand. When a Portuguese merchant-ship sent a message to Lancaster by way of a negro in a canoe, 'we took the negro along with us, because we understood he had been in the East Indies and knew somewhat of the countrie.' This became a regular practice among the English captains and the only sure way of finding the remote and isolated Spice Islands. Unfortunately, this particular 'negro' proved a disaster. Allowing the ship to be blown hopelessly off course, he missed the Laccadive Islands in the Arabian Sea where Lancaster had intended to revictual and decided to head to the Nicobar Islands instead. 'But in our course we were very much deceived by the currents,' and these islands also eluded the ship so that by the time she reached Penang off the coast of Malaysia the crew were once again in a desperate condition. Only thirty-three men were left alive, and eleven of these were so sick that they were unable to man the ship. After cruising the coastline for a few days, Lancaster spotted a large Portuguese ship sailing from Goa. To attack her was a great gamble but Lancaster was prepared to take the risk. Ordering the men to prime their cannon, he 'shot at her many shot, and at last shooting her maine-yard through, she came to anker and yielded'. The captain and crew escaped in little rowing boats leaving the English to ransack the vessel. She was loaded with a hotchpotch of cargo, including sixteen brass cannon, three hundred butts of Canary wine and a good supply of raisin wine 'which is verie strong', as well as red caps, worsted stockings and sweetmeats. As soon as these had been transferred onto the *Edward Bonaventure* Lancaster set sail in order to escape the danger of reprisals.

Sailing north-west towards Ceylon – and lost in the vastness of the Indian Ocean – the crew now decided that they had had more than enough adventure. With their captain languishing in his cabin, 'very sick, more like to die than to live', they refused to obey his orders and decided to head for England. Lancaster was reluctantly forced to agree.

Short of food and plagued with cockroaches, they safely rounded the Cape of Good Hope and, with the wind in their favour, headed straight to the island of St Helena where a group of men rowed ashore. Ever since the failure of Edward Fenton's mad scheme to proclaim himself king the island had been deserted. Ships occasionally stopped at the island to stock up on the 'excellent good greene figs, oranges, and lemons very faire', and the crew of one passing vessel had seen fit to construct a makeshift chapel on the island; but for the greater part of the year the island was uninhabited. It was with considerable surprise, therefore, and not a little fear, that Lancaster's men heard a ghostly chant emerging from the chapel. Kicking open the door, 'we found an Englishman, a tailor, who had been there 14 months.' His name was John Segar and he had been cast ashore the previous year by the captain of the *Merchant Royal* who, realising he was at death's door, reasoned that he stood a greater chance of survival on land than aboard the ship. But although the months on the island had cured his body, the loneliness, boredom and heat had begun to addle his mind. 'We found him to be as fresh in colour and in as good plight of body to our seeming as he might be,' wrote one witness, 'but crazed in mind and half out of his wits, as afterwards we perceived; for whether he were put in fright of us, not knowing at first what we were, whether friends or foe, or of sudden joy when he understood we were his olde consorts and countrymen, he became idle-headed, and for eight days space neither night nor day took any naturall rest, and so at length died for lacke of sleep.'

The journey home should have been almost over but as the crew set sail for home the wind dropped once again and they spent six weeks drifting helplessly in the mid-Atlantic. At last the breeze stiffened and Lancaster, who had by now recovered, suggested they let the winds carry them to the West Indies where they could obtain much-needed provisions. A chance encounter with a French ship enabled them to replenish their supplies of wine and bread but it was to be their last stroke of good fortune. A sudden storm arose which grew so fierce that 'it carried not only our sailes away, but also made much water in our shippe, so that wee had six foote water in holde'. The ship limped towards the outpost island of Mona and, relieved to have reached land, all but five of the crew rowed ashore. It was the last they would ever see of the *Edward Bonaventure*: at around midnight the ship's carpenter cut the moorings and, with a skeleton crew and a good measure of self-confidence, sailed off into the night leaving Lancaster and his men stranded.

Almost a month passed before a French ship was spotted on the horizon. Hastily lighting a bonfire to attract her attention the crew were eventually picked up and offered the passage home. By the time Lancaster and the pitiful remnants of his crew arrived back in England they had been away for three years, six weeks, and two days.

The voyage had proved a human and financial disaster. Of the 198 men who rounded the Cape, only 25 returned alive. Worse still, two of the three ships had been lost and the one that did manage to limp into port was carrying not spices but scurvy. Lancaster had proved – if proof was needed – that the spice trade involved risks that London's merchants could ill afford. It was not until they learned that the Dutch had entered the spice race, and achieved a remarkable success, that they would consider financing a new expedition to the islands of the East Indies.

The Dutch expedition had been planned in the utmost secrecy. For more than three years the inhabitants of Amsterdam's Warmoestraat, a genteel neighbourhood close to the city's main square, had watched an unusual amount of activity at the house of Reynier Pauw. This merchant, just twenty-eight years of age, had already made his fortune as head of an international lumber business. Now, it seemed, he had set his sights on a new and more ambitious project, for two of the regular visitors at his home, Jan Carel and Hendrik Hudde, were among the city's wealthiest merchants. There was a third man who joined them at their meetings – a bearded hunchback whose tight-fitting skull-cap emphasised his bulbous forehead. His name was Petrus Plancius, a gifted though dogmatic theologian who had studied in England before travelling to Amsterdam to preach his fanatical branch of Calvinism. But it was not

Cross staff was used to measure height of sun at noon and thereby determine latitude.

Expeditions set off to the Spice Islands with primitive instruments. Most navigational equipment was only useful in bright sunshine, and a common practice was to hire (or capture) a local 'pilot'. 'We took a negro along with us,' wrote James Lancaster, 'because we understood he had been in the East Indies.'

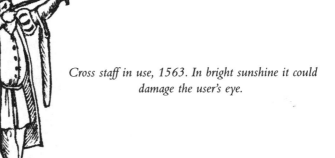

*Cross staff in use, 1563. In bright sunshine it could
damage the user's eye.*

theology that brought him to Pauw's house: Plancius had
come to show his maps of the Indies – maps that were said
to be the most accurate in existence.

Men of religion do not, as a rule, make great men of
science. Plancius was the exception and even when he
preached from the pulpit his mind would frequently
wander away from thoughts of God towards his fascination
with geography. 'I have been told,' wrote one critic, 'that

The back staff did not require the user to look directly at the sun.

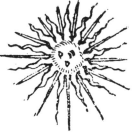

The astrolabe, also used to measure the height of the sun, was less accurate than the cross staff.

you frequently climb into the pulpit without having properly prepared your sermon. You switch then to subjects which have nothing to do with religion. You talk as a geographer about the Indies and the New World, or you discuss the stars.' This interest in geography strayed increasingly into his religious work. Commissioned to draw a map of Biblical sites for a new edition of the Bible, Plancius deftly crafted a map not of the Holy Land but of the entire world, including the Spice Islands. Soon he was concentrating more and more time on map-drawing until, in 1592, he published his important world map grandly entitled, 'A geographical and hydrographical map of the whole world, showing all countries, towns, places and seas under their respective degrees of longitude and latitude; capes, promontories, headlands, ports, shoals, sand banks and cliffs are drawn in the most accurate manner.'

Plancius drew on the work of two Dutch cartographers when he came to produce his maps. These men, Abraham Ortelius and Gerardus Mercator, had in turn derived their inspiration from the Roman geographer Claudius Ptolemy who had gone to immense lengths to determine the precise position of all known places. Ortelius's fascination with the science of cartography resulted in his magnificent *Theatrum Orbis Terrarum,* whilst Gerardus Mercator had been struggling throughout the 1560s to draw his pioneering world map on the projection that now bears his name. The finished work was similar in detail to that of Ortelius but differed in its novel projection, for although he drew all the lines meeting at right angles he pulled the parallels of latitude farther apart as they reached the poles. This, of course, distorted the distances to a huge degree, to the point that Greenland became the size of North America, but it also meant that the position of places relative to one another remained correct. His discovery gave Dutch cartographers a virtual monopoly on map-making for more than a century and enabled them to furnish their explorers with practical and up-to-date information when they set sail on their voyages to the East Indies.

Even with access to these maps, the Dutch merchants planning their first expedition remained cautious. They were aware that it took a huge sum of money to equip a fleet which, given the record of the English, was almost certain to suffer substantial losses on the long route to and from the East. But in the winter of 1592, Plancius arrived at Pauw's house with a new and unknown face whose weather-beaten features suggested that he had been abroad for some considerable time. The name of this stranger was Jan Huyghen van Linschoten and he had indeed been on a long voyage − nine years in the Indies − and had returned with reams of information about the spice ports of the East.

Linschoten was the antithesis of Fitch and, had the two men met in the souks of Malacca, they would have found little in common. The Dutchman's tales are a colourful mix of fact and fantasy and his book is filled with 'luxurious and unchaste women', rampaging elephants and giant rats 'as big as young pigges'. Most extraordinary of all is his tale of the monstrous fish of Goa which are 'in bigness as great as a middle sized dog, with a snout like a hog, small eyes, no eares, but two holes where his eares should bee'. As he tried to sketch this extraordinary creature, 'it ranne along the hall upon the floore and in every place snorting like a hog.'

Unlike Fitch, Linschoten was not travelling in order to research the cost and availability of spices; rather, his aim was to collect weird and wonderful fables from the East and he would quiz every merchant and mariner he met and transcribe their marvels into his bulging diary.

It was not until he returned to Holland and began to tell people of his travels that their true worth was realised. Unwittingly, Linschoten had compiled an immense encyclopaedia of knowledge about the islands of the East Indies. He knew exactly what the native merchants wished to exchange for their spices, had discovered that pieces-of-eight were the coins most sought after by traders, and had inadvertently researched all the most suitable ports for revictualling on the long journey to the East. The resulting book, the *Itinerario*, stretched to five weighty volumes, one of which included descriptions of the produce of every island in the Indies as well as a list of languages of most use to foreign traders. There were lengthy accounts of the nutmeg and clove trees along with a section on the healing and curative properties of these spices: 'nutmegs fortify the brain and sharpen the memory,' he wrote. 'They warm the stomach and expel winds. They give a clean breath, force the urine, stop diarrhoea, and cure upset stomachs.'

Linschoten's account and Plancius's maps convinced the three merchants that the time was now right to send an expedition to the East. Yet still they hesitated, deciding to await the return of a spy they had sent to Lisbon, a headstrong man named Cornelis Houtman whose unstable temperament was to cause so much trouble in the future. Exactly what Houtman discovered in Lisbon is not known, but it convinced the merchants that there was no time to be lost in entering the spice race and, 'after many discussions, it was finally resolved that, in the Name of God, a beginning should be made with the navigation and other affairs.' Six more merchants were summoned to help finance the project, four ships were built, and cannon were borrowed from various towns. Embarrassingly, not enough firearms could be found and an agent had to be despatched to England to buy some extra weaponry.

In stark contrast to the English expeditions, the Dutch voyage was meticulously planned. The ships were equipped with spare masts, anchors and cables and the begrudging pilots were compelled to have lessons in navigation from Petrus Plancius: 'five days a week, from Monday till Friday, from nine in the morning until five in the evening'. But in common with all the English voyages prior to that of James Lancaster, save that of Sir Francis Drake, the Dutch merchants made one critical mistake: they put unsuitable and inadequate men in command.

One of these was Cornelis Houtman, the very man whose clandestine activities in Lisbon had helped get the project off the ground. As a spy he was in his element; as a leader of men he was a disaster. Houtman was given the important post of chief merchant on the *Mauritius* which, had it been his only job, would have limited his potential to cause mischief. Unfortunately, he was also given a place on the ships' council with a special status that allowed him to speak first on any issue.

Setting sail in the spring of 1595, the expedition's four vessels headed first for the Cape Verde Islands in the mid-Atlantic and then set sail towards the equator. Here they entered the doldrums, drifting across the ocean for almost a month before the coastline of Brazil was sighted. From here, the ships changed course with the trade winds and let themselves be carried back towards southern Africa.

Many of the men were by now desperately sick and, as the ships rounded the Cape, good hope proved elusive for the seventy-one sailors who succumbed to scurvy. Worse still, discipline broke down completely as simmering discontent exploded into outright warfare. In normal circumstances, such unruly behaviour would have been treated with the utmost severity. According to a Dutch code of discipline, any fight that drew blood would result in the antagonist having one hand strapped behind his back and the other nailed to the mast. There he would remain until he tore himself lose. If the fight ended in death, the man was bound to his victim and tossed into the sea. Even pulling a knife in jest was a serious misdemeanour – the offender would suffer three lengthy dunkings from the yardarm. Refusing to obey the captain commanded the death penalty; desertion was rewarded with flogging, and the most serious offences were dealt with by keel-hauling – a terrible punishment which involved being hauled underneath the keel while the ship was moving. In the majority of cases, the victim's head was ripped off.

None of these deterred the crew of this pioneering Dutch expedition from indulging in the most violent and brutal behaviour. The troubles began when the skipper of the *Amsterdam* died of scurvy and the ship's chief merchant, a hothead named Gerrit van Beuningen, assumed control. The ships' council was furious and accused Beuningen of a series of crimes, including an attempt on the life of Cornelis Houtman, and demanded he be hanged from the ship's mast without further ado. Others supported Beuningen and vowed to defend him with force. Calmer counsel eventually prevailed and the merchant was clapped in irons instead. History has failed to record whether or not he regretted his action, but he was certainly given time to repent. When the *Amsterdam* finally arrived back in Holland two years later, Beuningen was still in irons.

Discipline now broke down completely and it was only when the ships reached Sumatra that the men called a temporary truce and patched up their quarrels. As they sailed through the shallow coastal waters, the natives rowed out in dug-out canoes and exchanged rice, water-melons and sugar-canes for glass beads and trinkets. Fresh food and water helped to heal the rifts but it was not long before new quarrels began. On arriving at the wealthy port of Bantam in Java, Houtman had hoped to buy spices for a song and was incensed when he discovered the prices to be sky-high. Worse still, all native authority in the town had disappeared as rival traders bickered and courtiers fought for possession of the throne.

Such an explosive situation was doomed to end in disaster. Angered by the escalating price of spices, Houtman lost his temper. 'And thus,' wrote one of the crew in a terrifyingly matter-of-fact entry in his journal, 'it was decided to do all possible harm to the town.' What followed was an orgy of destruction that was to set the pattern for the Dutch presence in the East Indies. The town was bombarded with cannon fire and prisoners were sentenced to death. A brief pause in the fighting allowed the Dutch commanders to debate the different means of disposing of prisoners (the choice was to stab them, shoot them with arrows, or blow them from cannons – unfortunately, no one recorded which method they settled for) and once this thorny question was resolved the battering continued. At one point the king's palace was hit; at another, a group of newly captured prisoners were tortured. 'And after we had revenged ourselves to the approval of our ship's officers,' wrote the same crew member, 'we prepared to set sail.' The ships proceeded to the nearby port of Sidayu where they were surprised by a group of Javanese natives who boarded the *Amsterdam* and hacked twelve men to death, including the skipper, before finding themselves under attack. The

Dutch 'then chased the natives back to the shore in our own rowing boats and executed the Javanese who had killed our colleagues'. Few paused to question why everyone was acting with such brutality. The voice of conscience is never loud in the journals of sixteenth-century mariners but one crew member did wonder why his fellow tradesmen had suddenly become such bloodthirsty cut-throats. 'There was nothing missing and everything was perfect except what was wrong with ourselves,' he wrote.

Events were to prove that the killing had scarcely begun. As the Dutch ships passed Madura, a low-lying island off the Javanese coast, the local prince (not yet privy to the events in Bantam) decided to put on a display of friendship, welcoming the Hollanders with a little flotilla of native prahus. The oarsmen rowed slowly and ceremoniously towards the Dutch vessels and at the centre of their display was a magnificent barge decorated with an elevated bridge on which stood the local prince, smiling broadly.

The Dutch grew agitated as more and more natives rowed out to the ships. Some whispered that it was an ambush; others were convinced there was treachery afoot and argued for a pre-emptive strike. Houtman agreed and, relying on the time-honoured principal that the best defence is attack, his ship 'opened fire and killed all on the big boat'. It was the signal for a general massacre. Within minutes, dozens of cannon were being fired into the flotilla, sinking boats and slaughtering the welcome party. No sooner had the floating parade been blasted out of the water than the Dutchmen lowered their rowing boats and concluded the day's business with hand-to-hand fighting. By the end of the battle, all but twenty natives were dead, among them the prince whose body was relieved of its jewels before being returned to a watery grave. 'I watched the attack not without pleasure,' admitted one Dutch sailor, 'but also with shame.'

The ships and crew were by now in a pitiful condition. Rival factions were at each other's throats while the various commanders – of whom Houtman was in the ascendant – were scarcely on speaking terms. Hundreds of men had died and those who were still alive were suffering from tropical diseases picked up at Bantam. Worse still, the ships themselves were in a sorry state of disrepair. Bearded with marine growth and encrusted with barnacles, they looked as if they had been raised from the depths of the ocean. Many were honeycombed with teredos (shipworms) which bored through the Dutch oak and allowed water to filter through the holes. On deck the tropical sun had so dried the timbers that the gaps between the planks were more than half an inch wide.

Then there was the question of spices. Despite many months at sea, Houtman had so far failed to buy any spices apart from the tiny quantity acquired when his ships first arrived in Sumatra. Having rejected trade with the merchants of Bantam, the Dutch were fast running out of suitable marketplaces.

A plan of action had to be made and a decision taken. Houtman argued that they should sail east to the Banda Islands where they were assured of a cargo of nutmeg at a reasonable price. But the captain of the *Mauritius*, Jan Meulenaer, disagreed. He said that the ships were virtually unseaworthy and that to make such a long voyage would be risking almost certain death. In the event, death came to Meulenaer rather sooner than he expected. Just hours after a particularly ferocious argument with Houtman he collapsed on deck and expired. There could be no doubt that there had been foul play. Two of the ships' on-board barbers proclaimed in front of the council that Meulenaer 'was completely blue and purple; poisoned blood came not only from his mouth but from his neck as well; and even his hair fell out at the slightest touch. A child,' they concluded, 'could tell he had been poisoned.'

A murder. A motive. And a body. It did not take long to find the suspect. The crew of the *Mauritius* accused Houtman of murder and promptly clapped him in irons. They then summoned the ships' council to convene for a second time and asked it to condemn him to death. But in this last demand they were to be disappointed for the council reasoned that there was insufficient evidence to execute Houtman and he was released.

The ships' crews now decided to abandon their quest for spices and sail for home. The *Amsterdam* was so rotten that she was emptied of supplies and set on fire. Then, making a final stop at Bali in order to take advantage of the amorous charms of local girls – and leaving behind two men who found those charms irresistible – the Dutch set sail for home.

When they finally reached Amsterdam more than two years had passed and two out of every three men on board had died. For the merchants who had financed the voyage the lack of spices was far more galling than the lack of men. They watched the ships' return to port fully expecting them to be laden with nutmeg, cloves and pepper. As it was, the cargo unloaded on that August day was silver reals – the same reals that they had watched being loaded two years previously. Incredibly, the price of spices had become so inflated while the ships had been in the East Indies that the tiny quantity Houtman carried home was enough to make the venture a profitable one. Had he been a more responsible commander he could have netted them a fortune.

The troubles that had plagued Holland's inaugural voyage to the East did little to deter Amsterdam's merchants from risking yet more of their money in the spice race. They argued that they had met with far greater success than the English who had not only lost two ships on their first expedition, one more than theirs, but had failed so far to reach the spice port of Bantam.

Less than seven months after Houtman's return, the merchants placed this unruly commander in charge of a second Dutch expedition to the East Indies, signalling that they had learned nothing from the mistakes of the previous voyage. But if Houtman was not up to the job, the chief pilot was more than qualified. His name was John Davis and he was an Englishman from Devon. A brilliant navigator, whose pioneering Arctic explorations had already carried him to the frozen shores of Greenland, he not only guided the ships to the East Indies and back, but also kept detailed notes on every coastline, port and harbour. Within weeks of completing the long voyage, Davis was hired for a second trip. But this time he was sailing on an English vessel under the command of the veteran James Lancaster. And this time, the two men were sailing as servants of the newly founded East India Company.

CHAPTER THREE

MUSIC
AND
DANCING DAMSELS

O N THE EVENING OF 24 September 1599, a loud
cheer was heard coming from the half-timbered
Founders Hall in London's Lothbury Street. For
much of the day the city's merchant adventurers had been
deep in discussion about sending a new fleet of ships to the
East Indies. Now they had at last reached a decision. With
a unanimous show of hands and a roar of excitement it was
decided to apply to Queen Elizabeth I for her assent to a
project that was 'intended for the honour of our native
country and for the advancement of trade of merchandise
within this realm of England'.

No painting survives to record the scene behind the
mullioned windows of Founders Hall on that September
evening but with the Company scribe recording every last
detail for posterity it is not hard to assemble a picture of the
historic events unfolding. Some fourscore men had
gathered to discuss the practicalities of the intended voyage.
These were not aristocrats nor landowners, nor were they
members of the courtly circle; most were merchants and
burghers, men who made their living by speculating on
trading ventures.

Some of the leading lights in this new enterprise had

considerable experience of international trade. Richard Staper and Thomas Smythe, for example, had been principal founders of the Levant Company and had helped to build a successful business in the eastern Mediterranean. Others, like Sir John Hart and Richard Cockayne were well-known faces in the City of London. Three of the men had held office as Lord Mayor of London and the chairman of the meeting, splendidly dressed in wig and robes, was Sir Stephen Soane, the present occupant of the Lord Mayorship.

Not all were merchants: among the aldermen and freemen of the London guilds were sailors and soldiers, bearded and weather-beaten sea dogs who wore gold rings in their ears and good-luck amulets about their necks. James Lancaster and John Davis could be seen among the crowds and so, too, could Francis Pretty, close friend of Thomas Cavendish. A few of Drake's crew pitched up for the meeting, as did some who had sailed with Fenton and Hawkins. Arctic explorer William Baffin put in an appearance as did the three Middleton brothers – John, Henry and David – who would all meet with disasters on the long voyage to and from the Spice Islands.

Such men were crucial to the success or failure of this, the Company's first venture. They were familiar with the sight of Portuguese carracks laden with costly spices and knew the best ports to obtain fresh water and new provisions. They also knew that although the Spanish and Portuguese had a vigorous commerce with the East, only a dozen or so ports were under their direct control. These were scattered over a huge area from Madagascar to Japan, and even Goa, the jewel in the crown of Portugal's eastern outposts, only housed a small settlement of traders and merchants. It scarcely deserved its suffix – dorado. In the 'riche and innumerable islands of the Mollucos and the

Spiceries', where nutmeg and cloves could be had for a song, the Portuguese influence was spread even more thinly. They had just two small forts on the islands of Tidore and Amboyna, leaving dozens of other atolls and skerries to be claimed, remote places like the nutmeg-producing Banda Islands.

Since it had become an axiom in international law that European nations could only claim such places as they had fortified or in which they had erected some visible symbol of possession, there were many who argued that it would make sense to head for these lonely outposts of the Spice Islands. If the flag could be raised in the Banda Islands, for instance, then England would have a toehold in the richest of all the islands in the East Indies.

When everyone had had the chance to speak Sir Stephen Soane called the meeting to order. There were important matters to be settled, not least of which was to prevent the large sum of money which had been subscribed just two days earlier from being contributed in any form other than cash. It was also decided to entrust the day-to-day running of the Company to fifteen directors who would organise and regulate the forthcoming voyage.

It was late by the time the meeting finally broke up. The sailors and adventurers trudged their way back to their homes in Shoreditch and Wapping, the merchants to their gabled dwellings in Charing Cross and Lincoln's Inn Fields. All must have felt that at long last they were on the brink of partaking in a successful trading enterprise to the East Indies.

To those subscribers who had gambled their money on the voyage there were huge riches to be had if it ended in success. Elizabethan London was home to an affluent aristocracy who clamoured for every luxury. Queen

Elizabeth herself determined the fashion of the age with her famous wardrobe of three thousand dresses, and the ladies of the court followed suit, cloaking themselves in brocades and satins trimmed with costly laces, sables and embroideries. The Queen loved the pomp, ceremony and luxuries that her state afforded her. In her palaces at St James, Greenwich, Windsor and Hampton Court she was surrounded by baubles, trinkets and precious objets d'art, as well as a magnificent library of Greek and Latin poets, richly bound in velvet.

Some of her more puritanical ministers reacted against the wanton extravagance of her court. At the wedding of one member of the aristocracy the celebrant priest, dismayed by the sight of so much finery, decided to speak his mind. Aware, perhaps, of the moves afoot for a great expedition to the East, he clambered into the pulpit and delivered a damning but topical sermon about the fripperies of Elizabethan fashion. 'Of all qualities,' he said, 'a woman must not have one quality, and that is too much rigging. What a wonder to see a ship under full sail, with her tackling and her masts, and her tops and top-gallants, with her upper deck and her nether decks, and so be-dekt with her streamers, flags, and ensigns ...' Pausing to survey the assembled ladies he continued: 'what a world of wonders it is to see a woman, created in God's image, so miscreate oft times with her French, her Spanish, and her foolish fashions, that He ... shall hardly know her with her plumes, her faunes, and a silken vizard, with a ruffle like a saile.'

The sermon fell on deaf ears. Elizabeth's courtiers were not about to abandon their new-found pleasures for this was an age that demanded excess. They needed to be richly clad for the pageants, masques and tournaments they attended and their frivolous needs were reflected in the trite ballads, odes and sonnets of the day. They loved curios and oddities, the unusual and the exotic, and it was to satisfy this vogue that had settled the merchants of London on their latest venture.

Queen Elizabeth herself was keen for the expedition to set sail at the earliest opportunity, especially when she learned that the Portuguese and Dutch had unexpectedly raised the price of pepper from three to eight shillings a pound. Pepper had become a basic commodity and with the price now beyond the means of all but the wealthy few it was imperative that a well-organised expedition be sent to seek it at its source. A handful of attempts had been made in the wake of James Lancaster's voyage but all had ended in disaster. The most recent, which had sailed under the captainship of Benjamin Wood, had disappeared without trace. It was, recorded Samuel Purchas, 'a double disaster; first in the miserable perishing of the fleet, and next in the losse of the historie and relation of that tragedie'. Rumours slowly filtered back to London reporting that the crew had been ravaged by disease and, one by one, perished at sea. 'Some broken plankes, as after a shipwracke, have yet beene encountered from the West Indies, which give us some notice of this East Indian disadventure.' Just four survivors managed to swim to a small island on the horizon and three of these were promptly despatched by a cut-throat Spaniard leaving just one man alive. Even he was not fated to live for long; fleeing the island aboard a passing ship, he soon succumbed to a dose of poison.

On 16 October 1599, less than a month after their first meeting, the London merchants received the Queen's official blessing. She instructed them to obtain from the Privy Council a warrant allowing them to proceed with the voyage, as well as a permit enabling them to carry overseas the five thousand pounds of bullion which the merchants needed for their proposed trade. The merchants were overjoyed at the Queen's enthusiasm, but the Privy Council, though outwardly enthusiastic, was determined to stop this voyage in its tracks. Delicate negotiations were just beginning with Spain and if this expedition were to set sail with the Queen's blessing – and against the wishes of the Pope – then Philip of Spain would be well within his rights to withdraw from the discussions. The merchants were warned in no uncertain terms that any voyage would have to be accommodated to the state of public affairs. Suddenly the expedition had been blocked at the highest level.

The merchants were furious to see their enterprise undermined by a handful of haughty lords in Elizabeth's court. They begged the Queen to intervene but although they had her full sympathy there was little she could do. The merchants now stiffened their resolve. Blithely ignoring the lords they 'did enter into the preparation of a voyage the next yeare following', poring over every map, chart and book of travels about the region they intended to visit. All this new-found information was then compiled into a document under the title: 'Certayne reasons why the English Merchants may trade into the East Indies, especially to such rich kingdoms and dominions as are not subjecte to the Kinge of Spayne and Portugal; together with the true limits of the Portugals conquest and jurisdiction in these oriental parts.'

Their reasoning as to why the voyage should go ahead was nothing less than a stoutly argued refutation of the Treaty of Tordesillas. 'Let the Spaniards,' they wrote, 'shewe any juste and lawful reasons ... why they should barre her Majestie and all other Christian princes and states, of the use of the vaste, wyde and infinitely open ocean sea, and of access to the territories and dominions of so many free princes, kings and potentates in the East.' These dominions, they argued, should be free to all merchants, 'for [the Spaniards] have noe more soveriegn comaund or authoritie, than wee, or any Christians whatsoever'.

The Queen read the document with great interest, then handed it to the learned Fulke Greville, Treasurer of the Navy, who concurred with every word and proceeded to strengthen its central argument by adding references to the spice trade from books in his impressive private library, 'espetially owt of the voyages of John Huighen [Lindschoten],' the man who had made possible the first Dutch voyage. Greville also provided a list of all the eastern kings already trading with Spain, leaving the inescapable conclusion that any potentates yet to sign a trading alliance were free to be exploited by whichever country reached them first.

When the London merchants held another meeting, on 23 September 1600, exactly a year had passed since their first gathering, yet they were no closer to setting sail for the East Indies. Increasingly impatient, they now resolved to 'goe forwards with the voiage' whether or not they had permission from the lords. Just two days after the meeting they bought their first ship, the *Susan*, for the princely sum of £1,600 and, on the following day, purchased the *Hector* and *Ascension* as well.

The obsequious courtiers, who had done so much to throw obstacles in the path of the merchants, now realised they had been wrong-footed. Instead of continuing their policy of refusing consent for the voyage they decided, instead, to wrest control from the merchants by placing one of their own in overall command. There was an obvious candidate: for months one of the chief players at court, the gentleman adventurer Sir Edward Michelborne, had been petitioning for an exclusive patent for trade to the Indies. Now, the Lord High Treasurer recommended Michelborne to the London merchants, politely instructing them to give him the position of 'principal commander'.

The merchants, mindful of Edward Fenton's disastrous expedition to St Helena, refused to be dictated to, even by so grand a luminary as the Lord Treasurer. They declined to take up his offer, explaining with considerable relish that they had resolved 'not to employ any *gentleman* in any place of charge', and added that they preferred to 'sorte their business with men of their own qualitye, lest the suspicion of the employment of gentlemen being taken hold of by the generalitie, do drive a great number of the Adventurers to withdraw their contributions'.

Michelborne was livid at this snub and refused to pay the subscription for which he had signed up. His name, in consequence, was removed from the Company's roll and, fuming and humiliated, he dropped from the scene to nurse his grievances. It was to be four years before he made his first independent foray into the eastern trade; when he did so, it had a devastating effect.

The merchants now settled on equipping a voyage to set sail in the spring of 1601 but the ships they had already bought were tiny, even by the standards of the time. Realising they would need a larger flagship if they were to have any hope of seeing off any war-mongering Portuguese carracks, they began to scout around for a more impressive vessel. The Earl of Cumberland had just the ship they needed: called the *Malice Scourge*, of 600 tons, she was offered for sale at the high price of £4,000. A deal was struck, she was bought for £3,700, and renamed the *Red Dragon*. She was a sturdily built and seaworthy vessel and although her construction was better placed for the chill waters of the north than for the tropics, she made an impressive sight on the Thames, her towering stern and carved poop betraying the large and comfortable living quarters for the captain and his lieutenants. Her low waist caused her to sit deep in the water, and she had a jutting prow adorned with an elaborate figurehead. She subsequently had a glorious career in the East Indies and was not sunk by the Dutch until a 'cruel, bloody fight' in October 1619.

After numerous arguments and deliberations the merchants settled on a mixed cargo of lead, iron (both wrought and unwrought), Devonshire cotton kerseys, broadcloth and Norwich woollens, as well as several boxes of trinkets and playthings suitable for presenting to the various potentates who would be encountered on the voyage. These included girdles, a case of pistols, ostrich plumes, looking glasses, spoons, glass toys, spectacles, and ewers wrought from silver.

The provisions were a subject of even more careful thought with every last pea and carrot calculated in individual portions. Food was not supplied for the time when the ships were in port: it would be up to the captains to barter from the natives enough to feed their crew. Even so, the detail that went into provisioning the ships is proof enough that the merchants were determined this voyage should succeed.

Bread for 16 months of 30 days p month

	c	lb		ll	s	d
at 24lb p man	1714	1 4	tons 150	1028	08	0

Meal for 4 months at 30 li p man p month

	c	lb		ll	s	d
	535	2 24	tons 30	267	17	4

Beer for 4 months at a pottle p man p day
the hoggeshead accoumpted clear of leakage 80 gallons

		ll	s	d
g 30000	tons 170	510	00	00

Cider for 8 months at a quart p day at the former rate

g 30000	tons 170	680	00	00

Wine for 8 months at a pint p day at the former allowaunce

g 15000	tons 80	960	00	00

Beef for 4 months at 1 li p man p day

c	q	li			
538	2	14	tons 30	428	10	00

Porke for 10 months at 1/2li p man p day

c	q	li			
669	2	16	tons 40	669	12	6.

And so the list continues. There were peas and beans to go with the pork, three months' supply of salted fish, oatmeal, wheat, 'olde holland cheese', butter, oil, vinegar, honey, sugar, and rice. The crew were even allowed a couple of pounds of nutmeg, cloves and pepper to help disguise the taste of rank meat, as well as fourteen hogshead of aqua vitae.

The merchants, though busy preparing the victualling of the ships, had not overlooked the appointment of the various captains and commanders. After electing Sir Thomas Smythe, a man of ripe experience, as the first governor of the Company, they next turned to the day-to-day running of the expedition itself. It came as no surprise that James Lancaster was named as 'General' or Admiral of the Fleet, nor that John Davis – only recently returned from the Dutch voyage – was appointed as pilot-major in charge of navigation. John Middleton, William Brund and John Heyward, all of whom had previously covered the route in various ships, were given command of the other three vessels.

There were also the on-board merchants, known as factors, to be chosen. These men were professional traders upon whose shoulders the financial success of the voyage would hinge. Selected with considerable care, they numbered 36 and would, all being well, settle in the East Indies and establish trading bases for future voyages. Those with foreign languages were particularly favoured, especially those who could speak Portuguese, Spanish or Arabic, the languages of trade in many of the larger ports in the East. Along with the crew the total tally came to 480 men, most of whom were experienced mariners.

Soon the wharves of London were alive with the clatter of ships being loaded with ropes, anchors, pennants, kegs of powder, and muskets. The cargo was loaded, the holds were filled and finally the heavy kegs of ale and cider were lashed to the decks.

There was one final business to attend to before the ships could set sail: the Queen's signature was still needed on the charter of what had now become known as the Governor and Company of Merchants trading to the East Indies. In this document, drawn up by the merchants themselves, they were to be granted a total monopoly of trade over 'traffic and merchandise to the East Indies, the countries and ports of Asia and Africa, and to and from all the islands, ports, towns, and places of Asia, Africa, and America, or any of them beyond the Cape of Bona Esperanza [Good Hope] and the Straits of Magellan'.

On 31 December 1600, it was at last signed by the

Queen. Valid for fifteen years, it conferred massive powers upon a small group of men – 218 in total. The merchant adventurers were given the exclusive right to trade with the East Indies – a vague geographical term which included the entirety of South-East Asia – without any interference from the Crown. They could take as much bullion out of the country as was necessary, found trading posts wherever they wished, and govern as they saw fit. In return for these sweeping powers they were to furnish a fleet of six ships annually.

The few regulations imposed upon this first trading expedition were drawn up by the merchants rather than the Crown. Lancaster was warned to be on his guard against any sailors who attempted to dabble in private trade and told that 'due inquisition shall be made into all and every ship, by search of all chests, boxes, packs, packets, writing, and other means whereby discovery may be made of this breach of present ordenance'. Unfortunately, this stricture proved impossible to enforce. Individual sailors were paid next to nothing for the long and hazardous voyage and many set sail with the full intention of smuggling home a sackful or two of nutmeg.

The Queen coined new money specifically for the Company. Minted at the Tower of London and bearing her arms on one side and a portcullis on the other, it soon became known as portcullis money. She also granted the merchants a new flag which, with its blue field and background of thirteen red and white stripes, prefigured the one adopted by the Thirteen Colonies of America some 175 years later.

On a cold February day in 1601, Lancaster's five ships slipped slowly down the Thames. They made a colourful sight as they passed the wharves at Woolwich. Bedecked with streamers, pennants and colourful bunting, they flew from their main mast the blood-red cross of St George. The banks of the river were lined with merchants, relatives and well-wishers, a crowd and a send-off not repeated until 1610 when Nathaniel Courthope would leave London on the greatest sailing ship ever built by the East India Company.

Scarcely had Lancaster's vessels reached the Thames Estuary than the wind dropped and for almost two months the sails hung loose. It was not until Easter that his fleet finally reached Dartmouth. Delayed again at Torbay, Lancaster sent instructions to each of the ships listing ports and harbours where they should rendezvous in the event of becoming separated. And then, with the wind once more filling their sails, the ships set off down the English Channel and had an uneventful passage all the way to Gran Canaria.

Here, the wind again died and for more than a month the fleet floated idly at sea, inching slowly towards the equator. Just two degrees short of the line Lancaster had a stroke of good fortune. A lone Portuguese ship, accidentally separated from her accompanying carracks, was spied on the horizon. The five English vessels circled her then closed for the kill. She was boarded, her crew disarmed and a team of men sent down into the hold. She proved to be a very rich prize: she was laden with 146 butts of wine and 176 jars of oil and her captured cargo was shared out among the English ships according to the number of men on board. And then, without further ado, they set sail once again.

As with Lancaster's first voyage men began to fall sick as soon as they crossed into the southern hemisphere and it was not long before 'the weakness of men was so great that in some of the ships the merchants took their turn at the helm and went into the top to take in the topsails.' But while men grew weaker on the smaller vessels, the diarist on board Lancaster's *Red Dragon* could not help noticing that her crew were completely immune to the illness. 'And the reason why the general's men stood in better health than the men of other ships was this; he [Lancaster] brought to sea with him certain bottles of the juice of lemons, which he gave to each one, as long as it would last, three spoonfuls every morning, fasting; not suffering them to eat anything after it till noon ... by this means the general cured many of his men and preserved the rest.' How Lancaster stumbled upon the cure for scurvy remains a mystery; it may be that he noticed the spectacular recovery that men made as soon as they were able to add fresh fruit and vegetables to their diet of salted food. On his first voyage the on-board chronicler Henry May had observed that one particularly ill crew member had made a full recovery after eating the oranges and lemons found on St Helena. Tragically Lancaster's cure was soon forgotten and more than 170 years were to pass before Captain Cook rediscovered the beneficial effects of citrus fruit in combating scurvy.

Although scurvy and sickness were a constant concern, life on board had its lighter moments. Journals and diaries make frequent mention of the play-acting, singing and clowning around that enlivened the tedium of the voyage. Music was extremely popular and on one vessel 'a virginal was brought for two to play upon at once.' This proved a great success for no sooner had the music commenced than 'the jacks skip up and down in such a manner as they will.' A later expedition even boasted a cornet player who used to regularly play for his colleagues. So accomplished was he at the instrument, and so wide was his repertoire, that on arriving in India he found himself blowing his brass for the Great Moghul himself.

The merry-making was helped along by the huge quantities of alcohol consumed by the crew. Although attempts were made to regulate the drinking, it was universally ignored until men began to drop dead of liver disorders caused by the 'inordinate drinking of a wine called tastie [toddy] distilled from the palmetto tree'.

After merry-making their way across the southern Atlantic, Lancaster's expedition finally slipped into South Africa's Table Bay on 9 September 1601, where the commander knew he could barter for fresh meat and provisions. As had happened on his first voyage the crew viewed the natives as wild barbarians who were laughably easy to exploit. Neither side was able to communicate with each other for, 'their speech is wholly uttered through the throat, and they cluck with their tongues in such sort that, in seven weeks which we remained here in this place, the sharpest wit among us could not learn one word of their language.'

Instead, the English sailors 'spake to them in the cattle's language'. When they wanted to buy oxen they would say 'moo'. When they wanted sheep, they would say 'baa'. The animals cost next to nothing: the natives did not demand silver or gold but seemed content with a couple of old iron hoops. After twelve days, the ship's company had bought more than a thousand sheep and several dozen oxen.

When his ships finally set sail Lancaster must have been pleased that his time in Table Bay had passed without incident. Aware that this was an essential revictualling point for ships heading east he did everything possible to ensure that negotiations with the natives progressed smoothly. Such a policy was in stark contrast to that of

Elizabethan sailors were fascinated by the primitive natives of southern Africa. 'The world doth not yield a more heathenish people,' wrote one Englishman. 'Their neckes were adorned with greasie tripes which sometimes they would pull off and eat raw. When we threw away their beasts' entrails, they would eat them half raw, the blood lothsomely slavering.'

Cornelis Houtman who had treated the natives of southern Africa with brutality and paid for it with the loss of thirteen crew.

Although every inch of space on the vessels was taken up with fresh supplies, the hot southern climate was still taking its toll on the crew and it was decided to land at the island of Cirne – now known as Mauritius – where lemons were said to be plentiful. Unfortunately, the wind unexpectedly changed direction and the little fleet was blown towards Madagascar instead. Arriving on Christmas Day in the bay of Atongill a reconnaissance party discovered a series of carvings on a rock close to the water. It had long been the practice to carve upon rocks the dates of arrival and departure of ships so that straggling vessels might know the fate of the rest of their fleet. From these carvings, Lancaster discovered to his dismay that five Dutch ships had called here just two months earlier. They had lost more than two hundred men to dysentery while they lay at anchor.

History soon began to repeat itself on the English ships. First the *Red Dragon's* master's mate died, then the preacher, the surgeon, and ten crew members. Others suffered more violent deaths: as the master's mate was lowered into the ground, the captain of the *Ascension* rowed ashore to attend the funeral. While doing so, he had the misfortune to enter the line of musket-shot that was frequently fired on such occasions and both he and the boatswain's mate were killed, 'so that they that went to see the buriall of another,' records the ship's diarist, 'and were both buried there themselves'.

It was a most unfortunate accident; Captain William Brund was popular among the sea dogs he commanded and was sorely missed. His death reinforced the growing feeling that Madagascar was not a place to linger, so as soon as the *Red Dragon's* little pinnace had been assembled (it was brought out from England in kit form) the fleet once more set sail.

The expanse of the Indian Ocean presented Lancaster with fewer problems than the Atlantic. A near-catastrophe was avoided when the pinnace detected the reefs and shoals surrounding the Chagos Archipelago and by the second week of May the ships had caught sight of the remote Nicobar Islands – missed on Lancaster's first voyage – where they resolved to revictual. To their surprise they discovered that the fantastical writings of medieval travellers, which spoke of men with horns and green faces, appeared to be correct. According to the ship's journal, the island priest 'had upon his head a pair of horns turning backward', while others had 'their faces painted green, black, and yellow, and their horns also painted with the same colour; and behind them, upon their buttocks, a tail hanging down, very much like the manner as in some painted clothes we paint the devil in our country'.

It is ironic that just as sceptics in England were beginning to question the veracity of accounts by medieval 'explorers' like Sir John Mandeville, genuine travellers were reporting sights that bore witness to their more outlandish tales. Sir Walter Ralegh was one of those sceptics who changed his opinion of Mandeville after hearing the reports filtering back from the mysterious East. 'Mandeville's reports were holden for fables many yeeres,' he wrote, 'and yet since the East Indies were discovered, we find his relations true of such things as heretofore were held incredible.'

On 5 June 1602, more than sixteen months after leaving Woolwich, Lancaster's fleet finally arrived at the Sumatran port of Achin. A rich, powerful and cosmopolitan city, its sea power enabled it to exert influence over the western approaches to the East Indies and the Malay Peninsula. Although its shipping proved unable to compete with the Portuguese fleet anchored off Malacca on the far side of the Straits, Achin was nevertheless a vibrant commercial centre.

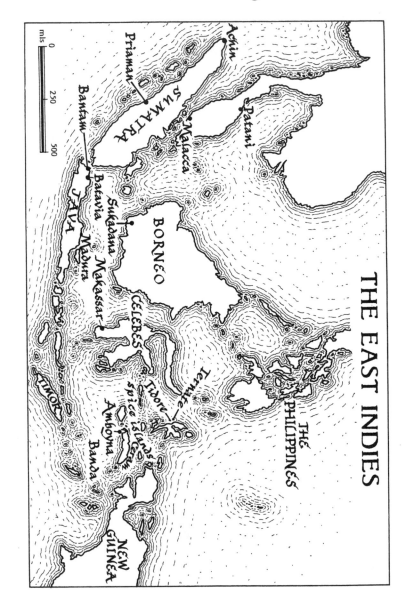

THE EAST INDIES

When Lancaster arrived here he counted no fewer than sixteen ships at anchor, including vessels from Gujarat, Bengal, Calicut and the Malay Peninsula.

Lancaster's chief pilot, John Davis, had visited Achin on his voyage with Cornelis Houtman and vividly recorded his meeting with the city's powerful ruler Ala-uddin Shah. The Sultan, he had discovered, was a keen Anglophile and had chatted enthusiastically to Houtman about England's seafaring victories – an enthusiasm not reciprocated by the Dutchman. When Ala-uddin learned that Houtman had a genuine Englishman on board he demanded to meet him immediately. 'He inquired much of England,' wrote Davis in his diary, 'of the Queen, of her Pashas, and how she could hold wars with so great a King as the Spaniard (for he thinks that Europe is all Spanish.) In these his demands he was fully satisfied, as it seemed to his great good liking.'

While in audience with the Sultan, Davis was gathering important information about Ala-uddin's personality and tastes; information which proved invaluable when he arrived back in England. Not only was the Company able to draft a suitable letter to the Sultan written in Queen Elizabeth's own hand, they were also able to buy him presents that were likely to find favour. He was a man of extravagant tastes; 'a lusty man, but exceeding gross and fat' – according to Davis – who was more than one hundred years old, 'as they say'. According to local tradition, he had been brought up a humble fisherman but, courageous and daring in wartime, was given command of the army and married to a relative of the reigning monarch. Ala-uddin promptly murdered the king and assumed the purple, ruling the country with an iron fist. Born to fight, he had held Queen Elizabeth in the highest regard ever since news of the Spanish Armada's defeat had filtered across the

Indian Ocean. Now, with Lancaster's fleet anchored in the bay, he was keen to meet one of her most trusted servants.

John Middleton, captain of the *Hector*, was the first to step ashore; he told the Sultan he had been sent by Lancaster to inform His Majesty that their fleet bore a letter from the Queen of England. The Sultan was most pleased and, presenting Middleton with a turban wrought with gold, he invited Lancaster to come ashore after he had rested himself for a day.

Lancaster acquitted himself well and, if the accounts are accurate, handled the Sultan with aplomb. Stepping ashore, he was welcomed by Ala-uddin's messengers who immediately demanded the Queen's letter so they could take it to the King. Lancaster refused, saying that such a letter, from so powerful a monarch, might be delivered only by himself.

The Sultan, too, was anxious to impress upon Lancaster the magnificence of his court and lavished every available resource on the English entourage:

> He presently sent six great elephants, with many trumpets, drums, and streamers, with many people, to accompany the generall [Lancaster] to the court, so that the presse was exceeding great. The biggest of these elephants was about thirteene or fourteene foot high; which had a small castle like a coach upon his back, covered with crimson velvet. In the middle thereof was a great basin of gold, and a peece of silke exceedingly richly wrought to cover it, under which Her Majestie's letter was put. The generall was mounted upon another of the elephants. Some of his attendants rode; others went on foote. But when he came to the court gate, there a nobleman stayed the

general, till he had gone in to know the king's further pleasure ... And when the general came to the king's presence, he made his obeysance after the manner of the country, declaring that hee was sent from the most mightie Queene of England to congratulate with High Highnesse, and treat with him concerning a peace and amitie with His Majestie, if it pleased him to entertaine the same.

First, Ala-uddin was presented with the gifts: a basin of solid silver with a fountain in the middle, a huge silver goblet, a rich looking glass, a case of fine pistols, a magnificent headpiece, and a finely wrought embroidered belt. The Sultan received all these graciously, but was particularly taken by the fan of feathers he was given. He called for one of his attendant mistresses and ordered that she fan him continually. This, the cheapest of all the gifts, was a runaway success: 'the thing that most pleased him'.

Now it was time to present the Queen's letter which, it was hoped, would make a favourable impression. Wrapped in silk, decorated with fabulous swirls of calligraphy and delivered to the Sultan in a gold ewer securely fastened to a huge bull elephant, it was given the most dramatic billing possible.

The letter's contents were, by turn, flattering, obsequious, anti-Portuguese and businesslike. Pandering to the Sultan's vanity, but at the same time imploring favourable trading privileges, it described Ala-uddin as 'our loving brother', recognising 'the honorable and truly royall fame which hath hither stretched'. After glorifying him for his 'humane and noble usage of strangers', it went on to attack the Portuguese and Spanish who 'pretend themselves to be monarchs and absolute lords of all these kingdomes and provinces'. Finally, after more than two pages of preamble, it arrived at the substance. Queen Elizabeth I, it said, would like to begin regular commerce with Ala-uddin, to settle merchants in his capital and open a warehouse for the stockpiling of provisions. 'Trade,' it grandiloquently informed His Highness, 'not only breeds intercourse and exchange of merchandise ... but also engenders love and friendship betwixt all men.'

Reading it in private Ala-uddin was captivated by the Queen's sentiments and found himself agreeing whole-heartedly. He told Lancaster that he was well pleased with what he had read and accepted all the Queen's requests. Once the deal had been signed it was time for the Sultan's banquet, a dizzying affair in which prodigious quantities of food and alcohol were followed into the banqueting room by a troupe of the Sultan's damsels and musicians. The food was served on beaten golden platters while the arak, a fiery and extremely alcoholic rice wine, was knocked back in copious quantities. Throughout the meal the Sultan, who sat aloft in a gallery, kept offering toasts to his new-found friend. Lancaster had to beg Ala-uddin that he might mix his arak with water, 'for a little will serve to bring one asleep'. The Sultan, gracious as ever, consented.

Next came the cabaret. Sultan Ala-uddin 'caused his damosels to come forth and dance, and his women to play musicke unto them; and these women were richly attired and adorned with bracelets and jewels'. This performance was a special treat, 'for these are not usually seene of any but such as the king will greatly honour.' But the entertainments did not end here; there were endless other activities to amuse the newcomers including a lengthy bout of cock-fighting, the Sultan's favourite sport. And although not recorded in the ships' journals, it is quite possible that some of the more daring crew members took part in the celebrated Achinese speciality, the sub-aqua drinking bouts in which guests perched on low stools in a river while court butlers served generous beakers of arak.

Although Lancaster was delighted by the Sultan's reception he soon grew concerned that he had yet to buy a single ounce of spice. Worse, he now learned that pepper – far from costing four pieces-of-eight for the hundredweight – was actually being sold for almost twenty. Realising that he could not hope to fill his ships in Achin, Lancaster returned to the Sultan and diplomatically asked for his permission to set sail for other ports. Ala-uddin agreed, but there was an important condition attached. 'Thou must bring me a fair Portugall maiden when thou returnest, and then I am pleased.' Lancaster smiled, the Sultan chuckled, and the English ships prepared to depart.

Lancaster sent the *Susan* to the port of Priaman on Sumatra's southern coast while he, together with the rest of the fleet, sailed into the Straits. Almost immediately he spied a huge Portuguese carrack heading for Malacca and opened fire with the *Red Dragon's* great guns. Six cannonballs were all it took to disable her; her main yard was split in two and crashed onto the deck with a tremendous boom. Completely marooned, the *Santo Antonio* gave up the fight and surrendered to the English. When Lancaster saw what he had captured he rubbed his eyes in disbelief: she was laden with Indian calicoes and batiks which, though almost valueless in England, were worth a small fortune in the ports of South-East Asia. Here, at last, was something which could readily be exchanged for nutmeg, cloves and pepper.

It took a full six days to unload the *Santo Antonio* and, by the time all her goods were stowed aboard the English

James Lancaster attacks the Portuguese Santo Antonio *in the Straits of Malacca. He was astonished when he saw what he had captured: she was richly laden with calicoes and batiks worth a fortune in the Spice Islands.*

ships, Lancaster realised it was imperative that he found a supply depot, a base for future trading, where the cloth could be stored. Achin, he now knew, was useless for although an important centre for trade it was not the source of the spices he was seeking. He decided to head for the spice port of Bantam on the north-west coast of Java, but thought it diplomatic to first return to Ala-uddin to bid him farewell.

The Sultan congratulated Lancaster on his success against the Portuguese, 'and jestingly said he had forgotten the most important business that he requested at his hands, which was the fair Portugal maiden he desired him to bring with him at his return. To whom the general [Lancaster] answered that there was none so worthy that merited to be so presented. Therewithall the king smiled and said: if there be anything here in my kingdom may pleasure thee, I would be glad to gratify thy goodwill.'

The request for maidens was not an unusual one among the potentates of the East. To ensure their harems retained an international flavour, they liked to procure youthful damsels from as far afield as possible. Ala-uddin's successor took his harem very seriously indeed and put in a request to London for an English rose or two. This put the Company's puritanical merchants into something of a quandary: if they sent two girls they would be seen to be condoning bigamy and that was unthinkable. There was also the problem of religion. Achin was an Islamic country and there was a theological objection to uniting a good Christian girl in holy matrimony with a Mohammedan. Ironically, the directors' most difficult task – that of finding a suitable virgin – was easily overcome. A London gentleman 'of honourable parentage' offered his daughter without further ado. She was, he explained, 'of excellent parts for musicke, her needle, and good discourse, also very beautiful and personable'. He even wrote a lengthy tract justifying mixed marriages. What the girl in question thought about all this has unfortunately not been recorded but she probably heaved a sigh of relief when King James I declined to sanction the presentation of such an unorthodox gift.

Lancaster was on the brink of departing from Achin when the increasingly eccentric Ala-uddin had an even stranger request. He asked the English captain if he possessed a book of the Psalms of David and, as soon as a copy had been produced, begged Lancaster that he and his court might sing one as a duet. This done, the Sultan wished the English crew his best wishes for the rest of their voyage. His last act was to present Lancaster with a letter addressed to Queen Elizabeth I and written in fine Arabic calligraphy. So magnificent was this calligraphy, in fact, that its eventual translator, Reverend William Bedwell of St Ethelburga's in Bishopgate Street, could scarcely read it. He did eventually produce a draft in English. It was absurdly grandiose and full of hyperbole and Queen Elizabeth was given a string of honorific titles. By the time the letter arrived back in England, she was no longer alive to read it.

Lancaster's fleet sailed from Achin in November 1602. The *Ascension*, by now fully laden with pepper and spice, set course for England while the rest of the ships headed towards Java, meeting with the *Susan* on the way. She had fared well in the port of Priaman and her captain had bought a large stock of spices for an extremely competitive price: in Bantam, Lancaster was to find the prices lower still.

Bantam's king was a boy of ten or eleven years. After showing him all the usual courtesies and presenting the customary gifts, Lancaster turned to his Protector to settle the finer points of trade. The English merchants were cordially received and prices for pepper and spice were fixed. A 'factory' or warehouse was established so that the English could unload their wares, and commerce was begun with enthusiasm. A problem of local thieving threatened to sour the buying and selling, but after Lancaster had slaughtered six robbers – a right he had been granted by the Protector – the thieving halted completely.

For five weeks spices were bought and bartered until two hundred and thirty sackfuls had been loaded onto the ships and there was not an inch of space left on board. The local natives were particularly curious to know why the

English required such huge quantities of pepper and there
was much scratching of heads until it was finally agreed
that English houses were so cold that the walls were
plastered with crushed pepper in order to produce heat.

One sad episode marred the stay in Bantam. The languid
heat was taking its toll on the men who had gone ashore,
while those who remained on their vessels, including
Captain John Middleton, 'fell sicke aboord his ship in the
road'. Middleton's fever grew steadily worse until
Lancaster, himself not well, became alarmed. Paying a visit
to his old friend, he watched Middleton pace slowly up and
down the deck, growing weaker with every step. That
night, the *Hector* lost its captain and Middleton was buried
at Bantam. The crew, though used to the sight of death,
wept openly.

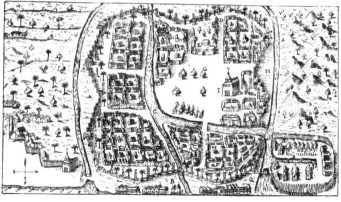

*The Javanese port of Bantam was the headquarters of the English in
the East Indies. Known as 'that stinking stew', the sailors had to
brave the constant threat of head-hunting, as well as malaria and
dysentery. 'Bantam is not a place to recover men that are sick,' wrote
one, 'but to kill men that come thither in health.'*

It was time to depart for England. Lancaster was aware that if trade between England and the East Indies was to succeed it was essential to establish a permanent base in the East. So, shortly before setting sail, he appointed eight men and three 'factors' or merchants to stay behind in Bantam, leaving in their charge all the goods he had so far been unable to sell.

He had also realised that the price of spices fell sharply the further east he sailed. The prices in Achin were astronomical while in Bantam they were much lower. He was certain that if he had been able to sail even further east, to the Banda Islands, the very source of nutmeg, those prices would dip still further. Before he left Bantam Lancaster therefore instructed the men staying behind to sail eastwards in the forty-ton pinnace left in their charge and buy as much nutmeg, mace and cloves as was possible.

In February 1603, the fleet set sail for England with a thunderous blast from their cannon. The first half of the return voyage proved remarkably uneventful and it was not until the ships reached Madagascar that they were buffeted by their first storm which so smashed their ships 'that they were leakie all the voyage after'. Two weeks later they were hit by a 'very sore storme which continued all the night, and the seas did so beate upon the ships quarter that it shooke all the iron-worke of her rudder'. Huge waves raged around the ships, lashing their weakened hulls and allowing water to seep into the holds. Early on the morning of the fourth the rudder of the *Red Dragon* 'brake cleane from the sterne of our shippe and presently sunke into the sea'. Unable to steer, 'our ship drove up and downe in the sea like a wrecke, which way soever the wind carried her.' Every attempt to make a new rudder failed and, as the rain turned to 'hayle and snow and sleetie cold weather', the men began to abandon all hope of surviving. 'It was a great miserie unto us,' wrote one, 'that pinched us exceeding sore, so that our case was miserable and very desperate.' Even Lancaster felt the end was near. Descending into his cabin, he penned a letter to the Company in London, a letter whose unfailing spirit would become legendary among the sailors of the East India Company. 'I cannot tell where you should looke for me,' he wrote, 'because I live at the devotion of the winds and seas.' And then, sending the letter over to the *Hector*, he bade her head for England leaving his own ship to her fate. The *Hector*'s captain refused and shadowed the *Red Dragon* until the storm finally abated. And so, side by side, the ships sailed first to St Helena and then into the English Channel.

On 11 September 1603, some two years and seven months after they had set sail from the Thames, the vessels finally anchored off the Downs, 'for which thanked be Almightie God, who hath delivered us from infinite perils and dangers in this long and tedious navigation'.

Compared to previous expeditions, this one had been an unqualified success. Wherever the Portuguese had been encountered in the Indian Ocean they had been of little threat – indeed the English were proving remarkably adept at disabling their unwieldy carracks. In the spice port of Bantam, Lancaster had found few difficulties in acquiring a full lading of spice and had even been allowed to build a small warehouse close to the harbour and leave behind a permanent staff. Even more impressive was the fact that all five of his ships had returned safely and more than a million pounds of spices had been successfully brought into the kingdom. But Lancaster had his misgivings. He had lost almost half his men, including his friends John Middleton and William Brund, and had failed to reach the islands far to the east of Bantam. As he kneeled before the King and received his knighthood, Sir James could only hope that the men he left behind – those eight crew and three merchants – would have the courage to sail to the Banda Islands in their tiny pinnace.

CHAPTER FOUR

IN THE PAWS
OF THE
LION

THE ENGLISH TRADERS left in Bantam watched the departure of Lancaster's fleet with deep misgivings. They had no idea when they might see their next English vessel but it was certain to be at least two years. In the meantime they were in a wholly unfamiliar environment, living in this fly-blown port on sufferance of the boy-king's Protector and terrified that they would soon succumb to the same sickness that had killed so many of their colleagues.

Lancaster had only reinforced their sense of vulnerability when he wrote down the hierachy of command to be adhered to if and when they died. William Starkey was put in overall charge with Thomas Morgan as his deputy, but 'if it please God to lay his hand upon you and take you out of this world' then Edmund Scott was to take control. In the event such caution proved all too necessary. Starkey died in June 1603, having already outlived Morgan by two months. Only Edmund Scott survived to see the arrival of the East India Company's second expedition and, to his evident relief, was allowed to join the fleet when it headed back to England.

Lancaster showed a similar concern for the moral well-being of his men. Bantam was infamous in the East for its loose women and lax morals and an air of profligacy hung over the town like the plague of typhoid that frequently descended on its inhabitants. He ordered Starkey that 'you meet together in the morninges and eveninges in prayer. God, whom ye serve, shall the better bless you in all your affairs.' He also begged them to 'agree together lovingly, like sober men [and] govern yourselves so that there be no brabbles among you for any cause'.

These men, who for so long had complained about the strict daily routine on board ship, now found themselves comforted by an ordered existence. The day began at dawn with William Starkey offering prayers of thanksgiving, and this was followed by a light breakfast. The main meal was at midday at which all the factors would sit together at a long table, seated in strict accordance with his position. The rice, mutton and tropical fruit which they ate, all of which was bartered in Bantam's souks, was washed down with locally distilled arak, a fiery spirit that was glugged in considerable quantity by these drink-hardened men. One captain who arrived in Bantam a few years later professed himself horrified at the drunken behaviour of the factors. 'If any be found by excessive drinking or otherwise like to prove a scandal to our nation,' he said, 'use first sharp reprehensions, and if that work not reformation then by the first ship send him home with a writing showing the reasons thereof.'

Once the English were familiar with life in Bantam they prepared to carry out Lancaster's instructions. Three of the factors were to remain in the city and buy pepper in preparation for the Company's second voyage. The rest of the men were to sail to the remote Banda Islands under the command of Master Keche and acquire as much spice as was available. Lancaster was most specific in his request

The native rulers of Bantam travelled in chariots pulled by white buffalo. Dissolute and quarrelsome, their irrational behaviour so terrified the English that 'our men in their sleepe would suddainely leape out of their beddes and ketch their weapons.'

for nutmeg: 'Have you a great care to receive such as be good,' he told them, 'for the smallest and rotten nutmegs be worth nothing at home.' Such a warning was born from experience. It had long been the custom of wily merchants to fill their sacks with old and rotten spices, as well as dust and twigs, in order to increase the weight and swell their profits.

The little pinnace hoisted its sails soon after the English fleet had departed from Bantam and gingerly headed east into uncharted waters. But no sooner had it come within sight of the 'spiceries' than contrary winds began to blow and the ship drifted off course. What happened next remains unclear for the report written by the men has been lost and only a couple of letters survive. Struck by 'contrarietie of wynde', the ship spent two months 'beating up and down in the seas' in a desperate attempt to reach the outlying Banda Islands. This proved wholly unsuccessful until a tremendous storm washed the boat up on Run's remote shores. The hardy English sailors were given a friendly welcome by the islanders who thought them too few to be of any threat. They were soon busily trading nutmeg with these storm-tossed sailors and even allowed them to construct a flimsy bamboo and thatch warehouse on the island's northern coastline.

Lancaster's fleet arrived back to a London steeped in gloom. The capital was in the grip of the plague and the streets and alleys around the Company's house in Philpot Lane were silent but for the rattle of tumbrels and barrows bearing corpses out of the city. The plague had not spared the Company directors: two had already succumbed to the disease while others had fled London for the safety of the countryside.

Hearing that the first of Lancaster's ships had arrived in Plymouth the Company directors bestirred themselves. Bestowing the princely sum of five pounds to the local courier 'for his pains in riding hither with the first report of the coming of the Ascension', they sent strict orders back to Plymouth that the ship's cargo was not to be touched until she was safely moored in the Thames. Even then they could not be too careful; the six porters charged with unloading the ship were instructed to wear pocketless

(Opposite) *James Lancaster returned to a London stricken with the plague. To the voyage-hardened crew, death was treated with a cavalier contempt. 'Walker died laughing,' reads one account. 'Woodes and I staked two pieces-of-eight on his body, and I won.'*

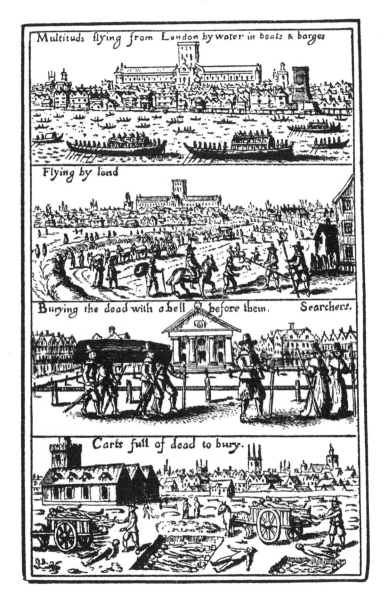

101

suits, just in case they should feel the urge to filch some spice.

The *Ascension* had made speedy progress back to England and arrived in advance of the other ships. Lancaster, together with the rest of the fleet, sailed up the Thames in September 1603, by which time almost 38,000 Londoners had fallen victim to the plague. There were none of the cheering crowds that had seen them off two-and-a-half years previously. The wharves lay silent and the dockyards were closed for Londoners were too scared to venture out of doors. The playwright Thomas Dekker summed up the sombre mood that hung over the city in his ironically titled *The Wonderfull Yeare*:

> No musick now is heard but bells,
> And all their tunes are sick mens knells;
> And every stroake the bell does toll,
> Up to heaven it windes a soule.

Even the physicians had fled for their lives, leaving only a handful of brave practitioners to sell their 'pomanders and what not' and reap enormous profits from their nutmeg potions: 'I confesse they are costly,' explained one doctor to his ailing client, 'but cheape medicines are as dear as death.'

To the voyage-hardened crew, death had become so commonplace that it was treated with a cavalier contempt. 'Walker died laughing,' reads one journal. 'Woodes and I staked two pieces-of-eight on his body, and after a long play, I won.' But one death caused many a sailor to shed tears: just a few months earlier Queen Elizabeth I, the last of the great Tudor monarchs, had passed away at her palace in Richmond. There was now a new ruler on the throne – Elizabeth's haughty Scottish cousin King James – who showed far less sympathy than his predecessor to the likes of the common burghers who formed the backbone of the East India Company.

Despite the general gloom, Lancaster was given an enthusiastic reception on his return and duly received his knighthood from the King. But the pressing problem facing the merchants was how, in the midst of the worst plague London could remember, to dispose of more than a million pounds in weight of pepper. Cash was desperately needed to pay off the sailors who had survived the voyage, the subscribers were anxiously clamouring for money, and preparations for the second voyage were unthinkable until the present stock had been sold.

Unfortunately, the financial institutions of the city had been paralysed by the plague for those dealers who were still alive had also fled to the country. Worse still, the King himself had recently acquired a huge quantity of pepper – probably the contents of a captured Portuguese carrack – and was keen to dispose of it as quickly as possible. Citing his kingly prerogative, and invoking a royal edict, he declared that the merchant adventurers could not sell a single peppercorn until he had first disposed of his own stock.

The Company was in dire straits and its future hung on a thread. It seemed ironic to many that it was so woefully short of funds as to threaten its survival at the very moment when the first voyage had ended in such triumph. A single event saved the day. When Queen Elizabeth had originally granted the merchants their charter she had specified that it was on the understanding that a trading expedition should be sent to the 'spiceries' annually. Now, sensing the merchants' vulnerability, the Privy Council threatened to hand over the Company's trading rights to another individual unless a second expedition set sail immediately.

No names were mentioned but it was clear whom they had in mind: Sir Edward Michelborne, whose name had been so humiliatingly deleted from the Company's lists, had nursed his grievances for long enough. He now wanted revenge.

The Company was shocked by the possibility of losing their privileges and acted with uncharacteristic decision, despatching a beadle to all the city merchants to collect subscriptions for a second voyage. The merchants were understandably reluctant to finance a new voyage before they had reaped the profits of the old and a mere £11,000 was subscribed. It was therefore decided that everyone who had invested £250 in the first voyage was obliged to subscribe a further £200 for the second. It was not a popular move but it saved the Company in its hour of need and within a few months preparations were under way for a second voyage.

Lancaster had no intention of commanding this new expedition: wealthy, knighted and understandably reluctant to tempt fate by sailing to the East Indies for a third time, he graciously accepted the desk-bound post of director. He was placed in charge of planning the new expedition and his influence is everywhere apparent: although the ships were to call at Bantam in order to rendezvous with the English factors, their mission was to sail east to the 'Molloccos', or Spice Islands, which Lancaster himself had failed to reach. Here, the ships were to buy the most valuable of the spices, nutmeg and cloves, and leave factors behind in anticipation of the Company's third voyage. Lancaster's instructions once again placed special emphasis on the crews' spiritual well-being and asked that concern be shown for the men he had left behind, particularly chief factor William Starkey who was to be 'provided for and well placed in such ship as he shall be shipped as a man that we hold in good regard and to be respected accordingly'. He did not know that Starkey was long since dead.

The man charged with leading this second expedition was Henry Middleton who had sailed under Lancaster's command on the first venture and proved himself to be both capable and trustworthy. Energetic and resolute, he was always respected by his subordinates and his leadership never came under fire, even when he guided his fleet through dangerous and uncharted seas. Although given to impetuosity and hot-headedness, he dealt with both the Dutch and Portuguese, as well as the native chieftains, with considerable diplomacy.

With no shortage of funds to finance the voyage it was decided to send four ships to the East – the *Hector, Ascension* and *Susan*, with the trusty *Red Dragon* once again serving as flagship. Following Lancaster's instructions to the letter, Middleton headed directly to Bantam where he found the few remaining Englishmen in a desperate plight after receiving much harsh treatment from the local traders. The arrival of his ships on 22 December 1604 was the best Christmas present these men could have asked for. 'Towards evening we descried our ships coming into the road, to all our extreaordinary great joy.' So wrote Edmund Scott, by now the most senior Englishman still alive in the city. 'But when we came aboard of our admiral, and saw their great weakness, also hearing the weakness of the other three ships, it grieved us much.'

Middleton went straight to business on his arrival at the port. Presenting the boy-king with a hotchpotch of presents – including two gilt cups, a spoon and six muskets – he struck a deal, loaded the *Hector* and *Susan* with pepper, and sent them directly back to England. His last task before bidding them farewell won him widespread popularity from his crew. Having listened to endless complaints about the tiresome habits of Master Surfflict, the preacher on the *Red Dragon*, Middleton decided to despatch him back to England. He had proved completely useless on the outward journey and few tears were shed when he dropped dead on the return.

More deaths were soon to follow. Middleton continued eastwards to the Spice Islands as instructed but no sooner had he left Bantam than his ship was afflicted by the 'blody flux' – a life-threatening strain of dysentery. With the list of casualties growing by the day, the ship's journal becomes little more than a roll-call for the dead: 'The seventeenth day died of the flux William Lewed, John Jenkens, and Samuel Porter ... the twentieth dyed Henry Stiles our master carpenter, and James Varnam, and John Iberson, all of the fluxe. The twenty-second day died of the fluxe James Hope; the twenty-fourth dyed John Leay and Robert Whitthers.' The atmosphere on board was sombre indeed and still the men kept dying. Three more succumbed on the following day, then another two, and by the time the ships sighted land another five men had died of the 'flux'. It was with considerable relief that the ships at last arrived at Amboyna, a clove-fringed island that lay at the very heart of the 'spiceries'.

Middleton stepped ashore to greet the local king and entreat him for a trading deal but was promptly informed that all trade was forbidden without prior permission of the Portuguese garrison stationed on the island. The English commander now showed his colours as an accomplished diplomat. Aware that the Portuguese were unlikely to part with their cloves, especially to their old adversaries the English, he sent a letter to their captain informing him that there was at last peace between the two nations and that he 'desired that the like might be between us, for that our comming was to seeke trade with them'. What he said was true: King James I and King Philip III had indeed signed a peace treaty but Middleton can hardly have been aware of this for it had been agreed more than five months after he left England.

The news had the desired effect and the Portuguese commander, safely ensconced in the stout bastion that guarded Amboyna's natural harbour, sent word of his agreement to a deal. But before the two men even had the chance to shake hands, they learned that there was trouble on the horizon. In the far distance, and fast disappearing into the twilight, a formidable fleet of vessels could be seen approaching the island. To Middleton's dismay, these were neither Portuguese nor English: this veritable armada was flying the Dutch colours from its flagship.

When the sun rose the following day there were no less than nine ships in the offing, together with an auxiliary fleet of pinnaces and sloops. These slowly sailed into the harbour and 'came to an anker within a musket shot of the fort'. The Portuguese commander immediately ingratiated himself with his Dutch counterpart, asking him 'wherefore they came thither' and stating that 'if they came in friendshippe they should be welcome'. But the Dutch had certainly not come in friendship and their general 'made answer that his comming thither was to have that castel from them; and willed them to deliver him the keyes [which,] if they refused to do, he willed them to provide for themselves to defend it, for he was minded to have it before he departed'.

Middleton now found himself in an unenviable position. It was clear that his fleet was no match for the

Dutch, but if he went ashore and joined forces with the Portuguese there was a slim chance that together they could successfully defend the island. If so, the dividends would be rich indeed for Amboyna's mountainous interior was thickly forested in clove trees. But before he had time to reach a decision he learned that the battle for Amboyna was over. Although the Portuguese bragged that 'they would never yeild up their fort, but fight it out to the last man', they capitulated after a short bombardment and the only death occurred when their commander mysteriously expired. His unhappily married wife later took credit for his death, explaining that she had poisoned him in order to save his honour and reputation.

With Amboyna lost to the Dutch, Middleton put to sea with not a single clove on board. He was growing increasingly concerned by the difficulties of trading in the 'spiceries' and wisely decided that his two vessels, the *Red Dragon* and the *Ascension*, should separate and sail for different islands. While the *Ascension* headed south to the unknown Banda Group, he directed his own ship to the most northerly of the Spice Islands, Ternate and Tidore, which had been loosely under the control of the Portuguese for some decades.

As the *Red Dragon* approached these islands, Middleton heard the crack of musket-shot split the air and saw two galleys 'making all the speed possible toward us'. The foremost vessel contained the King of Ternate while behind him, and hot on his heels, were dozens of pirates rowing furiously and firing with their guns. Realising that the king would be an invaluable ally should his life be saved, Middleton immediately ordered the *Red Dragon*'s sails to be hauled down and ropes to be thrown over the side. In the nick of time the king was pulled aboard the vessel, but not before his oarsmen had been captured by the pirates and 'put to the sword, saving three men which saved their lives by swimming'.

Middleton for once had the upper hand. Leading the King down to his private quarters, he handed him one of the letters of trade and friendship drafted by King James and, without even having time to affix the King of Ternate's name to the top, kindly requested him to sign it. Although quaking with fear, the king hesitated for he had only recently signed a secret agreement with the Dutch in which he promised to reserve all his spices for their merchants. But he soon realised that he was in no position to bargain and scrawled his signature on Middleton's treaty, even taking the trouble to write a personal missive to King James explaining how 'we have been informed that Englishmen were of bad disposition, and came not as peaceable merchants, but as thieves and robbers to depose us of our countries. But by the coming of Captain Henry Middleton we have found to the contrary, and we greatlie rejoice.'

Middleton's luck was not to last. Just a few hours after his triumph a small Dutch fleet stormed the island of Tidore, capturing its sturdy bastion from the Portuguese and threatening to repeat the exercise on neighbouring Ternate. They had been extremely fortunate in the ease of their conquest for 'the Portugals manfully defended their honour against the assailants, till an unfortunate fire (how or whence uncertaine) lighting in their powder blew up a great part of their castle with sixtie or seventie of their men.'

Middleton watched these events unfold with a growing sense of anger. 'If this frothy nation [the Dutch] may have the trade of the Indies to themselves,' he wrote, 'their pride and insolencie will be intollerable.' The victory of the Dutch gave them control of both the northern and central groups of the Spice Islands, leaving the Banda Islands as the only group of 'spiceries' that still offered the possibility of trade without competition.

It was to the Bandas that Captain Colthurst had steered the *Ascension*, ordered by Middleton to 'seeke a lading of nutmegs and mace'. Hoping to trade in peace, he watched in disbelief as a flotilla of Dutch ships followed in his wake. Unfortunately, there are few records of Colthurst's time here – save for a brief account which gives depth readings and soundings of various harbours in the archipelago – and it is necessary to turn to later accounts for a description of these verdant and grandiose islands.

Dominating them all was Gunung Api, a classically shaped volcanic island with steep sides and a hole at the top. At the beginning of the seventeenth century, it was entering one of the more energetic periods in its history, 'yeelding nothing but cinders, fire and smoake' and frequently erupting with such violence that 'it carried stones of three or four tunnes weight from the one iland into the other.' These boulders would rain down upon neighbouring Neira Island which, although not the largest in the group, had long been the centre for the nutmeg trade. It was to Neira that Captain Garcia had steered his Portuguese carrack in 1529 and, without consulting with the native chieftains, had attempted to construct a castle. Although Garcia was driven away by the local warriors, Neira remained popular with captains and traders on account of its fine natural harbour – once the volcano's caldera – which provided a safe anchorage for far larger vessels than the *Ascension*.

Less than half a mile from Neira was the kidney-shaped

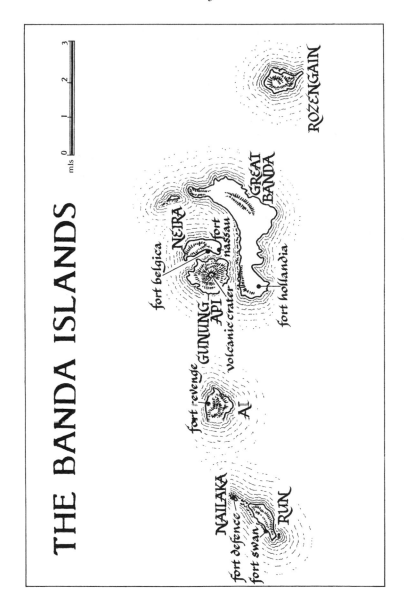

THE BANDA ISLANDS

mls 0 1 2 3

ROZENGAIN

GREAT BANDA

NEIRA

fort belgica

fort nassau

fort hollandia

GUNUNG API

volcanic crater

fort revenge

AI

NAILAKA

fort defence

fort swan

RUN

*The Banda Islands' volcano, Gunung Api, had a habit of erupting
every time a Dutch fleet arrived. 'The hill cast forth such hideous
flames,' wrote one observer, 'such store of cinders and huge streames
that it destroyed all the thicke woods.'*

island of Great Banda, 'strong and almost inaccessible, as [if]
it were a castle'. Great Banda's rocky backbone was covered
in a mantle of greenery – almost all nutmeg trees – and
there was 'scarce a tree on the iland but beareth fruit'. These
fruits were jealously guarded by the native inhabitants, an
aggressive and warlike people who had built an elaborate
system of defensive fortifications around the island's
shelving coast.

The other two islands, Ai and Rozengain, were less than
an hour's sailing from Great Banda. Rozengain had little
nutmeg and was therefore of no interest to Captain
Colthurst, whilst Ai had an extremely treacherous shoreline
which deterred all but the most foolhardy of mariners.
Nevertheless, it was 'the paradice of all the rest [for] there
is not a tree on that iland but the nutmeg, and other

delicate fruits of superfluitie; and withall, full of pleasant walkes so that the whole countrey seemes a contrived orchard with varieties'.

The only other island of note was Run, a tiny and outlying atoll whose cliffs and mountain were so tangled with nutmeg trees that they yielded a massive third of a million pounds of the spice every year. But Run, more than two hours from Neira, was the most dangerous of all the Banda Islands for its small harbour was ringed by a sunken reef which had claimed the timbers of many a vessel attempting to put in to port. Such dangers appear to have deterred Colthurst from landing on the island and he returned to Neira where the Dutch commander generously invited the English captain to dinner. According to Dutch records, Colthurst arrived bearing a freshly baked chicken pie, not out of courtesy but because he disliked Dutch food.

He left the Bandas with a valuable cargo of spice, as well as a friendly letter from a local headman offering King James I a generous gift of nutmeg. It was several years before this headman received a reply, but when he did he was overjoyed. The King, courteous as ever, thanked him for his kind present which, he said, 'we accepted with all kindness.'

Middleton and Colthurst sailed together for England, following in the wake of the *Hector* and the *Susan*. The *Susan* was destined never to make it home. Caught in a ferocious storm off southern Africa, she sank with the loss of all hands. The *Hector* almost shared a similar fate; stricken by sickness she was spotted by the *Red Dragon* 'in lamentable distress' and drifting helplessly in the waters around Table Bay. With just fourteen men left alive, the captain was about to scupper her when Middleton arrived on the scene. He oversaw her repair, waited until her surviving crew had been nursed back to health, and eventually accompanied her back to England, arriving in the spring of 1606.

The joyous welcome that greeted Middleton and his surviving men on their arrival home was to prove short-lived. For no sooner had his ships' cargo of nutmeg, cloves and pepper been unloaded than a vessel arrived in London bearing news of appalling happenings in the harbour at Bantam: ships had been ransacked, cargoes stolen and men indiscriminately slaughtered. At first it was thought that only the Dutch or Portuguese could wreak such terror, but London's merchants were soon to learn otherwise. The perpetrator of these outrages was none other than the 'gentelman' adventurer Sir Edward Michelborne.

Sir Edward had made good his promise to have his revenge. Flattering King James with his patrician charm and bad-mouthing the East India Company in the same breath, he persuaded the King to grant him a royal licence for a voyage of discovery to the Far East, a licence that was valid 'notwithstanding any grant or charter to the contrary'.

The Company were incensed at this sudden loss of their monopoly but not unduly surprised. Unlike his predecessor, King James had failed to grasp the fact that trade with the East Indies could only succeed if it was carried out by a monopoly and with the full backing of the Crown. He was also blind to the problem of the occasional ship sailing into eastern waters, even when that ship was captained by a loose cannon like Sir Edward. It was with the King's sanction and blessing, therefore, that the *Tiger*, together with a pinnace christened the *Tiger's Whelp*, set sail from the Isle of Wight on 5 December 1604.

The *Tiger* was a minuscule ship of just two hundred and forty tons and the East India Company directors might reasonably have hoped that she would be lost in the first storm. But Michelborne had a trump up his sleeve. Catching them unawares he announced that his chief pilot was the hugely experienced John Davis, veteran of James Lancaster's expedition and survivor of two difficult voyages to the East Indies. The Company was most surprised to hear this and wondered how Michelborne had managed to seduce Davis on board. In fact, the intrepid navigator had not needed much persuading for he was still angry at having returned from Lancaster's expedition under a cloud. Lancaster himself had complained about Davis, informing the directors that he was 'not a little grieved' that his navigator had been wrong about both the ease with which pepper could be bought in Achin and also the price. Davis was unfairly made a scapegoat and, offered the chance by Sir Edward Michelborne to have his revenge, he promptly signed up to join the *Tiger*.

No sooner had they reached Bantam than the mayhem began. Spotting a fully laden vessel on the horizon Michelborne 'fell in fight with her' and she was captured. She was a poor prize, a rice-laden cargo boat, and a dismayed Michelborne recorded that she 'was not suffering the worth of a penny to bee taken from them'. Other ships were stopped and searched in the shallow coastal waters around Bantam until the natives of one vessel, indignant at this blatant act of piracy, set upon the Englishmen and inflicted terrible injuries before leaping overboard and 'swimming away like water spaniels'.

Undeterred, Sir Edward next waylaid an Indian vessel of eighty tons and ransacked her. Emboldened by his success he now sailed into Bantam harbour where five enormous vessels, all Dutch, were riding at anchor. Chuckling at his own audacity he sent a message to each captain informing them 'that hee would come and ride close to their sides, and bad the prowdest of them all that durst to put a piece of ordnance upon him'. There was a warning attached to his message: if any ship so much as loaded a musket 'hee would either sinke them or sink by their sides.'

The Dutch were most upset to find themselves at the receiving end of such threats and complained to the King of Bantam that all Englishmen were the same, 'being thieves and disordinate livers'. Yet they steadfastly refused to take up Michelborne's challenge, cowering below deck as Sir Edward tacked up and down the harbour and, 'whereas the Hollanders were wont to swagger and keep great stirre on shore all the time before our being there, they were so quiet that wee could scarcely see one of them.'

Sir Edward had so far been lucky; he had acted with daring and bravado and no one had called his bluff. But he was shortly to meet his match. As the ship drifted in calm waters off the Malay Peninsula, a cry was suddenly raised from the look-out. A mysterious ship was approaching, a huge junk, whose decks were lined with more than eighty men. They were strange-looking fellows: short, squat, and with an almost total lack of expression on their faces. Sir Edward despatched a heavily armed boat to discover if these people were friend or foe and, after a brief exchange in which the English learned that the vessel was 'a junke of the Japons', they were invited on board and shown around. When they enquired of the Japanese as to their line of business the men made no bones about their trade. The junk, like the *Tiger*, was a pirate ship and the men were proud of her devastating progress through the waters of South-East Asia. She had pillaged the coasts of China and

Cambodia, plundered half a dozen ships off Borneo, and was now heading back to Japan laden with spoils.

When the English party were safely back on the *Tiger*, Sir Edward weighed up his options. Trusting to his previous good fortune, he decided to ransack the junk and, to this end, sent a second band of Englishmen on board to stake her out. Although it was clear to the Japanese that Michelborne's buccaneering sailors were assessing the strengths and weaknesses of the vessel, they welcomed the English with open arms and allowed them free access to the ship's hold. They even pointed to the choicest items on board, astonishing the crew of the *Tiger* who had never met with such an odd race of men. 'They were most of them too gallant a habit for sailors,' wrote one, 'and such an equalitie of behaviour among them that they all seemed fellows.' When they asked to visit the English vessel all agreed that it would be impolite to refuse.

Here Michelborne's inexperience told for the first time. He was unaware that the Japanese had the reputation in the Indies for being a 'people so desperate and daring that they are feared in all places' and was ignorant of the fact that all eastern ports demanded that any Japanese sailor coming ashore must first be disarmed. Davis, too, was 'beguiled by their humble semblance'. Not only was he of the opinion that disarming them was unnecessary, he offered them the run of the ship and let them freely fraternise with the crew. As more and more Japanese clambered aboard, beakers were raised and the two crews joked and chatted among themselves.

In a flash everything changed: unbeknown to the English, the Japanese had, in the words of Michelborne, 'resolved with themselves either to gaine my shippe or to lose their lives'. The smiles vanished, the laughter died and the Japanese suddenly transformed themselves into brutal 'rogues' who stabbed and slashed at their English adversaries. The crew of the *Tiger* had never faced such hostility and scarcely had a chance to resist before the deck was swarming with Japanese wielding long swords and hacking men to pieces. Soon they reached the gun room where they found Davis desperately loading muskets. 'They pulled [him] into the cabbin and giving him sixe or seven mortall wounds, they thrust him out of the cabbin.' He stumbled on deck but the sword wounds had severed one of his arteries and he bled to death. Others, too, were in their final death throes and it seemed inevitable that the *Tiger* would shortly be lost.

It was Michelborne who saved the day. Thrusting pikes into the hands of his best fighters he launched a last-ditch attack on the Japanese soldiers 'and killed three or four of their leaders'. This disheartened the Japanese who slowly found themselves at a disadvantage. Armed with knives and swords, they were unable to compete with Michelborne's pikemen and found themselves driven down the deck until they stood en masse by the entrance to the cabin. Sensing their predicament, they let out a terrific scream and dashed headlong into the heart of the ship.

The English were at a loss as to know how to evict them. Not one man volunteered to follow them into the cabin for to do so would be to court certain death. It was equally hopeless to send a large group down. The passageway was low and narrow and the men would end up wounding themselves rather than the Japanese. Eventually, a bright spark on board had a simple but devastating solution. Two thirty-two-pound demi-culverins were loaded with 'crosse-barres, bullets, and case-shot' and fired at point-blank range into the most exposed side of the cabin. There was a deafening crash as the shrapnel tore through the woodwork and 'violently marred therewith boords and splinters'. A terrible shriek followed, a cry of agony, and then there was silence. When the smoke cleared and the dust settled, the cabin was entered and it was found that only one of the twenty-two Japanese had survived. 'Their legs, armes and bodies were so torne, as it was strange to see how the shot had massacred them.'

It was now time for Michelborne to have his revenge. Training every last cannon on the Japanese junk, he fired shot after shot into her sides until the men on board begged for mercy. When this was refused they vowed to go down fighting and the battle raged until all resistance was quelled and the junk fell silent. Only one Japanese attempted to surrender. Diving into the water he swam across to the *Tiger* and was hauled aboard. When quizzed by Sir Edward as to the motive for the attack he 'told us that they meant to take our shippe and to cut all our throates'. Having said this, and terrified by the crowd of hostile onlookers, he told Michelborne that his one desire was 'that hee might be cut in pieces'. Michelborne preferred a less bloody method of execution and ordered the man to be strung up at the yardarm. This sentence was duly carried out but the rope snapped and the man dropped into the sea. No one could be bothered to haul him in and as the coast was not far away it was presumed that he escaped with his life.

The English crew were by now weary of their piratical adventure and elected to return home, eventually sailing back into Portsmouth in the summer of 1606. Michelborne was totally discredited by his conduct and retired in disgrace, but far more serious than the damage to his own career was the damage he had done to the reputation of English shipping. The Dutch in particular seized on his acts of piracy and used them to blacken the name of England among the native princes of the East. The English traders living in Bantam were in particular peril, for the King of Bantam was furious about what had happened. So damaging was Michelborne's voyage, in fact, that the Company sent a protest to the Lords of the Privy Council calling upon them to seize all the goods that Sir Edward had pillaged and reminding them that 'Sir Edward Michelborne has taken and spoiled some of our friends there, whereby not only the utter overthrow of the whole trade is much endangered, but also the safety of our men and goods.'

The spice race had by now been under way for more than ten years; time enough to judge who had gained the upper hand. Although London's merchant adventurers were flushed with success after Middleton's return, they had a nagging suspicion that they were steadily losing the race. They had so far despatched three fleets to the East (including the ships of Lancaster's maiden voyage) with a combined total of twelve vessels. Of these, one in three had either sunk or simply disappeared without trace. The loss in men was an even greater cause for concern. Of the approximately twelve hundred men who had sailed on these expeditions, some eight hundred had died either of scurvy, typhoid or the 'blody flux'. Two captains had been lost – one accidentally shot by his crew – and only one ship, the *Ascension*, had reached the distant Banda Islands. The profits, of course, had been enormous, even given the difficulties of disposing of Lancaster's cargo of pepper; and the Company warehouses were currently filled with sweet-smelling nutmeg and cloves. But the report that Middleton had submitted on his return suggested that it might be the last cargo they received. For the Dutch, latecomers to the spice race, were proving formidable rivals. Within a few years of Houtman's return they had managed to despatch a staggering fourteen fleets comprising sixty-five ships. Unlike the English commanders, who preferred 'a quiet trafficke', the Dutch had entered the race with cannons blazing. They had achieved a remarkable success against the Portuguese, ousting them from virtually all the 'spiceries' in which they had an interest. Now they were turning their attentions to the Banda Islands and seemed poised to capture these by force.

Faced with such a threat the Company took the view that they needed to expand their activities with all possible haste. They still had only one 'factory' or warehouse in the East, at Bantam in Java, and this was on a much smaller scale than those belonging to either the Dutch or Portuguese. If they were going to compete successfully against their rivals this factory needed to be expanded and new factories established right across the region.

There was a good case for expansion. One of England's most important exports, woollens, was understandably unpopular in the stifling climate of the Spice Islands. Instead of cloaks and blankets, the natives wanted cottons and calicoes which could be picked up cheaply in the ports along India's west coast. Already there was a brisk trade in these cottons and local ships regularly plied their trade between Gujarat and Bantam. Since India was believed to present a more favourable market for English woollens (as well as lead, iron and tin), the London merchants reasoned that if they could exchange these goods for cottons, then barter cottons for spices, they would have established a triangle of trade which would benefit everyone. Better still, they would be able to dramatically reduce the amount of gold being exported from England.

But there was a problem with trade with India. Much of the subcontinent was under the control of the mighty Moghul Emperor, Jehangir, the self-styled 'Conqueror of the World' who had already granted extensive and exclusive trading rights to the Portuguese – rights which they jealously guarded. Since a military assault on their fortified factories was out of the question, the only solution was to send an ambassador to Jehangir and beg his permission to build a factory on the western coast of India. If the Emperor agreed, the Portuguese would be powerless to intervene.

The governors began to search around for a suitable candidate to bear their petition to the Moghul Emperor. There were, they soon realised, few men qualified for the task and after several weeks of searching, their shortlist still contained only one name, William Hawkins, a sea captain whose background remains obscure but whose name links him to one of the most distinguished seafaring families of the Elizabethan age. He may have been the Hawkins who travelled across the Atlantic with Edward Fenton; he may also have put to sea in the *Griffin* against the Spanish Armada. But there were so many of the Hawkins family at sea during this period – including four named William – that it is not possible to untangle their exploits. Why the Company alighted on this particular Hawkins is easier to ascertain. Having spent some years trading in the Levant he was able to speak Turkish, an invaluable aid in any eastern country. He was also familiar with the customs and manners of the Orient and would be able to make an impression on the Moghul Emperor.

Hawkins set sail in the *Hector* in 1607 and arrived at

Surat on India's north-western coastline some sixteen months later. The journey was apparently uneventful for Hawkins makes scant mention of the storms, hunger and sickness that invariably afflicted the Company's voyages. Even the first sighting of the lush Gujarat coast, watered by the recent monsoons, failed to move him.

The town of Surat lay some twenty miles up the River Tapti and was reached by way of a muddy estuary which was only navigable by the smallest of vessels. The *Hector* therefore anchored off the sandy bar that blocked the estuary's mouth and Hawkins – accompanied by several of his crew – rowed upstream towards the town, watched by a crowd who had gathered to stare at these new and unfamiliar faces. The town's governor was too drunk to speak with Hawkins so he and his companions made his way to the Custom House where their personal possessions were 'searched and tumbled to our great dislike'.

While Hawkins explained that he wanted to establish a trading base his companion, Will Finch, set off to explore. The city, he discovered, was a pleasant one and home to a large number of merchants. Keeping a look-out for a suitable residence Finch noted that the finest houses were those fronting the river and those next to the castle where, to his surprise, he stumbled across 'a pleasant green, in the midst of which is a maypole'.

The customs' official spoke kindly to the English but was wary. He informed them that he was powerless to grant trading rights – that was the prerogative of the Moghul official in overall charge of the Gujarat ports – but assured Hawkins he would make their stay as comfortable as possible. Assigning them sleeping quarters in the porter's lodge of the Custom House, a room that Finch considered rather 'poore lodging', he then secured them an invitation to dinner at the home of one of the richer merchants in town.

Unfortunately what should have been a jovial meal proved to be painfully embarrassing. The merchant was none other than the owner of one of the ships that Sir Edward Michelborne had seized a couple of years earlier. Although he was gracious when he noticed their embarrassment and tactfully pointed out that 'there were thieves in all countries', Hawkins and Finch could not help but feel their mission had got off to a poor start.

It was soon to take a turn for the worse. While the two Englishmen awaited the return of the Moghul official whose permission they sought, the Portuguese took matters into their own hands. They were most upset when they heard of Hawkins' request to set up shop in the town and, seizing an English skiff packed with crew from the *Hector*, they arrested the men and threatened to pack them off to Goa to be dealt with by the Portuguese Viceroy.

Hawkins was annoyed but placed his trust in tact and diplomacy. He sent a polite but firm letter to the Portuguese commander reminding him that their two countries were at peace and asking that 'he release my men and goods, for that we were Englishmen.' The commander was in no mood to be lenient and sent Hawkins a return letter 'vilely abusing His Majesty [King James I] terming him King of Fishermen, and of an island of no import'. Worse still, he described Hawkins as 'a fart for his commission'. Hawkins exploded when he read that last insult. Labelling him a 'base villain and a traitor to his king', he immediately challenged 'the proud rascal' to a duel. The commander ignored the challenge and promptly despatched the English prisoners to Goa.

The *Hector* had by now sailed for Bantam leaving

Hawkins and Finch in a particularly vulnerable position, the more so when Finch fell 'extreme sick of the blody flux'. 'After the departure of my ship,' wrote Hawkins, 'I was so misused that it was insuferable. [I was] environed with so many enemies, who daily did nothing else but plot to murther me and cosen me of my goods.' The arrival of the Moghul official, Mukarrab Khan, did little to further his cause. Proud, arrogant and avaricious, Mukarrab had originally entered the emperor's service as court physician, only to be elevated to the governorship after curing the Emperor of a particularly nasty disorder. With the lucrative port of Surat now under his control, he proceeded to milk any arriving trader. Hawkins was not exempt from this policy – Mukarrab impounded the Company's wares, pocketed the choicest articles that had been brought ashore, and listened attentively to the lies and deceits told him by the Portuguese. 'He outwardly disembled and flattered with me almost three moneths,' wrote Hawkins, 'feeding me with faire promises and kindnesses. In the meantime he came to my house three times, sweeping me cleane of all things that were good so that when he saw that I had no more good things left, he likewise by little and little degraded me of his good looks.'

With enemies in every camp the two Englishmen were now in the gravest of dangers. 'I could not peep out of doors for fear of the Portugals,' records Hawkins, 'who in troops lay lurking in by-ways to give me assault to murder me.' Soon, they chose more direct action. Learning that the English captain had been invited to dinner with a friendly Moghul official they hatched a plot to murder him. While a company of Portuguese troops fanned out along the shoreline, three soldiers bristling with weapons stormed the marquee. Hawkins reacted quickly, grabbing his musket and stopping them in their tracks. The Moghul official then shouted to his followers and the Portuguese, suddenly outgunned, fled from the scene.

It was not long before they tried again. A band of forty men, egged on by Portuguese monks, tried to storm Hawkins' home, 'but I was always wary, having a strong house with good doores'. The man engineering the attacks was a Jesuit priest called Father Peneiro. Fanatically anti-English and a close friend of 'the dogge Mocreb [Mukarrab]' he did everything he could to whip up hatred against Hawkins and Finch throughout their stay in India.

By February 1609, Hawkins realised he would achieve nothing by staying in Surat and set out for Agra, the imperial capital, leaving behind a much-recovered Finch. To protect him during the ten-week journey he hired fifty Pathan horsemen, 'a people very much feared in these parts', though not so feared as to stop two more attempts on his life before he reached the capital. News of his arrival had preceded him, causing quite a stir at court. The Emperor wished to meet this curiosity immediately and 'presently charged both horsemen and footmen in many troupes, not to leave before I was found, commanding his knight marshall to accompany me with great state to the Court as an ambassador of a king ought to be'. So keen were they to bring Hawkins to his audience with the Emperor that he was scarcely given time to change into clean clothes. He was unprepared in another respect. It was well known that Jehangir expected anyone to whom he gave an audience to arrive with a large bag of presents. Paintings, toys and trinkets were his favourites, but he had a keen eye and did not take kindly to gifts of an inferior quality. Hawkins had arrived in India with half a cartload of presents but all had been stolen by 'the dogge' in Surat.

Rummaging through his baggage for a gift, the only item he could find was a small bundle of cloth; 'a slight present,' he admitted later, 'and not esteemed'.

Despite all the setbacks Hawkins found himself heartily welcomed by Jehangir and chatted to him for two hours in Turkish, informing him of all the problems he had faced in Surat. Despite their different stations in life, the two men struck up an instant friendship and the Emperor 'spake unto mee in the kindest manner that could be [and] with a most kind and smiling countenance'. Jehangir loved curiosities and an Englishman at his court was something truly exotic. Hawkins was given lodging and instructed to appear before the emperor every morning.

Each day Hawkins questioned him about the possibility of opening an English factory in Surat. Each day Jehangir stalled for time and urged him to be patient until, tiring of the constant petitions, he suggested that England would be best served if Hawkins stayed at his court on a semi-permanent basis. As an inducement he offered an annual pension of £3,200 a year, four hundred horses and the title of Inglis Khan: 'the title for a Duke'. It was a tempting offer and the captain-turned-duke weighed up the options. Eventually he agreed to stay for 'halfe a doozen yeeres', deciding it would be foolish to turn down this opportunity to 'feather my nest'.

He now became an intimate member of the Emperor's inner circle. Not only did he take part in the ceremonial duties that accompanied the daily durbar, where he sat in the little railed enclosure reserved for the highest nobility, but he also became a regular guest at the nightly wassails that filled the inner recesses of the palace with debauched laughter. It was at one of these drinking binges that Jehangir was struck by a brilliant idea. 'He was very earnest

with me to take a white maiden out of his palace' – not as
a mistress, but as a wife. For a free spirit like Hawkins the
idea of settling down to a life of domesticity was far from
appealing but he knew that he would have to be diplomatic
when refusing the Emperor's kind offer. Quick-thinking as
ever, he told Jehangir he was theologically opposed to
marrying a Muslim, but jested that if the Emperor found
him a good Christian girl, why, he would be up the aisle in
a trice. 'At which speech,' says Hawkins, 'I little thought a
Christian's daughter could be found.' Nor did he realise
that he had thrown down the gauntlet. It became a matter
of honour for the Emperor to find Hawkins a wife and
after much searching he learned of an Armenian Christian
who had recently lost her father and was all alone in the
world. Hawkins found himself unable to refuse. 'Therefore
I took her,' he writes, 'and for want of a Minister, before
Christian witnesses, I married her.' He later discovered that
such a marriage was unlawful, 'upon which news I was new
married again'. Surprisingly, the couple fell head over heels
in love and 'for ever after I lived content and without feare,
she being willing to goe where I went and live as I lived.'

Throughout his time in Agra, Hawkins gives almost no
description of the place, save to mention that it was 'one of
the biggest cities in the world'. Although the Taj Mahal had
yet to be built, the city was nonetheless adorned with
outlandish public monuments, none of which was more
beautiful than Jehangir's palace built inside the walls of
Agra Fort. From here, richly caparisoned elephants would
carry the imperial court up into the hills for numerous
hunting expeditions. Here, too, a steady stream of courtiers,
sycophants and imperial flatterers from all over India would
arrive to pay homage to the Emperor. And as word got
around of the influence of the Englishman at court – and

as jealousies flared – the web of intrigue grew ever more complex.

'The Jesuits and Portugalls slept not,' recorded Hawkins with evident relish, 'but by all means sought my overthrow; and to say the truth, the principal Moslems near the king were exceeding envious that a Christian should be so close unto him.' Hawkins was shrewd enough to hold his own against men like Mukarrab Khan and the Portuguese Jesuits, and this latter group received a stern warning from the emperor that if Hawkins 'died by any extraordinary casualty, they should rue for it'.

He was fortunate to be invited to partake in the numerous daily drinking binges at court for they brought him ever closer to the Emperor. Jehangir liked to spend the greater part of every day completely drunk and was quite open about his love of alcohol, stating in his memoirs that he began to drink wine at the age of eighteen and increased his consumption day by day until it no longer intoxicated him. Then he moved on to spirits until, by the end of his life, his hand shook so much that he could no longer drink from his cup.

The imbibing would begin as soon as the day's official business was over. Jehangir would eat his main meal of the day, then retire to his private quarters with a few of his closest friends. These invariably included Hawkins, who describes how the Emperor would drink himself into a stupor. Then, after consuming a large quantity of opium to heighten his sense of well being, he 'layeth him down to sleep, every man departing to his own home'.

Hawkins knew that if he was ever to acquire the elusive trading privileges so desperately sought by the East India Company he needed to have a constant supply of novelties and trinkets to present to the Emperor. He wrote several letters to London urging them to send high-quality presents, a call that repeatedly fell on deaf ears. Several times the directors sent paintings of inferior quality and letters had to be despatched to London warning them 'to be very wary what they send'. In the end Jehangir took matters into his own hands, writing a list of his favourite presents which included 'any figures of beasts, birds, or other similes made of glass, or hard plaster, or silver, brass, wood, iron, stone or ivory'.

It was the expectation of more gifts that at long last led Jehangir to grant Hawkins his request for an English factory in Surat. Learning of the imminent arrival of the *Ascension*, he gave his approval for the establishment of an English trading base and allowed Hawkins to send a message to William Finch with the good news. Finch was most impressed with Hawkins' work and was duly deferential in his reply, addressing him as 'my Lord' and 'my Worship', rather than 'the captain'.

The Moghul officials and the Portuguese now redoubled their efforts to revoke the Emperor's licence. They proved successful for hardly had Jehangir's order reached Surat than it was inexplicably countermanded. There was more bad news in store for Hawkins and Finch. The *Ascension* 'was cast away' off Gujarat, presumably after striking a reef and, although many of the crew were saved, the 'disorder and riot committed by some of them' caused Finch untold trouble, especially when a certain Thomas Tucker butchered a cow in the street – 'a slaughter more than murder in India'.

Hawkins, meanwhile, was trying to mend his fences with the emperor, all the while making observations about Jehangir's unpredictable character. Most afternoons he accompanied him to lion and elephant fights which were of a scale and brutality akin to those of imperial Rome. Relishing the quantities of blood spilt, Jehangir took increasing delight in gladiatorial contests between man and beast, as Hawkins relates in a particularly gruesome anecdote.

A Pathan warrior from the frontier approached one of the Emperor's sons for a job but, when asked what pay he expected, said he would not work for less than 1,000 rupees a day. The prince was taken aback and asked how he could justify asking for such a huge salary. 'Make trial with me with all sorts of weapons,' he said, 'and if I do not perform as much as I speak, then let me die for it.'

Later that evening, the prince went to visit his drunken father and repeated this amusing story. The Emperor immediately commanded that the Pathan be brought before him and also asked for the strongest and most savage lion he possessed to be led into the palace. When asked by the emperor why the Pathan thought he was worth such a great salary, the man repeated his earlier challenge. Jehangir, bleary-eyed from drink and by now slurring his words said, 'That I will … go wrestle and buffet with this lion.'

The Pathan protested, saying that to fight a lion without a weapon was no test of strength. But Jehangir was in no mood to change his mind. 'The King,' writes Hawkins, 'not regarding his speech, commanded him to buckle with the lion, who did so, wrestling and buffeting … a pretty while: and then the lion being loose from his keepers, but not from his chaines, got the poore man within his clawes, and tore his body in many parts: and with his pawes tore the one halfe of his face, so that the valiant man was killed by this wilde beast.' The Emperor so enjoyed the spectacle that he called for ten of his horsemen to wrestle with the lion, three of whom lost their lives.

He was no less unpredictable with his ministers. One of Hawkins' friends at court, the Chief of the King's Wardrobe, had the misfortune to smash one of Jehangir's favourite Chinese dishes. Knowing the Emperor would be furious if he discovered the accident, he sent a servant to travel over the whole of China to find a replacement. The man searched in vain. Two years after the accident – and with still no sign of the servant – the Emperor asked the Chief of the King's Wardrobe for the dish and was told it was broken. 'Now when the king heard [this] he was in a great rage, commanding him to be brought before him and to be beaten by two men, with two great whips made of cords: and after he had received one hundred and twenty of these lashes, he commanded his porters, who he appointed for that purpose, to beate him with their small cudgels till a great many of them were broken. At least twenty men were beating him, till the poore man was thought to be dead, and then he was hauled out by the heels and commanded to prison.'

The following morning the Emperor demanded to know whether the man was still alive; when told that, yes, the man had survived the ordeal, he ordered that he spend the rest of his days in prison. At this point Jehangir's son intervened, secured the poor man's release and nursed him back to health. But still the Emperor was angry. Summoning the trembling fellow into his presence once again, he dismissed him from his court and told him 'never to come again before him until he had found such a like dish, and that he travel through China to seek it'. The man voyaged the length and breadth of the country for fourteen months but had no success in finding a copy. At length he discovered that a similar dish was owned by the King of Persia who sent it to him out of pity.

Hawkins eventually tired of the constant bloodshed and debauchery and grew fearful that the capricious Emperor would turn against him. One minute he was in favour, the next minute he was despised: 'Thus', he writes, 'was I tossed and tumbled in the kind of a rich merchant, venturing all he had in one bottom and, by casualtie of storms or pirates, lost it all at once.' When he was told his allowance had been annulled Hawkins knew it was time to pack his bags. He headed back to Surat with Mrs Hawkins and found himself in luck. A new English fleet under the command of the recently knighted Sir Henry Middleton had just arrived from Arabia and was presently at anchor off the bar at Surat.

Hawkins sailed home a disappointed man. He had been sent to India with high hopes of striking a deal with the emperor but, after almost three years of constant petitioning, he had left the court empty-handed. On a personal level, the mission had also failed. Jealous of Hawkins' influence over the Emperor, his fellow sailors did their utmost to undermine his reputation on their return. Purporting to be scandalised by his drunkenness, they told the East India Company directors that his debauchery at court had led to his disgrace. It was an unlikely charge but it stuck. In any case, Hawkins was in no position to defend himself for he fell sick on the long journey home and died shortly before arriving in England. The loyal Mrs Hawkins was distraught. Unable to live on her own she sold a very valuable diamond, married a factor called Gabriel Towerson, an experienced East India trader, and accompanied him back to the East.

CHAPTER FIVE

'ADMIRAL,
WE ARE
BETRAYED!'

TO THE HANDFUL OF observers gathered on Dover's cliffs there had rarely been a more magnificent sight. A flotilla of ships was flying up the Channel, the wind filling their sails and their pennants streaming behind them. But these were not English vessels, nor were there any English sailors on board. The fleet was commanded by a Dutchman, Jacob van Neck, who was about to bring untold wealth to his mercantile masters in Amsterdam.

Rarely would expeditions pass as smoothly as Jacob van Neck's, which returned to Holland in the summer of 1599. He sailed to the East without any untoward incident and successfully bought an enormous quantity of spices in Bantam before heading for home. On later voyages he would find himself accused of sodomy, would lose his hand in a gun battle and eat a poisonous fruit which temporarily afflicted him with 'madnesse, seeing angels, devils, serpents, all things and nothing'. But on this occasion he was spared such troubles and his return was a cause for joyous celebration, for 'as long as Holland has been Holland there have never arrived ships as richly laden as these.' Indeed they were: nearly a million pounds in weight of pepper and cloves as well as half a ship-load of nutmeg, mace and cinnamon. The commander and his men were fêted as heroes: led by a band of trumpeters they were paraded in triumph through the streets of Amsterdam while the city's church bells rang out in celebration. The merchants presented van Neck with a glittering golden beaker (a generosity somewhat marred by the discovery that it was only gold-plated) and the crew were given as much wine as they could drink.

The success of the voyage was due to van Neck's skill in dealing with the natives in Bantam. Three years previously the choleric Cornelis Houtman had battered the town with his formidable firepower, slaughtered hundreds of the local population, and even had the audacity to train his largest cannon on the King's palace. Van Neck was a shrewd enough operator to realise that any redress for Houtman's behaviour would be welcomed. Not only did he agree to the King's prices, he boldly suggested that he pay over the odds for the goods in order to cement their new-found relationship. 'Some may think', he wrote in his journal, 'that we are a bit too liberal with the money of our masters. But if they will look at it soberly, they will have to agree that, at places where our nation previously left as an enemy, a certain amount of goodwill is not misplaced.' He was aided in his task of mending fences by Bantam's merchants who had recently captured three Portuguese vessels, stripped them of everything of value, and set fire to them. Aware that the Portuguese were sure to avenge this wanton act of piracy, the Bantamese were desperately in need of a powerful ally.

A brisk trade followed van Neck's arrival and within four weeks the three ships under his direct command were filled with spices. His only concern was what had happened to the second squadron of his fleet, not sighted since Madagascar. But as New Year's Eve approached and van Neck planned festivities for his crew, these other ships, commanded by the splendidly named Vice Admiral Wybrand van Warwyck and the Arctic explorer Jacob van Heemskerck, sailed into view. 'They were joyously received,' records the ship's journal, 'and made welcome.'

None was happier than Jacob van Heemskerck who, just two years earlier, had been stranded in the Arctic when his search for the fabled North-East Passage was brought to an icy halt. Now, basking in the tropical heat of Bantam, Heemskerck found himself in considerably more genial surroundings. Back among old friends, he threw himself into the festivities. His own voyage had been better than many; stumbling across a paradisal island in the middle of the Indian Ocean – which he named Mauritius – his men stuffed their bellies with the easy-to-catch wildlife and amused themselves by lounging on the beaches and riding four-abreast on giant tortoises. Realising that Mauritius could be a valuable port of call for Dutch ships Heemskerck put a rooster and some hens ashore and planted orange and lemon seeds, invoking 'the Almighty God's blessing that He may lend His power to make them multiply and grow for the benefit of those who will visit the island after us'.

Jacob van Neck's frantic buying had left the port of Bantam bereft of spices. Before sailing for home he suggested that the rest of the fleet sail east to the Spice Islands where it was certain they would be able to procure a full cargo of nutmeg and mace. This they duly did: Warwyck headed for the northernmost island of Ternate where he fired so many rounds of ammunition in celebration of his safe arrival that the very island was said to quake. Heemskerck, meanwhile, had sailed into even remoter seas. Fearless and daring, he had his eye on the Banda Islands – as yet unvisited by either the Dutch or English – and sailed eastwards with a bravado that was not always appreciated by his on-board merchants. When one of their number suggested that the captain should be more careful with his ships, Heemskerck exploded: 'When we risk our lives,' he said, 'the Lords of the Company may damn well risk their ships!'

He also had to risk a monster, a creature of 'devillish possession' which was said to live in the Banda Islands and prey on passing ships. Fortunately his Indian pilot knew just the method of dealing with such monsters: 'With a terrible ghastly countenance [he] thrust forward the boat-hook' as if to kill the devil. This did the trick, the monster remained out of sight and in mid-March, 1599, Heemskerck dropped anchor at Great Banda and petitioned the local chieftain for trade.

The Bandanese were less than happy to see this band of Dutchmen arrive at their shores. Almost ninety years of contact with the Portuguese had taught them to treat all foreigners with mistrust and the arrival of the Dutch seemed to portend some new and menacing threat. Scarcely had Heemskerck's vessels dropped anchor in the huge natural harbour at Neira than Gunung Api, a volcano which had lain dormant for centuries, suddenly burst into life and sent a spectacular display of fireworks into the tropical sky. 'The hill cast forth such hideous flames, such store of cinders, and huge streames that it destroyed, burnt, and broke downe all the thicke woods and mightie trees, overwhelming them as it were her owne vomiting so that a greene leafe could not be seene in all that part of the iland.' The locals were reminded of a prophecy, told them five years earlier by a Muslim holy man, that an army of white strangers would shortly arrive at the islands and take them by force. Since the Dutch ships were heavily armed, and Heemskerck appeared to take a keen interest in the local feuding, it was widely agreed that this was that white army.

After the presentation of lavish gifts, and repeated assurances from Heemskerck that he was a sworn enemy of the Portuguese, his men were allowed to land on Great Banda and barter their knives and mirrors for nutmeg and mace. The Dutchmen spent almost a month buying spices and were allowed to trade peacefully and undisturbed, though not without quarrels: 'A man needs seven eyes,' recorded Heemskerck, 'if he does not want to be cheated. These people are so crooked and brazen that it is almost unbelievable.' Nevertheless, the prices they paid for nutmeg were laughably low (less than one English penny for ten pounds of nutmeg) and their cargo would increase many thousand-fold in value by the time they arrived back in Holland.

A house was rented on Great Banda and soon local boats began arriving from the neighbouring island of Neira. Trading was temporarily halted when the Banda Islands were plunged into war as rival chieftains embarked on a series of ambitious head-hunting expeditions. The menfolk of Neira, together with their allies on nearby Ai Island, went on the rampage, killing their enemies and adorning their boats with the bloody trophies of battle. They even chopped off women's heads, contrary to tradition, although they had the good grace to 'burie these heads in cotton clothes'. On their return, 'with their swords yet bloody, [they] made glorious muster of themselves four or five days together.'

Such localised wars were a recurring feature in the

Banda Islands and the Dutch were soon to exploit them to devastating effect. But for the moment Heemskerck was happy to watch from the sidelines and gather intelligence for future expeditions. When he finally set sail on his homeward journey he left behind a party of twenty-two Dutchmen and instructed them to stockpile nutmeg in preparation for the next Dutch fleet. His parting conversation with the headman of Great Banda provoked an unusual request: drawing Heemskerck to one side the headman confessed to an abiding passion for horology and begged the Dutch commander to return to the island with a large grandfather clock, adding the proviso that any representation of man or beast must be removed since it would cause offence to his Muslim islanders. Heemskerck agreed, but as there is no further mention of the clock, the request seems to have been conveniently forgotten.

The Dutch captain finally arrived back in Amsterdam in the spring of 1600 and was accorded a welcome no less rapturous than had been given to van Neck. When his nutmeg was finally unloaded into the city's warehouses, 'the air of the whole neighbourhood was sweetened by their savoury smell.'

'But before the returne of any of these ships, in the yeere 1599, the Dutch set forth another fleet.' Much to the chagrin of Amsterdam's merchants, this new expedition had been despatched by their trading rivals in Rotterdam and Zeeland who had long been keen to involve themselves in the spice trade. Amsterdam responded by toughening its stance, informing its commanders to deal harshly with any competitors. 'You know as well as we do what losses it would cause us if the Zeeland ships were to arrive before ours are fully loaded. Therefore, buy. Buy everything you

*Nutmeg-traders in the Banda Islands, 1599. Local merchants added
grit to their spices to increase the weight and swell their profits.
'Have you a great care to receive such nutmegs as be good,'
Lancaster warned his merchants, 'for the smallest nutmegs
be worth nothing at home.'*

can lay your hands on, and load it as quickly as possible.
Even if you have no room for it, keep on buying and bind
it to yourselves for future delivery.'

Their advice came too late. With more and more ships
heading for the 'spiceries', and with prices rising by the
month, the merchants of Amsterdam petitioned their
delegates in the States General, the body that represented
all the provinces of the United Netherlands, for a total and
exclusive monopoly on the spice trade. 'For many and
varied reasons,' they wrote, 'it is advisable that this
commerce be conducted by one administration.'

It was an outrageous demand and it was soon thrown
out. Yet the man who led the opposition, Johan van
Oldebarnvelt, who as Advocate or Attorney-General of
Holland was the most powerful man in the land, realised
that some sort of monopoly was essential if the spice trade

was to flourish. He rejected Amsterdam's proposal, insisting instead that small-time investors from the entire country should be included 'so that these men can discuss ways and means whereby this aforementioned navigation and trade shall be secured for many years to come'. It was not a popular move and was bitterly opposed by the Amsterdam merchants, but on the evening of 20 March 1602, an agreement was struck and the Dutch East India Company officially came into being. Known as the VOC (Vereenigde Oost-Indische Compagnie), or more colloquially as the Seventeen after its seventeen-strong council, it was given a total monopoly over the spice trade for a period of twenty-one years. It was to prove a formidable rival to its English counterpart.

The Seventeen wasted no time in sending their first fleet to the East Indies. Just eleven days after putting their signatures to the charter, they despatched three ships under the robust command of Sebald de Weert whilst the rest of the fleet, under Wybrand van Warwyck, left the Texel some two months later. The men were ordered to establish trading links with scores of countries and princedoms including Java, Sumatra, Ceylon and the 'spiceries'. As if that was not enough, van Warwyck was also instructed to sail to China and open trading bases up and down the coast. Military action was both permitted and expected: 'attack the Spanish and Portuguese wherever you find them,' read the instructions, and it was not long before the Dutch ships found themselves embroiled in local hostilities. No sooner had Sebald de Weert arrived at Ceylon than the maharajah 'protested much his hatred to the Portugall and began to explore the possibilities of a joint assault on their castles'. De Weert struck up an instant rapport with this candid but jovial ruler who, he learned, had been brought up by the Portuguese, converted to Christianity and taken the name Dom Joao. Now, his friendship had turned sour and he was planning his revenge, suggesting to de Weert that if the Dutch vessels blockade the island's principal port, he would attack the Portuguese castle with his land forces. They could then repeat this exercise up and down the coastline until the Portuguese had been decisively trounced. In return, he promised to turn over the Portuguese battlements to the Dutch and 'reserve his merchandising for them'. This was too good an offer to turn down and de Weert whole-heartedly embraced the project.

The good humour was not to last. De Weert's crew were exhausted after their long journey and although there was plenty of fresh fruit on the island, the humid climate made them jumpy and irritable. 'They were disquieted with flies and gnats which would not suffer them to sleepe.' Even more annoying were the natives 'who made fire and smoake all the night'. But what really angered the Dutch crew was the fact that they were still living off the by now putrid salt beef loaded onto the ships in Holland. 'The king entertained them well,' records one journal, 'but their religion prohibiting to eat beefs and buffals – whereof they had great plenty – they would not sell any to the Hollanders.' This was all the more galling since the surrounding fields and meadows, and even the streets, were crowded with plump cattle and buffalo. To the Singhalese, these were holy animals who harboured the souls of their deceased relatives. But the Dutch, sick of gnawing rancid gristle, saw juicy steaks in every cow that passed. De Weert listened politely as Dom Joao explained why he could not sell any cattle but privately he scoffed at the suggestion of sacred cows and allowed his 'unruely' men to go on the rampage, butchering cows and roasting the meat over camp-fires.

The natives were horrified when they saw what was happening and none more so than Dom Joao. 'The Portugals had never offered such indignitie,' he stormed. De Weert's apologies did little to dampen the fury over the 'sacriligious murther of beefs', nor did his offer of payment for the butchered cows. 'From that time on,' wrote Dutchman Jacob Rycx, 'we were on a bad footing with the king and his subjects.'

The incident was temporarily forgotten when the military campaign against the Portuguese was resumed, but resentment towards the Dutch continued to simmer and when Dom Joao learned that his son had been allowed to fall into enemy hands he decided that it was time to act. With an outward show of friendship he invited de Weert and his staff to a fabulous banquet and there had his bloody revenge:

> While the Vice-Admiral and the King discussed various matters, there was quite a bit of drinking. Suddenly the King berated the Vice-Admiral for having allowed the Portuguese to escape. By then De Weert was pretty drunk. He denied the accusation heatedly and insisted that the King and his retinue pay him a courtesy visit on his ship, adding: 'The Dutch are not accustomed to bend their knee without receiving some respect in return.' This added fuel to the fire and the King apparently convinced himself that the Dutch were not to be trusted, and that the invitation was for the sole purpose of taking him prisoner. At a signal the King's followers drew their swords, slaughtering the Vice-Admiral and all

those who were with him. There were three hundred Singalese hidden in the woods near the beach, and when they learned what was happening in the palace they attacked those of us who were ashore. In all we lost forty-seven men and six wounded ... And so it was all enmity and we knowing what had caused this because we thought we were all friends.

Dom Joao soon tried to mend fences with the Dutch but there was an understandable lack of goodwill on the part of the survivors. 'We are sailing for other lands where we shall be treated less treacherously,' they informed the maharajah.

Long before news of the massacre reached Holland, yet more ships had been despatched eastwards under the command of Steven van der Hagan. These headed straight to the Banda Islands where the commander intended to build a fortified factory. He had expected to be greeted by the party of Dutch traders left behind by Heemskerck but as he stepped ashore and knocked on the factory gates he was most surprised to find himself answered by a cheery English voice. It was Christopher Colthurst, captain of the *Ascension*, who extended a gleeful welcome to van der Hagen. The Dutchman quizzed Colthurst about the fate of the Dutch settlers, only to learn that they had all been murdered by the natives after a fiery argument. The cause of their quarrel 'was a strangenesse', according to the records. Two of the Dutchmen were said to have renounced Christianity shortly after arriving in the Banda Islands and had adopted the Islamic beliefs of the natives. 'They were slaine by three Hollanders which, in revenge, were slaine by the natives.' This led to a blood feud which ended only when all the Dutchmen were dead.

Van der Hagen was outraged by what he heard and

made veiled threats to the Bandanese. 'Stormie weather followed,' writes Samuel Purchas in his colourful account of the event, '... wherein all the beasts of the forrest crept forth, the young lions roared after their prey; the ghastly ghosts walked abroad in the darke, and the rulers of the darknesse ... domineered at pleasure.' Gathering the island's headmen together, the Dutch commander duped them into signing a document that granted him a total and permanent monopoly over their supply of nutmeg. To the native chieftains, such a document was scarcely worth the paper it was written on, but the Dutch treated it as a legally binding agreement and would later use it as the justification for their annexation of the Banda Islands.

By the time van der Hagen set sail for Holland the Dutch could boast three forts in the Spice Islands which gave them a virtual monopoly on the world's production of cloves – and had secured a written agreement with the Banda Islands, theoretically capturing the priceless nutmeg supply as well. But van der Hagen's mistake was to leave behind insufficient forces to guarantee this treaty he had concluded. Scarcely had he left the Banda Islands than a fleet equipped by the English East India Company sailed into port and experienced few difficulties in buying nutmeg from the local islanders.

News of Holland's success was a cause of grave concern to the directors of the English East India Company. Less than four years after launching themselves into the spice race they found that most of the 'spiceries' were already lost to the Dutch. This caused panic among the Company directors who resolved to challenge the Dutch authority by building factories on the clove-producing islands of Tidore and Ternate as well as on the nutmeg-producing Bandas.

They reasoned that having 'factors' or merchants permanently living on these islands was an essential requisite to trade in the Spice Islands; not only could these factors stockpile spices at the time of harvesting when prices were low, they would also be able to keep an eye on the movements of the Dutch and appraise newly arrived fleets of the current situation.

In 1607 they despatched their third expedition to the East, supplying it with £17,600 of gold bullion (but just £7,000 of home-produced merchandise). The captains were urged to stay one step ahead of the Dutch. 'Take your speedy course along the coast of Malabar,' read their orders, 'that you may come [to Bantam] before the Hollanders ... for they will do what they can to anticipate you at the Molluccas.' The directors also took the opportunity to remind all crew members that gambling and swearing was strictly prohibited, and this time an extra clause was added. With the thought, perhaps, that cleanliness is next to godliness, men were asked 'that there be a diligent care to keep the lowest decks and other places of the ships clean and sweet, which is a notable preservation of health'. This sudden concern for on-board hygiene owed less to a concern for the crew's health than to the fact that the Company had learned that 'the Dutchmen do far exceed us in cleanliness, to their great commendation, and to the great disgrace of our people.'

The directors had one other request – a trifling matter, really, but one they felt obliged to fulfil. 'Remember to do your best to bring for the Lord of Salisbury some parrots, monkeys, marmasetts, or other strange beasts and fowls that you esteeme rare and delightful.' The Lord of Salisbury was the celebrated Robert Cecil, Secretary of State, who had been pestering the Company for months for exotic animals to add to his collection. The leaders of the third expedition surpassed themselves when it came to meeting this request, for when the *Hector* at last docked at the Thames-side wharves onlookers were amazed to discover a 'blacke savage' gazing wistfully across the London landscape. His name was Coree, a native of Table Bay, who had made the mistake of clambering on board ship as she revictualled in southern Africa. Realising what a stir he would cause in London, the acting captain Gabriel Towerson took Coree captive and carried him back to England. He proved tiresome company, for 'the poore wretch' moaned throughout the long voyage, not through lack of creature comforts but – according to the ship's journal – 'merely out of extreme sullenness, for he was very well used'.

Sir Thomas Smythe strode down to the Thames to extend a personal welcome to Coree and to assure him that the East India Company would do everything in its power to make his stay as enjoyable and comfortable as possible. Despite these promises, the homesick Coree caused the London merchants much disquiet for he singularly failed to offer them any word of thanks. 'He had good diet, good cloaths, good lodging and all other fitting accommodations,' they said, 'yet all this contented him not.' Indeed the longer he stayed in London, the less he appeared to like the city and 'would daily lie upon the ground and cry very often thus in broken English, "Coree go home, Saldania go, home go." '

It was a surprise present of a suit of chain mail, including a brass helmet and breastplate, that gave Coree a change of heart. He was overjoyed with his gift and would don his 'beloved metal' every morning and clatter through the capital's markets proudly displaying his armour to astonished passers-by. When he was at last shipped back to southern Africa having escaped an undignified end as a stuffed accompaniment to Lord Salisbury's collection of hunting trophies, Coree was still wearing his suit of chain mail. However, the novelty of the armour soon wore off, 'for he had no sooner sett foot on his own shore but did presently throw away his cloaths, his linen and other covering and got his sheepskin upon his back and guts aboute his necke'.

It had long been intended that the Company's third expedition should consist of three ships under the overall command of William Keeling, but the irrepressibly energetic David Middleton, captain of the diminutive *Consent*, tired of the slow progress of the *Red Dragon* and *Hector* and decided to press on without them. It was a wise decision for by the time Captain Keeling reached the Spice Islands, Middleton had already returned to England and was planning his next expedition to the East Indies.

David Middleton was the youngest of the intrepid Middleton trio and the most impatient and businesslike of them all. Never one to dawdle in foreign ports, his overriding concern was to conduct his business in as short a time as possible. Travelling at breakneck pace across the Atlantic he arrived at Table Bay with the loss of just one man, 'Peter Lambert [who] fell off the top-most head, whereof he died.' He paused briefly to stock up on fresh food and was soon under way again, this time heading towards Madagascar. Here Middleton stopped to inspect the island but, after a cursory glance, decided 'there was nothing on it' and continued with his voyage, arriving in Bantam less than eight months after leaving Tilbury.

Almost every expedition that made it to Bantam did so in poor shape. Men on board would be sick and dying while the factors living in the town were generally found

to be in an advanced state of degeneracy. Not so on this
occasion. The ever-efficient David Middleton headed
straight ashore for a meeting with Gabriel Towerson, the
factor left behind by his brother Henry in 1604, and 'found
the merchants in very good health and all things in good
order'. Towerson expressed concern that the youngest
Middleton lacked in experience what he made up for in
enthusiasm and warned him that any dealings with the
Spanish or Portuguese would be viewed with hostility by
the Dutch. But Middleton needed no lectures on how to
conduct business: although sailing in a tiny vessel and
without an accompanying fleet he was full of bravado and
informed Towerson that he 'cared little for their threats and
brags'. Towerson recorded all this in a lengthy letter to his
superiors in London and although scrupulously impartial
when writing about this youngest Middleton, his verbatim
report of Middleton's behaviour does the captain few
favours. Towerson clearly felt that Middleton's headstrong
nature betrayed his youth. But Middleton was no fool and
played a clever game of cat and mouse when he reached
the spice-rich Moluccas. Having dashed across the Indian
Ocean to get here, he now spent more than two months
wining and dining the Spanish and Portuguese, apologising
for not participating in sorties against the Dutch but
explaining that it would run contrary to his orders. He
cared little that the Spanish steadfastly refused to sell him
spices for, in the words of Samuel Purchas, his men 'had
privy trade with the people by night, and were joviall and
frolicke by day with the Spaniards'.

Setting sail from Tidore, his next port of call was the
island of Celebes where he found himself royally
entertained by the King of Butung or, as the jovial crew
nicknamed him, the King of Button. This island was almost

unknown to the English but Middleton enjoyed his stay here and found the King a curious fellow who was only too keen to entertain his guests with banquets and sweetmeats. Some meals were novel affairs; the ship's purser found himself eating in a room whose interior decor consisted entirely of rotting human heads dangling from the ceiling.

Scarcely had the English made their final farewells to the King of Button than they had a stroke of good fortune. The captain of a passing junk sent a message to Middleton that he was laden with cloves which were for sale. Middleton jumped at this piece of news. He bought the lot and, not bothering to sail to the Banda Islands to buy nutmeg, immediately returned to England. One mishap marred their leaving: 'Our captain had bought some slaves from the king,' records the ship's journal, 'and as we were busy this night, one of them stole out of our captain's cabbin door and leaped into the sea, and swum ashore, and was never heard of.' The few captains who later followed Middleton's lead and bought slaves all met with similar problems. They either escaped when the ships reached port or died en route. Slaves apart, the *Consent* had a trouble-free return to England. Middleton had spent just £3,000 on cloves but when they were sold on the London market they reaped more than £36,000.

The rest of the fleet was making painfully slow progress towards the East Indies. Setting sail from England on April Fools' Day, 1607, it was beset by troubles from the very beginning. So numerous were the 'divers disasters', in fact, that its commander, William Keeling, tired of describing them and contented himself with a list: 'Gusts, calms, rains, sickness, and other marine inconveniences.' Keeling was the antithesis of the businesslike David Middleton. In the journal of his voyage he cuts a flamboyant figure whose erratic behaviour was to cause many problems for the Company directors. On a later trip he smuggled his beloved wife on board ship, contrary to Company rules, and kept her hidden in his cabin. She was discovered soon after the ship left England and a rowing boat was sent to bring her back to land, though not before Keeling had written dozens of letters to the exasperated directors in London informing them that he loved his wife dearly and thought their actions to be mean-spirited.

Keeling's other great passion was the plays of William Shakespeare and, as his ship drifted listlessly in the mid-Atlantic, he spent his leisure time planning a magnificent performance of one of the bard's plays. While the men on the *Hector* were busy mending ropes and caulking the decks, the crew of Keeling's vessel were learning speeches, sewing costumes and performing dress rehearsals. Finally, the big day arrived. Dropping anchor off the coast of Sierra Leone the dilettantish Keeling watched a final rehearsal and decided that his men were as good as they would ever be. A select audience was invited from the *Hector* and the play performed under the star-studded African sky. 'We gave,' wrote the proud captain, 'the tragedie of Hamlett.' If this is correct it must have been one of the earliest amateur performances of the play, staged not in the Globe Theatre but on the mangrove-tangled shores of equatorial Africa.

What Keeling's crew thought of these dramatics has passed unrecorded. More certain is that the spills and adventures of English mariners provided Shakespeare with an endless supply of material for his plays, and it was surely one of the East India Company's sailors, mimicking the strictures of his superiors, who put the words into the mouth of Shakespeare's Clown in *Twelfth Night*: 'I would have men of such constancy put to sea, that their business might be everything and their intent everywhere; for that's it that always make a good voyage of nothing.' Other plays echo the risks that investors took when they ploughed money into the spice trade and many merchants must, like Antonio's friend in *The Merchant of Venice*, have spent their waking hours thinking,

> of shallows and of flats;
> And see my wealthy Andrew dock'd in sand
> Vailing her high-top lower than her ribs
> To kiss her burial. Should I go to church
> And see the holy edifice of stone,
> And not bethink me straight of dangerous rocks,
> Which touching but my gentle vessel's side
> Would scatter all her spices on the stream,
> Enrobe the roaring waters with my silks;
> And, in a word, but even now worth this,
> And now worth nothing?

Drama was not the only diversion provided by Keeling. Realising the importance of keeping his men busy he organised a fishing expedition for his crew who, spurred on by his enthusiasm, managed to catch six thousand fish in a single hour. Never one for half measures, he then rowed ashore for a shopping trip and returned with three thousand lemons. He also carted back a massive elephant tusk as a wall-hanging for his cabin. It cost him eight pounds of iron and a couple of yards of cloth.

This last purchase set him thinking: if the natives could slaughter an elephant with their primitive spears, then he would certainly be able to kill one with his musket. And so, 'on the seventh of September in the afternoon, we went all together ashore to see if we could shoot an elephant.' Trekking through the African bush they spied an enormous bull elephant and Keeling and his men immediately opened fire with their muskets: 'We shot seven or eight bullets into him, and made him bleed exceedingly as appeared by his track, but being near night we were constrained aboard without effecting our purposes on him.'

With his men restored to good health it was time to set sail once more. No sooner was the *Red Dragon* clear of the land than Keeling and his men were rehearsing Shakespeare's *King Richard II*. By the end of September the captain thought them sufficiently good to send a boat across to the *Hector* and once again invite Captain Hawkins aboard to watch the play. Keeling was in his element and ordered an elaborate fish dinner to be cooked in honour of the event. Mindful that such entertainments were discouraged by the Company's directors, he justified his actions by explaining that amateur dramatics 'keeps my people from idleness and unlawfull games or sleep'.

After almost nine months at sea the *Red Dragon* and *Hector* at last neared the Cape of Good Hope. They had still received no word from Middleton, but putting into Table Bay to revictual Keeling stumbled across a rock carved with the words: '24 July, 1607: David Middleton in the Consent.' Since then, half a year had passed yet still Keeling was in no hurry. After allowing his crew a leisurely few weeks ashore, he reluctantly put to sea, only to drop anchor again as soon as they reached Madagascar. This time Keeling paused to give his men a chance to wash their clothes, an attention to cleanliness that cost one man dear. Stepping ashore, a certain George Evans was 'sore hurt with a crocodile, or alligator, which had siezed upon the man's leg [as] he had been washing a shirt by the boat's side'. This unfortunate man had been tugged into shallow water where he managed to kick the crocodile so hard that it momentarily released its jaws. Even so, Evans was 'sorely wounded, and recovered the boat, making no other account but that his foot was gone, till he saw that the hind part of the small of his leg was bitten clean asunder both flesh and sinews to the bone; and had the alligator got him into deep water, assuredly he had been carried clean away'.

Another stop, another Shakespeare play, and the ships made their stately progress towards Socotra, a parched island off the Horn of Africa. Even the unhurried Keeling could find little to detain him here and after buying a huge supply of aloes, noted for their efficacy against constipation, he again set sail, this time for Bantam.

Bantam held good news and bad. Keeling was less than happy to be greeted by six Dutch ships in the harbour but overjoyed when the king told him that he was desperate to 'have commerce with so great a king as his Majesty of England with whom, he understood, the King of Holland was not comparable'. True to his word, he allowed the *Red Dragon* to be loaded immediately and, two days before Christmas 1608, she set sail for England. Keeling was not on her: just a few days earlier, he transferred all his goods onto the *Hector* which he now intended to sail to the Banda Islands.

The first of these islands that came into sight was the tiny outpost of Run. Instead of stopping here Keeling sailed east for another ten miles until he reached the larger islands of Great Banda and Neira where there was 'a very fair and spacious harbour' and a safe anchorage was assured. Scarcely had he entered this huge natural harbour than a party of Dutchmen rowed out to his vessel, intrigued by the unexpected arrival of these Englishmen. At first they

Bantam market, circa 1600. It was here that one Englishman, William Clarke, was attacked by a Dutch gang who stripped him naked and 'cruelly cut his flesh, and then washed him with salt and vinegar.'

were cordial in their greetings; they blasted their cannon in Keeling's honour and even invited him to a feast. But their friendship soon turned sour when they discovered that Keeling had presented the local headman with a letter from King James I, along with a gilded beaker, an ornamental helmet and a first-class musket. Resorting to underhand tactics, they sent a message over to the *Hector* informing Keeling that there were plots against his life and that he should set sail immediately.

The English captain was unmoved and, after paying some four hundred pieces-of-eight to the headman of Great Banda, his men began buying large quantities of nutmeg from the local growers. He was unhurried in his trade for he knew that the winds which had carried him to the Banda Islands were on the brink of shifting direction and, with the imminent arrival of the monsoon, was confident that no more Dutch ships would be able to sail east from Bantam. It was with considerable surprise, therefore, that he opened the curtains of his cabin on the morning of 16 March 1609, and saw three Dutch vessels sail into view.

The crew of these new ships came to visit the *Hector* and were outwardly friendly, but 'an Englishman [serving on one of the ships] reporteth that they mean to surprise us ere a month expire'. They were, in fact, already hampering Keeling's business and within days of their arrival the price of nutmeg had rocketed. Abandoning trade with Great Banda, the English captain 'made a secret accord with the chief of Ai Island' and prepared to send a factor there. But less than a week had passed before there was further bad news. Not only had the Dutch learned about this secret deal and vowed to undermine it, they had also received reinforcements in the shape of six more vessels. This was an entirely unexpected development and left Keeling with very few options. 'Sixty-two men against a thousand or more could not perform much,' he wrote. Outnumbered and outgunned, he realised that friendship was his only option and as the Dutch ships approached he lamely ordered his men to welcome them with a burst of cannon fire. Keeling also discovered that he was fast developing an allergy to nutmeg and that far from curing sickness it was actually making him ill. 'I went aboard,' he writes irritably, 'to cure mine eyes which, by the heat of the nuts, were very sore.'

He was by now thoroughly dispirited. The Dutch were treating him 'most unkindlye, searching his boate disgracefullye ... and not suffering him to have any further trade, not to gather in his debts, but with a peremptory comaund, to be gone'. Keeling held a secret meeting with the ruler of Neira and tentatively suggested that he surrender his authority to King James I in return for trade and protection. He was pleased to learn that the headman was interested in the proposal but, 'doubted their inconstancies'. He continued to play his game of bluff with the Dutch, warning them that 'his majesty of England, our sovereign, would not permit his subjects to sustain any damage by their means without special and sound satisfaction.' The Dutch simply ignored him for they were getting a perverse enjoyment in goading Keeling. When they filched some sacks of rice from under his nose, the English commander lost his temper. Grabbing the Dutch admiral's messenger, 'I requested [him] to tell his admiral ... that if he were a gentleman, he would not permit his base people to abuse me as I walked among them.' The messenger sniggered when he heard this and replied that his admiral was not a gentleman but a weaver.

Keeling was in a hopeless position. Denied spices and spied upon day and night, he could have been forgiven for abandoning the Company's orders and setting sail for England. But no sooner had he considered such an option than the entire situation changed. Yet another Dutch fleet arrived in the Banda Islands, and it was carrying new and wholly unwelcome orders.

★

The commander of this latest fleet, Peter Verhoef, was a spirited fighter who had first acquitted himself at the Battle of Gibraltar two years previously when he masterminded the annihilation of the Spanish fleet. Now, he was despatched on a mission which, although ostensibly to buy spices, had an unambiguously military objective. 'We draw your special attention to the islands in which grow cloves and nutmeg,' wrote the Seventeen in their instructions, 'and we instruct you to strive to win them for the Company either by treaty or by force.'

Following their instructions to the letter, Verhoef sailed directly to the Banda Isles with his impressive fleet which carried at least a thousand Dutch fighting men, as well as a contingent of Japanese mercenaries. On his arrival at Great Banda he ceremoniously presented the headman with his credentials and summoned all the local chieftains to a meeting 'under a greate tree'. Reading from a prepared script, first in Portuguese and then in Malayan, he admonished them for breaking their promise 'to have trade only with them, who had now traded there six yeares ... and were often much abused'. He went on to explain that he intended to construct a castle on Neira Island 'to defend themselves and the whole countrey from Portugals'. This news was greeted with 'uprore' by the natives who, 'but for feare of their shipping would have slaine the Hollanders'.

Verhoef found it impossible to negotiate with the chieftains who seemed to lack any overall authority. Although numerous documents refer to a 'King of Banda' there was no such person. Instead, every island and every village had its own headman whose authority extended over a few hundred people at most. In informing more than two hundred headmen of his intentions, Verhoef had at a stroke made himself a common enemy.

Ignoring their threats, he promptly landed 750 soldiers on Neira and instructed them to start digging the foundations. The building, whose massive walls are still visible beneath a curtain of creepers, was constructed on the site of a Portuguese fort which had been abandoned almost a century previously. The headmen watched with alarm as the fort's outer walls grew in height and on 22 May 1609, they asked for a meeting with the Dutch commander. Verhoef immediately agreed, hoping that they would at last consent to his plans.

After the passing of almost four centuries it is hard to piece together exactly what happened next. The Dutch records suggest that William Keeling helped instigate the ensuing massacre, but this accusation contradicts his own diaries. Although he had certainly struck a number of secret deals with the natives, there is nothing to suggest he was actively inciting them to violence. Indeed, he was busy buying nutmeg at Ai Island, a day's sailing from Neira, when rumours of a plot began to circulate.

The first hint of trouble was conveyed to Keeling by the chief of the island. He was told that on no account should he set sail for Neira unless he wanted to be henceforth regarded as an enemy. Keeling was intrigued and took to his bed in order to puzzle over this cryptic message. The following night things became clearer. 'As I was going to bed, there came a command upon our lives that we should not stir out of doors. And presently I heard that the Dutch were upon their knees to the people.' Throwing on his clothes, 'I armed myself and went out among them, where I found the Dutch overcome with fear.' One of their colleagues had been shot in the leg while the others had been threatened with their lives.

If the situation on Ai was unsettled, on Neira it had

turned murderous. Verhoef had sailed to the island's eastern
coastline in order to meet the native headmen, but when
he stepped ashore he discovered that the headmen were
nowhere to be found. This was strange. He had certainly
got the right day and he knew for certain that this was the
village where the two sides had agreed to meet. As he
pondered what to do next, a lone native appeared from the
woods and 'told the admiral that the orang-kayas, and other
chiefs of the isles, were nearby in the woods but were so
frightened by the soldiers that the admiral had with him
that they feared to come unto him'. The native messenger
asked Verhoef and his advisors if they would leave the
soldiers and weapons on the beach and step into the woods
for the meeting. Amazingly, Verhoef agreed and led the
cream of the Dutch command into a deadly trap. 'And
being entered among them he found the woods
replenished with armed blackamoores, Bandanese, and
orang-kayas who instantly encircled them and without
much conference between them passed, were by them
treacherously and villainously massacred.'

The last words Verhoef heard were those of his
subordinate, Jan de Bruin, who cried in panic, 'Admiral, we
are betrayed!' Defenceless and unarmed, there was nothing
the men could do. All forty-two Dutchmen who entered
the grove were butchered and their heads severed from
their bodies. The Bandanese then attacked the soldiers on
the beach before inciting a general uprising.

The Dutch now found themselves in a perilous
position. An emergency council was summoned and
elected a new leader, Simon Hoen, who hurried back to
the half-built castle and urged his men to work even harder
to complete the construction. Hoen did not waste any time
in taking his revenge; the blood-flag was hoisted from his

flagship and the Dutch made a formal declaration of war against Neira Island and began to 'execute and practise all revenge possible'. Villages were burned, vessels destroyed and natives butchered.

On 10 August 1609, a peace treaty was at last signed on board Hoen's flagship. This pact, agreed by only a handful of orang-kaya, stated that henceforth Neira Island was to be placed under Dutch dominion and 'to be kept by us forever' – the first territorial acquisition by the Dutch in the East Indies – while the rest of the islands were to suffer similar losses to their freedom. Furthermore, the headman was forced to 'sweare that they would thereafter have trade with none other nation whatsoever it were but sell all their nuts and mace to the Hollanders only'. Hoen sent a letter to Captain Keeling informing him of this fact and commanding him to sail from the Banda Isles within five days and never to return – the beginning of 'the warres betwixt the English and Dutch'.

Keeling, having suffered so many indignities at the hands of the Dutch, now felt he was in a position to act defiantly. He sent a reply stating that there was no question of him leaving the Banda Islands since he had just managed to procure a large batch of spices which would take a full twenty-five days to load on board. He also informed Hoen that he intended to leave a permanent English factory on Ai Island.

Keeling's bluff worked. He was well aware that 'oftentimes rash men threaten to kill which they durst not for life perform': so it was on this occasion. He loaded his spices in peace and, happy to bid farewell to the Banda Islands, set sail for England. At last, after months of hardship, he had time to perform some Shakespeare again.

CHAPTER SIX

A REBEL
AT SEA

I N THE SUMMER OF 1558, almost five years after Sir Hugh Willoughby's fateful expedition to the Arctic, a piece of disconcerting news filtered into London. It was rumoured that a resourceful young explorer from Brussels called Oliver Brunel had travelled a considerable distance along the northern shores of Russia and claimed he was on the verge of discovering the North-East Passage. Confident of success, he was now planning to board a Russian ship and continue sailing until he reached the Spice Islands – a route that would slash two thousand miles and more than a year's sailing time off the long journey east.

This news was a cause of great anxiety to London's merchants for Brunel's sympathies lay with the Dutch and any discovery would be to their benefit. It was imperative that Brunel's exploration should be stopped in its tracks and, to this end, the merchants of the newly formed Muscovy Company promptly denounced him to the Russians as a spy and the unfortunate Brunel spent the next twelve years in prison.

Lesser men might have found their enthusiasm for foreign travel dampened by this experience. Not Brunel: no sooner had he been released from jail than he set off eastwards again, this time in the employ of the Strogonov family. Exploring the ice-shattered coastline of Arctic

Russia, he compiled endless notes and charts and eventually returned to Holland to find a string of geographers waiting to meet him, including the distinguished Gerardus Mercator. Mercator was overjoyed to discover that Brunel brought the news he had been waiting so long to hear; for years a constant trickle of hearsay and rumour had reached both Amsterdam and London suggesting that there was indeed a navigable North-East Passage that led to the Spice Islands. Many of these stories were decades old, and even more were complete fiction, but each new finding saw geographers redrawing their charts of the Arctic, much of which remained a vast white blank known only as Terra Incognita.

What was particularly interesting about Brunel's findings was that he claimed to have reached the fabled River Ob which, it was believed, wound a golden route in the direction of the Indies. 'It is,' wrote one trader, 'a common received speech of the Russes that are great travellers, that beyond the Ob to the south-east there is a warm sea, which they express in these words in the Russe tongue: "Za Oby reca moria Templa;" that is to say, "beyond the River Ob is a warm sea." '

No one could be sure whether or not this was true and even Brunel had not managed to sail down the River Ob, but a persistent stream of rumours suggested that the Ob did indeed lead to the tropics. Certainly the dependable merchants of the newly formed Muscovy Company believed the stories and often added their own tales to the increasing dossier of evidence. Chief merchant Francis Cherry told his London bosses that he had eaten a sturgeon from the Ob; others, more tantalisingly, declared that they had seen 'great vessels, laden with rich and precious merchandise, brought down that great river by black or swart people'.

This caused great excitement among London's spice merchants; the more so when they learned that the people living on the shores of the Ob appeared to be of Chinese descent for 'whenever they make mention of the people named Carrah Colmak (this country is Cathay) they fetch deep sighs and, holding up their hands look to heaven signifying, as it were, and declaring the notable glory and magnificence of that nation.'

Despite all the evidence, the English were wary about furnishing a new expedition in search of the northern route to the 'spiceries'. A handful of bold adventurers continued to try their hand at sailing into the Arctic and an expedition despatched in 1580 managed to sail a considerable distance across the Kara Sea before finding its path blocked by pack-ice. But the mission was not a complete failure for the crew returned to England with a strange horn, some six feet long and decorated with a spiral twirl. Ignorant of the existence of the narwhal – that strange member of the whale family that has a single tusk protruding from its head – the rough English mariners confidently declared that this odd piece of flotsam had once belonged to a unicorn, a highly significant find, for 'knowing that unicorns are bred in the lands of Cathay, China and other Oriental Regions, [the sailors] fell into consideration that the same head was brought thither by the course of the sea, and that there must of necessity be a passage out of the said Oriental Ocean into our Septentrionall seas.'

The English were urged on in their Arctic endeavours by Samuel Purchas who called upon all intrepid and adventurous men to set sail in search of a passage, reminding them that their journey towards the 'spiceries' would shorten with every step they took towards the Pole, 'where that vast line at the Circumference itself becomes no line anymore, but a Point, but Nothing, but Vanitie'. Purchas's poetry failed to stir his English compatriots but his enthusiasm was echoed in Holland by the more practically minded Mercator who gave repeated assurances that Arctic exploration was not as dangerous as was commonly supposed. 'The voyage to Cathay by the east is doubtless very easy and short,' he wrote dismissively, 'and I have oftentimes marvelled that being so happily begun it hath been left off, and the course changed to the West, after more than half of the voyage was discovered.'

Advice of a more concrete sort came from Petrus Plancius, the man who would help to despatch the first Dutch expedition to the Indies in 1595 and who was as keen as ever on sending a fleet over the top of the North Pole. Arguing that fresh water froze more easily than salt, he maintained that the coastline of Russia was continually choked with ice because of all the water pouring into the sea from freshwater rivers such as the Ob. His advice to the Dutch explorers was to sail further north, away from the land, where they would find a sea completely free from ice.

In the wake of such demonstrable logic three fleets set sail in succession. The first, which left the Texel in 1594, was so confident of success that it carried letters in Arabic to be handed to the eastern potentates on arrival in the Spice Islands. Splitting into two groups, the first squadron was commanded by an accomplished mariner called William Barents who was destined to go down in history as one of the greatest of all polar explorers. But even his navigational skills were useless in the frozen wastes of the Arctic and it was not long before his ship reached a 'great store of ice, as much as they could descry out of the top, that lay like a plain field of ice'. He sailed more than fifteen hundred miles in search of a passage through this ice but was eventually forced to admit defeat.

Cornelis Nay, commander of the second group, was more fortunate. Sailing through the Strait of Vaygach to the south of Novaya Zemlya, he had a trouble-free passage into the Kara Sea and would have continued eastward if summer had not come to an abrupt end. He returned to Holland and boldly pronounced that he had discovered the North-East Passage, informing the Dutch merchants that it was 'ready-made and certaine'. Nay was fêted as a hero. Northern Russia was renamed New Holland, the Kara Sea became the New North Sea, and the Strait of Vaygach was rechristened Strait Nassau.

There was no time to lose for other nations, particularly the English, were certain to hear such momentous news. The following summer a second fleet was sent with the full expectation of it reaching the Spice Islands by Christmas. It was not to be. Strait Nassau was choked with ice and the New North Sea was frozen solid. Morale plummeted when two men, caught stealing pelts from natives, were disciplined in accordance with the rules of the ship. This involved being keel-hauled three times in a row – a brutal enough punishment in the warm waters of the Indies but even more dangerous when performed in the glacial Arctic. The first man had his head ripped off as he was pulled under the vessel. The second survived only to be cast ashore where he froze to death. A small mutiny followed, resulting in the hanging of five men, and by the time the expedition arrived back in Holland, the crew had lost their enthusiasm for their Arctic adventure.

The States of Holland and Zeeland decided to abandon the project, arguing that they had already spent a fortune on an increasingly futile venture. But the merchants of

The Dutchmen built a shelter and survived by eating bear-meat. One bear 'did us more hurt than her life, for after we ripped her belly we dressed her liver and ate it ... but it made us all sick.'

Amsterdam were undeterred by the repeated failures and promptly equipped a third fleet of two ships which set sail in the spring of 1596 under the overall command of William Barents, with Jacob van Heemskerck as captain. Trapped in ice somewhere to the north of Novaya Zemlya, the two men were convinced that their experience of Arctic climes would enable them to survive the winter. Building a temporary shelter out of logs and driftwood — a shelter so well constructed that it was still standing three centuries later when visited by Englishman Charles Gardiner — they hibernated for eight months. Good humour helped them win their battle for survival. In January they feasted on flour after crowning their ship's constable King of Novaya Zemlya whilst in February they shot a polar bear 'that gave us a hundred pounds of fat'. In June the ice at last began to thaw revealing that the ship had been crushed beyond repair. Two small craft were hastily built by the remaining survivors who were encouraged in their endeavours by the jocular Barents. Although desperately sick he kept everyone in good spirits: 'Our lives depend on it, boys,' he jested. 'If we cannot get the boats ready we shall have to die here as burghers of Novaya Zemlya.'

A few days later he expired, leaving Heemskerck to guide the little boats through the ice. Nearly two months passed before the survivors spied a Dutch ship close to the Kola Peninsula, which came to the rescue. When Heemskerck and his men eventually reached Holland and had an audience with their Amsterdam financiers they betrayed a considerable cynicism about any northern route to the Spice Islands. To reinforce the message that the North Pole was no place to go looking for spices, they pitched up at the meeting dressed in full Arctic clothing, including 'fur caps made of white foxes'.

With the failure of this third expedition, enthusiasm for the northern project waned. Although a prize of 25,000 guilders awaited anyone who did break through the ice, more than a decade was to pass before any ship, Dutch or English, ventured further east than the White Sea port of Archangel. The Reverend Purchas was distraught: 'That which I most grieve at,' he wrote, 'is the detention of further discovery of the Pole and beyond.' He believed that it was the duty of rich merchants to finance polar exploration, for 'they might get the world and give us the world better if Charitie were their Needle, Grace their Compasse, Heaven their Haven, and if they would take the height by observing the Sun of Righteousness in the

As the temperature plummeted, 'it froze so sore within the house that the walls and the roof thereof were frozen two fingers thick with ice.'

Scripture-astrolabe, and sounding their depth by a Leading Faith, and not by a leaden bottomless Covetousness.'

In 1608, word reached Purchas that an English explorer by the name of Henry Hudson had made two journeys northwards, setting sail with the intention of crossing the pole and continuing on to the 'islands of spicerie'. Although he had failed in both these aims he had covered considerable distances, touching land at Novaya Zemlya, Spitzbergen and even the eastern coastline of Greenland. But what really excited Purchas was that Hudson had travelled further north than any mariner before him; sailing, indeed, to within less than ten degrees of the Pole.

The London merchants expressed interest in Hudson's findings but were too preoccupied with bringing their ships home around the Cape of Good Hope to entertain the idea of equipping a new expedition to the north. Not so their Dutch counterparts; learning of Hudson's voyage and fearing that the North-East Passage might be discovered by their English rivals, they instructed their wise old consul in London, Emanuel van Meteren, to make contact with Hudson and bring him back to Holland.

Hudson arrived in Amsterdam in the winter of 1608 and was immediately granted an audience with the directors of the Dutch East India Company, to whom he presented his discoveries as the eighth wonder of the world. He told them of his conviction that there was an open sea at the North Pole, as Plancius had suggested, explaining that the further north he had sailed the warmer the climate became; and that instead of being confronted with ice and snow he had found land covered with grasses and wild flowers as well as many different species of animals living solely from the produce of the land.

The merchants were intrigued and asked Hudson why their own mariners had failed to find this temperate land. To this the English explorer had a ready explanation. In order to reach the mild climate of the North Pole, he said, it was necessary to push beyond 74 degrees latitude – the point at which the Dutch ships had always found their path blocked by ice – into the open sea where the great depth of the water and the swell of the waves prevented any ice from forming. Furthermore, he confidently asserted that if 83 degrees latitude was reached – somewhere to the north of Franz Josef Land – it would be possible to turn eastwards and break through to the warm seas of the East Indies.

Hudson's theory sounded plausible but the merchants had suffered so many failures in their Arctic exploits that they demanded further evidence. Summoning Petrus

Plancius to their meeting, they asked for his opinion of Hudson's findings. Not only did Plancius concur with every word, he actually reinforced the Englishman's claims with his own evidence. He argued that although the heat of the sun is extremely weak at the North Pole, the fact that it shines uninterrupted for almost five months of the year enables a permanent warmth to build up at the top of the world. To prove his point he reminded the directors that a small fire kept alight for a long time in the same place gives out considerably more heat than a large fire that is constantly extinguished.

The Amsterdam directors were impressed with this explanation but hesitated in equipping a fleet immediately, largely because Company rules dictated that an expedition to the Spice Islands could only set sail with the unanimous consent of the Council of Seventeen. Since that only met two or three times a year they would not be able to agree to any project until its next meeting which was scheduled for late spring 1609. Unfortunately this would be too late in the season to send an expedition across the Arctic, so Hudson would have to wait a further year before he could set sail.

This uncharacteristic hesitation nearly cost the directors dear. The charter of the Dutch East India Company gave them a monopoly on any trade passing by way of the Cape of Good Hope or the Magellan Straits, but there was no mention of any northern route to the Spice Islands, leaving the inescapable conclusion that if any dissident merchant were to go in search of the North-East Passage it would be beyond the power of the Seventeen to stop him. By the time Hudson visited Amsterdam just such a situation had arisen. Isaac Lemaire, one of the city's wealthiest merchants, had grown increasingly dissatisfied with what he considered to be Holland's overly cautious approach to trade and, in 1605, promptly withdrew his support. He was now their enemy, and a dangerous one at that, for he vowed to do everything in his power to undermine his former partners. When he heard that they had effectively turned down Hudson's proposal for an immediate voyage to the North he made contact with the English navigator and suggested the two men form a partnership. Lemaire had powerful backing: King Henry IV of France had watched with growing jealousy the Dutch ships sail up the Channel and was anxious to have his share of the riches of the East Indies. When he learned of Lemaire's rift with his erstwhile partners the King made contact with the Dutchman through his ambassador, Pierre Jeannin.

The ensuing negotiations had to be conducted in the utmost secrecy lest the Seventeen, who were 'fearful above all things of being forestalled in this design', should learn of the plan. A meeting was sought with Hudson, and the English explorer, irritated that the Seventeen were dragging their feet, placed his Arctic research at the disposal of the two men.

As soon as Jeannin had read these findings he wrote to the French King urging him to finance a Hudson-led expedition to the Arctic. He predicted that the return journey to the Spice Islands would take just six months, with the added advantage that not a single foreign carrack would be met en route. 'It is true,' wrote Jeannin, 'that the success of this undertaking cannot be promised with certainty, but Lemaire has long been making inquiries as to what results could be expected from this enterprise and he is regarded as a prudent and industrious man.' He added that 'it is the opinion of Plancius and other geographers that there are other lands which have not yet been discovered and which God may be reserving for the glory and advantage of other princes ... Even if nothing should come of it, it will always be a laudable thing, and the regret will not be great since so little will be risked.'

The King acted promptly on receipt of this letter. Although sceptical about the project he was sufficiently enthused to send a draft for four thousand crowns. Unfortunately the money arrived too late. Learning of Lemaire's secret meetings with Hudson, the Seventeen urgently recalled the Englishman and this time acted swiftly. A contract was drawn up in which Hudson was named as captain of an expedition to discover the northern route to the Spice Islands and which included details of the route he was to take, the payment he would receive, and the obligations placed upon him. 'The above named Hudson shall about the first of April, sail, in order to search for a passage by the North, around by the North side of Nova Zembla, and shall continue thus along that parallel until he shall be able to sail Southward to the latitude of sixty degrees.' Throughout the voyage he was to 'obtain as much knowledge of the lands as can be done without any considerable loss of time and, if it is possible, return immediately in order to make a faithful report and relation of his voyage to the Directors, and to deliver over his journals, log-books and charts, together with an account of everything whatsoever which shall happen to him during the voyage without keeping anything back'. In return for his services, 'the Directors shall pay to the said Hudson ... the sum of eight hundred guilders; and in case (which God prevent) he do not come back or arrive hereabouts within a year, the Directors shall further pay to his wife two hundred guilders in cash; and thereupon they shall not be further liable to him or his heirs.'

The contract throws light on the considerable risks that

explorers like Hudson were prepared to take. The vessel he was to sail in was tiny – sixty tons is scarcely bigger than a modern yacht – and poorly equipped for seas littered with icebergs. The financial reward, too, was paltry, whilst payment for any success was left entirely in the hands of his employers who 'will reward the before named Hudson for his dangers, trouble and knowledge in their discretion'. Nor was he offered any assurance of future employment; the contract was for a single exploratory voyage only. Even more surprising is that Hudson should agree to such a pitiful sum being paid to his wife in the event of him dying while at sea. Possibly he could not persuade the Seventeen to part with any more money, but more probably he had supreme confidence in his own abilities.

A curious set of additional instructions were handed to Hudson shortly before he set sail. These stated in even greater detail the route that he was to take and explicitly ordered him 'to think of discovering no other routes or passages, except the route around by the North and North-East above Nova Zembla'. Why the Seventeen added this last clause remains a mystery but perhaps, even now, they had an inkling that Hudson would ignore all their instructions once he had set sail. Certainly there was some disquiet about this headstrong Englishman for one of the Company letters, referring to a dispute over the crew's wages, states: 'If he begins to rebel here under our eyes what will he do if he is away from us?'

Subsequent events were to prove that they were right to be concerned about Hudson's behaviour and were fully justified in mistrusting his leadership. But what the Dutch merchants could never have imagined was that his 1609 voyage would have such a profound and lasting consequence on the spice race.

A Rebel at Sea

The *Half Moon* set sail in March of that year with a mixed crew of Dutch and English mariners. The vessel was built with a high forecastle and poop, and resembled in appearance the shallow-bottomed *vlie* boats used in the calm waters of the Zuider Zee. Few who watched its slow progress towards the North Sea, and fewer still among its crew, could have guessed that Hudson had no intention of sailing along the northern coastline of Russia; and that unbeknown to anyone he had set sail with his cabin piled high with charts and maps relating not to the North-East Passage, but to the North-West Passage, and it was this western waterway that he now wished to research.

Hudson's own account of the voyage has been lost but two contemporary journals have survived. One, written by Robert Juet, Hudson's mate, is a colourful and personal account of events on board; whilst the other, by Emanuel van Meteren, is drawn from conversations with Hudson's crew on their return. Juet provides little information about the early weeks of the voyage and records scant detail until the *Half Moon* had edged her way towards the Arctic pack-ice. He does mention a 'black fortnight' and refers to 'much trouble' although whether this is due to the crew or the 'close stormie weather, with much wind and snow', is not clear.

Emanuel van Meteren tells a more intriguing story. He relates that even in these early weeks there were bitter quarrels between the Dutch and English sailors and that some of the crew staged an abortive mutiny against their captain. The appalling weather only increased their discomfort for some of the Dutch crew were only recently returned from the Indies and were used to sailing in the languid heat of the tropics. Now they were heading into altogether colder climes where it was necessary to chip blocks of ice off the ropes before they could be hauled through the pulleys.

At exactly noon on 21 May 1609, the crew of the *Half Moon* were called on deck to watch something peculiar happening to the sun. 'We observed the sunne having a slake', says Juet, 'and found our height to be 70 degrees, 30 minutes.' The word 'slake' means 'an accumulation of mud or slime', suggesting that Juet was describing a sun spot. If so, this is the earliest recorded sighting, for the observation of astronomer Thomas Hariot – usually considered the first on record – was not until the winter of 1610.

Troubled by tempestuous winds and snow showers, as well as a rebellious crew, Hudson now decided to abandon his search for the North-East Passage and instead head westwards across the Atlantic. According to van Meteren, 'Master Hudson gave [the crew] their choice between two things': to head to the Spice Islands by way of the Davis Straits far to the north of Baffin Island, or to sail down the eastern seaboard of America until they reached the 40 degrees latitude at which point he hoped to force his passage through to the Pacific. This latter route, Hudson's preferred option, had been drawn to his attention by the English navigator George Weymouth who had explored America's eastern coastline in 1602 and 1605 and had, on at least one of these expeditions, reached the entrance to the Hudson River. Weymouth himself would have proceeded upstream had it not been for 'the imbecility of his crew' who forced him to return home.

How Weymouth's charts and maps came into Hudson's possession remains unclear. According to a Dutch account, 'the journals of George Weymouth, which fell into the hands of Domine P Plancius ... were of the greatest service to Hudson in his exploration of this famous strait, for in the year 1609, when he was negotiating with the Directors of the [Dutch East] India Company ... he begged these journals from D P Plancius.' This suggests that even as Hudson was signing up for an expedition to discover the North-East Passage, his real interest was in sailing westwards across the Atlantic.

A week after Hudson's crew had chosen the second option – an attempt on the supposed southerly passage – the *Half Moon* came in sight of the jagged silhouette of the Faroe Islands. Hudson had visited these islands before and knew they were a good place to revictual. Anchoring far from the shore for fear of the treacherous rocks and dangerous whirlpools, he sent a small party ashore to fill the ship's casks with fresh water. On 30 May 1609, the weather brightened and the crew caught a glimpse of the sun, prompting Hudson to lead all the men ashore for some exercise. Unfortunately Juet, keeper of the journal, stayed aboard so there is no record of what the sailors made of these primitive, cormorant-eating islanders who traded seal skins and still spoke a peculiar dialect of ancient Norse.

Setting sail once again they kept a sharp look-out for Busse Island, discovered thirty years previously by Martin Frobisher, but the rolling sea mists had grown too thick. Storms and gale-force winds plagued them for days on end and at one point grew so ferocious that the foremast cracked, splintered and was hurled into the sea. It was with considerable relief that the crew sighted through the mist the coast of Newfoundland – a vague geographical term in Hudson's day – at the beginning of July. They dropped anchor in Penobscot Bay, some one hundred miles west of Nova Scotia.

It was not long before the Indians on shore caught a glimpse of the vessel and, 'at ten of the clock, two boats came off to us, with six of the savages of the country, seeming glad of our coming. We gave them trifles, and they ate and drank with us; and told us that there were gold, silver and copper mines hard by us; and that the Frenchmen do trade with them; which is very likely, for one of them spoke some words of French.' The French, in fact, had been fishing these rich waters since the days of the Cabots and often ventured ashore to barter knives, hatchets and kettles for beaver skins and other furs. They must have treated the natives well for the *Half Moon* was given a warm welcome, a reception not reciprocated by Hudson's crew who headed ashore armed with muskets and stole one of the Indians' small boats. Realising that the Indians were powerless to defend themselves, they rowed ashore for a second time armed with 'two stone pieces or murderers', drove the 'savages' from their houses and 'took the spoil of them'.

Such barbarous and confrontational acts repeatedly stain the pages of Juet's journal. Throughout his account he views the native Indians – always described as 'savages' and usually treacherous ones at that – with a distrust approaching hatred and sees nothing untoward in firing at approaching canoes. What Hudson made of such behaviour can only be guessed at. His personality is shadowy in the extreme and much that is known of him is derived from the writings of others who usually bore a grudge against their captain. He was, perhaps, morose and suspicious, and quite possibly indulged his favourites at the expense of others, yet in the few surviving fragments of his own writings he always speaks kindly of the native Indians and appears to have held them in the highest respect. He and his crew seem to have disagreed entirely on how the Indians should be treated and while his personal acts of kindness to the natives were reciprocated with friendship, his crew's hostility was met with mistrust. Hudson's weakness was that he was unable to keep his subordinates under control, and it comes as no surprise that his eventual end, on his next voyage west, should be not at the hands of an irate Indian but of his own mutinous crew.

The *Half Moon* now headed south towards Cape Cod pausing briefly to allow a particularly jolly Indian to come on board, plying him with so much liquor that he 'leaped and danced and held up his hands'. As the ship passed the English colony of Virginia, the captain's cat mysteriously ran from one side of the ship to the other, wailing and mewling all night and causing considerable anxiety aboard.

Towards the end of August 1609, the *Half Moon* reached Cape Charles, the southernmost point of its voyage, and the men caught their first glimpse of Chesapeake Bay, 'a white sandy shore [which] sheweth full of bays and points'. From here they headed north once more and, two days later, reached Delaware Bay. They had now entered the region in which Hudson thought he might find the channel that would lead their ship to the Spice Islands and all the men were told to keep a watch for any inlet or estuary that looked promising. Juet climbed the mast several times to look for the elusive channel but each time he was disappointed. A forest fire broke the darkness on 2 September but the shoreline remained indistinct and even when the first rays of the sun rose above the horizon it was hard to chart the coastline for it was 'all like broken islands'. At last the light strengthened and Harbour Hill on Long Island hove into view followed, a few hours later, by the gleaming flats of Sandy Hook. When the *Half Moon* finally dropped anchor, Hudson found himself in 'a very good harbour, and four or five fathoms, two cables length from the shore'. According to American tradition, he had arrived at Coney Island at the mouth of the Hudson River.

★

Hudson was not the first explorer to discover the Hudson: that honour goes to Giovanni da Verrazano, a navigator in the service of the French King François I who had sailed into the natural harbour some eighty-five years earlier. Like Hudson, he was searching for a passage through to the Pacific and had also been struck by the natural beauty of the landscape. In a letter to the King he wrote that 'we found a very pleasant situation among some steep hills, through which a very large river, deep at its mouth, forced its way to the sea; from the sea to the estuary of the river, any ship heavily laden might pass, with the help of the tide, which rises eight feet.' Verrazano would have continued upstream had it not been for a 'violent contrary wind' which suddenly blew in from the sea and forced him to depart. 'I did not doubt that I should penetrate by some passage to the eastern ocean,' he recorded in his journal. It was this passage that Hudson now hoped to discover, a passage that would slash thousands of miles off the journey to the 'spiceries'.

After dropping anchor off Coney Island, Hudson sent a small party ashore on a reconnaissance mission. They returned with a band of curious natives who had watched with wide-eyed astonishment as the *Half Moon* had approached their island. Dressed in deer skins and proffering green tobacco, they expressed an interest in acquiring knives and glass beads. The following day the crew rowed ashore again though this time they headed towards either New Jersey or Staten Island. Here they were amazed by the 'very goodly oaks' that were 'of a height and thickness that one seldom beholds'. Indeed everywhere they landed they were astonished by the abundance of fruit that grew without cultivation: the blue plums, red and white vines, and whortleberries, not to mention the poplars, linden trees, 'and various other kinds of wood useful in ship building'.

So far the trigger-happy crew had been well received by the native Indians but they were soon to discover that their arrival was not everywhere greeted with the same enthusiasm. Hudson had sent Englishman John Coleman with a party of four others through the Narrows, and as the men chatted about the beauty of the landscape and savoured the 'very sweet smells' that came from the flowers on the foreshore, a hail of arrows descended without warning upon their boat, piercing Coleman's throat and killing him instantly. The others rowed desperately away from the shore but dusk descended before they could regain the *Half Moon* and they spent the rest of the night fighting the current with their grapnel and trying to stop their boat being dragged out to sea. It was not until ten o'clock in the morning when they finally rejoined the ship, and almost noon by the time they buried their colleague at Coleman's Point, close to Sandy Hook.

Incensed by the attack, and now fearful of stepping ashore, the crew weighed anchor and set sail up the Hudson River. On the way they bartered with the natives for provisions and even brought a small party of 'savages' aboard the *Half Moon*. This was not done in a spirit of friendliness: mindful of Sebastian Cabot's famous advice that 'if [a native] may be made drunk with your beer or wine you shall know the secrets of his heart', Hudson now plied his Indian guests with 'so much wine and aqua vitae that they were all merrie'. Unfortunately, they soon became so 'merrie' that they were unable to tell him anything about the supposed passage that led to the Indies and it was only with considerable difficulty that they managed to row back to the shore. But although Hudson learned nothing about the geography of the region from his impromptu drinks party, the gathering did help to restore relations between the crew and the natives and the next day saw the two groups once again bartering their goods. Continuing upstream the *Half Moon* soon arrived at 'that side of the river that is called Manna–hata'. Some six months after leaving Holland, and more than four thousand miles from where he was supposed to be, Hudson had arrived at the island of Manhattan.

Although most of Hudson's writings have been lost, a fragment of his journal was transcribed by a Dutch merchant called John de Laet. De Laet quotes Hudson's account of being paddled ashore by an elderly Indian, a passage that throws considerable light on the English captain's personality. There is none of the intolerance shown by Juet and his men. Instead, Hudson seems intrigued by the Indian customs and impressed by their kindness. 'I sailed to the shore in one of their canoes with an old man who was the chief of the tribe,' he writes, 'consisting of forty men and seventeen women; these I saw there in a house well constructed of oak bark, and circular in shape, so that it had the appearance of being well built, with an arched roof.' Hudson was surprised at the abundance of food, for the house 'contained a great quantity of maize or Indian corn, and beans of last year's growth, and there lay near the house for the purpose of drying, enough to load three ships, besides what was growing in the fields'. He was immediately made welcome by the Indians who, 'on our coming into the house, [spread] two mats … and immediately some food was served in well made red wooden bowls'. It soon became apparent that Hudson was to partake in a lengthy feast:

Two men were also despatched at once with bows and arrows in quest of game, who soon after brought in a pair of pigeons which they had shot. They likewise killed a fat dog, and skinned it in great haste, with shells which they had got out of the water. They supposed that I would remain with them for the night, but I returned after a short time on board the ship.

The land is the finest for cultivation that I ever in my life set foot upon, and it also abounds in trees of every description. The natives are a very good people, for when they saw that I would not remain they supposed that I was afraid of their bows, and taking the arrows, they broke them in pieces and threw them into the fire.

The journals and letters written by men like Hudson and Juet, along with the accounts preserved by the English East India Company, form an invaluable record of the first European contact with native tribes. Much rarer are the records of what the natives thought of the unshaven English mariners who pitched up on their shores. Hudson's arrival at Manhattan is the exception, a result of the work undertaken by a diligent American missionary called Reverend John Heckewelder. In January 1801, almost two centuries after the *Half Moon* dropped anchor on Manhattan's western shoreline, Heckewelder wrote to a friend in Jerusalem explaining that he had spent several years working with native Indians and had struck up friendship with many of the chieftains. As he chatted about their early history he was surprised to learn that Hudson's arrival had long ago entered tribal lore. Learning that the story had been handed down from father to son, but was nowhere written down, Heckewelder reached for his notebook: 'A long time ago,' he wrote, 'when there was no such thing known to the Indians as people with a white skin, some Indians who had been out a-fishing ... espied at a great distance something remarkably large swimming or floating on the water, and such as they had never seen before.' Immediately returning to their homes, the men gathered their bravest warriors and set out to discover what it might be. But the closer they got to this strange object, the more puzzled they became. 'Some concluded it either to be an uncommon large fish or other animal, while others were of opinion it must be some very large house. It was at length agreed among those who were spectators, that as this phenomenon moved towards the land, whether or not it was an animal, or anything that had life in it, it would be well to inform all the Indians on the inhabited islands of what they had seen and put them on their guard.'

The various chieftains duly arrived to discuss this strange object and there was a great deal of argument. At length they agreed that it was a giant canoe in which Mannitto, the Supreme Being, lived and that he was coming to pay them a visit. This sent the assembled crowds into a panic: men were sent to search for meat for a sacrifice, women were ordered to prepare fine victuals, idols were repaired and repainted and a grand dance was organised in order to please their god.

While preparations were under way, news arrived from the fleet of runners sent to monitor the floating object. Having observed it for some hours they confidently declared it to be a large house painted in different colours and filled with people. Not only were these of a different colour to them, but they wore peculiar garments around their bodies. The one dressed in red, they said, was Mannitto himself who was behaving in a most undignified manner, shouting and bawling to those on the shore and creating the most ungodly noise.

At length, Hudson came ashore with two colleagues and saluted the chieftains and wise men. The chieftains returned the salute, all the while studying this strange character and wondering what type of cloth would shimmer so brightly in the sunlight. (It was Hudson's lace ruff.) They watched in astonishment as Mannitto opened a bottle of pure alcohol, poured it into a glass beaker, and gulped down the lot. He then handed the bottle and glass to the nearest Indian chieftain and instructed him to drink.

'The chief receives the glass but only smells it, and passes it to the next chief who does the same. The glass thus passes through the circle without the contents being tasted by anyone; and is upon the point of being returned again to the red-clothed man when one of their number, a spirited man and great warrior, jumps up, harangues the assembly on the impropriety of returning the glass with the contents in it.' He argued that Mannitto had offered them the glass in the spirit of friendship and for the peace of their people, 'and that as no-one was willing to drink it he would, let the consequence be what it would. He then took the glass and bidding the assembly a farewell, drank it off. Every eye was fixed on their resolute companion to see what an effect this would have upon him, and he soon beginning to stagger about, and at last dropping to the ground, they bemoan him. He falls into a sleep, and they view him as expiring.'

But after a few minutes the man suddenly leaped to his feet and, to gasps of amazement from the crowd, declared that he had never felt so happy in all his life and demanded that he be given another glassful. 'His wish is granted, and the whole assembly soon join him, and become intoxicated.'

This last detail gives the story the ring of authenticity. Juet's journal frequently records how only a tiny quantity of alcohol was needed to get the Indians drunk, 'for they could not tell how to take it'; and tales of the drunkenness that greeted Hudson's arrival persisted among the native Indians until the last century. Indeed Heckewelder claims that the name Manhattan is derived from the drunkenness that took place there, since the Indian word *manahactanienk* means 'the island of general intoxication'.

When the Indians had sobered up Hudson stepped ashore once again to distribute beads, axes, hoes and stockings. The Indians were overjoyed with their presents although they had no idea of their use. It was a cause of much mirth when it was later discovered that they were wearing the axes and hoes as jewellery and using the stockings as tobacco pouches.

On 19 September 1609, the *Half Moon* continued its journey upstream in search of the passage that, it was hoped, would lead to the warm waters of the Pacific. Hudson anchored somewhere in the region of Albany and sent his Dutch mate and four others upstream in the ship's small boat. They returned at dusk bearing bad news. The channel narrowed and the water became shallow; it was clear to all on board that this mighty river did not lead to the spices of the East.

Their return journey was marred by a series of violent interludes. Dropping anchor 'down below the mountains', presumably the Highlands near Peekskill, Hudson's crew invited a band of natives on board and proudly showed off their weaponry. All was amicable until Juet spotted an Indian, who had been paddling his canoe around the stern of the ship, clamber onto the rudder and filch a pillow and two shirts from his cabin. The guns that had caused so much wonder were now demonstrated with deadly effect. Taking aim at the Indian, Juet blasted him in the chest, killing him instantly. His action caused a sudden panic and the Indians dived into the water, many of them still clutching items they hoped to buy, while the crew of the *Half Moon*, furious at losing their goods, jumped into their little boat and forcibly recovered their possessions, shooting several Indians in the process. When all were back on ship, the *Half Moon* set sail down the Hudson with the ill-tempered Juet still fuming over the treachery of the natives. To assuage his anger he fired indiscriminately at Indians gathered on the banks of the river, noting in his diary whenever he had success. The gratuitous violence makes for distasteful reading: 'We discharged six muskets and killed two or three of them ... I shot a falcon at them, and killed two of them ... I shot at [a canoe], and shot it through, and killed one of them.'

The ship soon reached the mouth of the Hudson and, with clear weather and a blustery wind, 'we set our main sail, and sprit sail, and our top sails, and steered away.' Less than five weeks later they had recrossed the Atlantic and caught sight of the English coastline.

Had Hudson followed his instructions he should have continued up the Channel and not stopped until he reached Amsterdam. Instead, he dropped anchor in Dartmouth and sent notice to his Dutch employers informing them of his return. There was no mention of his travelling to Amsterdam; indeed his letter requested a further fifteen hundred florins to be forwarded to Dartmouth so that he could set sail once again, this time to explore the northern coastline of Newfoundland.

The Dutch directors were incensed by Hudson's behaviour and ordered him to return immediately. But the English government, hearing rumours that Hudson had actually discovered a passage through to the Spice Islands, issued an Order in Council accusing him of undertaking a voyage 'to the detriment of his own country', and forbidding him from leaving England. This proved too much for Emanuel van Meteren, the Dutch consul in London: 'Many persons thought it rather unfair that these sailors should have been prevented from laying their accounts and reports before their employers,' he wrote in his official report. In his private correspondence he was less diplomatic. 'The English,' he declared, 'are inconstant, rash, vainglorious, light and deceiving, and very suspicious, especially of foreigners whom they despise. They are full of courtly and affected manners and words, which they take for gentility, civility, and wisdom.'

Reports of Hudson's discovery of a 'groote noordt rivier' slowly filtered back to Holland where it was greeted with a mixed reception. Van Meteren himself was dismissive of the discovery, recording that the Englishman had merely stumbled across a river in Virginia; whilst others, though interested in Hudson's route down America's eastern seaboard, state that he 'achieved nothing memorable by this new way'. Nevertheless, wrote one, 'it was thought probable that the English themselves would send ships to Virginia to explore the aforesaid river.'

Although the Dutch East India Company showed little interest in Hudson's findings, a handful of individual merchants were intrigued to learn that 'the land is the finest for cultivation that I ever set foot upon', and extremely interested to read of the abundance of skins and furs. Less than a year after Hudson's return, 'some merchants again sent a ship thither, that is to say, to the second river discovered, which was called Manhattes.'

These merchants soon found that Hudson had not exaggerated the richness of the countryside around Manhattan. They informed the Indians that 'they would

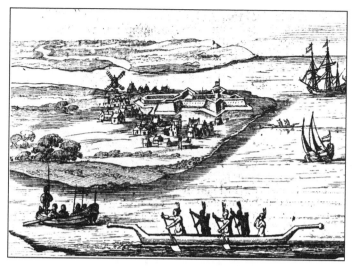

Half a world away, Fort New Amsterdam on Manhattan Island was a carbon copy of Fort Belgica in the Banda Islands. Its capture by the English was a response to the 'inhuman proceedings' in the Spice Islands four decades previously.

visit them next year again' and would bring gifts and trinkets, but added that because 'they could not live without eating, that they should then want a little land of them to sow seeds in order to raise herbs to put in their broth.' Had the native Indians been able to foresee the future, they would not have been so obliging to these Dutch sailors. Within a few years the English and Dutch were squabbling over land rights and the Hollanders had built a couple of shacks on the island's southern tip. These would become a castle, then a town, and, within a decade, New Netherland. But little did anyone realise, least of all Hudson, that its future would be inextricably entwined with the nutmeg-producing Banda Islands.

CHAPTER SEVEN

THE CANNIBALS'
COUNTRY

S CARCELY HAD WILLIAM KEELING sailed away from the Banda Islands in the autumn of 1609 than David Middleton arrived on his second voyage to the East. 'He passed us in the night,' noted Keeling with bitterness, 'else we should have surely seen him.' More than two years had passed since he had last spoken to his mercurial colleague and he must have been seriously wondering if he would ever hear from him again.

Middleton had made a brief stop at Bantam and learned from the English factors that the situation in the Banda Islands was not good. The Dutch were deadly serious about enforcing the treaty they had imposed on the islanders and were muttering dark threats about defending their monopoly at all costs. A governor had been left behind on Neira to monitor the coming and going of all shipping and a strong garrison posted in Fort Nassau to safeguard Dutch interests. Any vessel arriving at the Banda Islands was ordered to anchor close to the Dutch castle and submit to inspection, and no foreigner was allowed to settle without a Dutch permit. Even inter-island trade, upon which the survival of the outer islands depended, was forbidden unless authorised by the Dutch.

These laws and strictures sounded harsh but they proved

impossible to enforce and were soon being openly flouted by the Bandanese who realised that the Dutch were in a far weaker position than had first appeared. The fleet of ships commanded by Simon Hoen, Verhoef's replacement, had been plunged into chaos shortly after the imposition of the treaty and the morale of the crew had never been lower. Few showed any respect to their new master and when Hoen dropped dead, presumably from poison, his ship was left in the hands of an uncontrollable rabble. Life was little calmer on land where the garrison left to guard the Banda Islands found itself under a constant state of siege. There were numerous tales of 'the blacks killing divers Hollanders in a wood; of a kinde of siege of their castle; [of] bloody fight; the castle almost famished; all in the same yeere that this peace was concluded'.

News of the Dutch woes came as music to David Middleton's ears. Never short on confidence, he sped eastwards across the Java Sea and arrived at Neira displaying the 'flag and ensign, and at each yardarm a pendant, in as comely manner as we could devise'. To make his presence felt, he blasted every cannon and musket on board the *Expedition* and provocatively moored well within gunshot of the Dutch vessels riding at anchor.

The Dutch governor, Hendrik van Bergel, was infuriated by Middleton's effrontery and despatched a messenger to demand the reason for his coming. Ordered to surrender his commission from London, the English commander refused, consenting only to read the first paragraph to prove, as he put it, that he came as an authorised trader and not a pirate. When the messenger asked Middleton to clarify if he was a merchant or a man-of-war the English captain gave an equivocal answer, saying that 'I would pay for what I take' and 'defend my selfe' if attacked.

The Dutch retired to their castle to plan their response but Middleton had already won the war of words and the natives, who had watched the chicanery from the shore, rowed out to the *Expedition* to greet the English commander. Middleton was in his element and 'knowing well that in troubled waters it is good fishing', wasted no time in cultivating his friendship with the native merchants. Within a few days he had struck a profitable deal with a nutmeg trader from Ai Island who agreed to sell to the English all the spice he could gather.

Middleton could have saved himself any further argument with the Dutch by setting sail for this outlying island, but he was rather enjoying his new-found status as irritant and antagonist. Although warned by the Dutch governor not to remain anchored so close to their ships, he sent reply that 'I would ride there until I found the inconvenience [too great to bear] and then I would come into the best of the harbour.'

He then despatched a second letter informing van Bergel of the deal he had struck with the merchants of Ai and explaining that he was writing not out of courtesy but because he was keen to know whether the Dutch would be challenging him or not. After reminding the governor that both Ai and Run maintained their total independence from the Dutch (their headmen had steadfastly refused to sign the 1609 agreement), he insolently offered any assistance that the governor might require. 'If your worship stand in need of any thing that I have,' he wrote, 'I pray you make bold to demand it, and I will be as ready to perform it to my power.'

This last sentiment so angered van Bergel that he began to plot his revenge. The *Great Sunne*, a dilapidated Dutch vessel which was no longer seaworthy, was to be towed

towards the *Expedition* under cover of darkness, chained to
its hull, and 'there set her selfe a fire'. She was loaded with
thirty kegs of gunpowder so it would not take long for the
fire to spread to the English ship. As a precaution against
failure, van Bergel suggested that the rest of his vessels spray
the decks of the *Expedition* with musket shot.

Middleton's spies brought news of this plot and the
English captain, never one to shy away from confrontation,
'thought it fit to goe and speake with the Governour my
selfe, and before wee would try it with battaile, to see what
hee would say to my selfe'. After all the bluffs and threats
the two men met in Fort Nassau and were surprised to
discover a mutual respect for each other. 'So there passed
words between us, some sharpe and some sweet; but at the
length they began to be more mild, and [the governor]
called for a cup of wine, then the company rose all up,
drank a cup of wine, and went to walke and to view the
castle.' Having expected to be expelled after a fiery
argument, Middleton ended the day examining suits of
armour with van Bergel and discussing the varied merits of
different types of musket.

With the hostilities postponed Middleton assured the
governor that he did not wish to cause any trouble and, in
return for the right to buy spices, offered a large sum of
money 'which often maketh wise men blind'. The
governor seemed genuinely sympathetic to Middleton's
request but 'he told me plainly that he durst not give me
leave to deal for any spice, under pain of losing his head.'
When he heard this Middleton knew the time for talking
was over. Although he left the castle in friendship and 'the
governor caused all the ordnance to be shot off', he realised
that buying spice would almost certainly lead to
confrontation with the Dutch. This caused him not the

slightest worry, but he was concerned that his men might not have the stomach for the fight. So, 'I called all my company to know their minds, and told them plainly that if they would stand by me, I meant to set up my rest, to make my voyage to those islands [Ai and Run], let the Hollander do what he could: and promised them that if any man were maimed, he should have maintenance during his life.' The men did not hesitate to place their trust in Middleton and shouted their assent to a man.

As they prepared to head for Ai, the wind suddenly changed direction and it proved impossible to sail west in the cumbersome *Expedition*. So Middleton sent his assistant, Augustus Spalding, in the ship's pinnace to establish a factory on the island while he and the rest of the crew set up base on the rugged island of Ceram, some one hundred miles to the north. From here they could run a shuttle of pinnaces to and from Ai, enabling Middleton to lade his ship with little danger of attack from the Dutch.

The strategy proved a great success. With Spalding successfully established on Ai, the little *Hopewell* plied its hazardous way to and from the island with its cargo of nutmeg and mace. It was wearisome work and Middleton cursed the Company directors who, although aware of the great difficulties of buying nutmeg, were as fussy as ever about what he spent their money on. 'Make choice of such nutmeg as be large and sound,' they had told him before he left London, 'and at the lading therof [do not] lime them too much, for that doth burn them.' They were no less concerned about his treatment of the mace. 'Lay [it] in cannisters in some fit place by itself so that it be not spoiled by the heat of the other spice, taking good heed to buy that which is bright, and not withered or red or dark brown.'

After making no fewer than nine exhausting trips in the

Hopewell Middleton needed a rest. Electing a new crew to man her – not an easy matter, for he was desperately short of men – he bid her God's speed as she sailed on her tenth journey. He fully expected her to be back within seven days, but a week passed, and then a fortnight, and still there was no news of the *Hopewell*. Each day Middleton scanned the horizon for the tiny craft until a third week had gone by and he decided to lead a search party, hoping to find her adrift in the treacherous currents that surround the Banda Islands. 'Having not a sound man with me that could stand on his legges, I hired three blacks and put to sea. Being out of sight of land, there arose a grievous storme that I was fain to spoone afore the sea, to save our lives.' Middleton was fortunate to be blown back towards Ceram, but with the velocity of the wind increasing by the hour he found it increasingly difficult to stop the boat being dragged onto the rocks. 'Night being at hand, we strove all we might to keepe her upon the sea till day, the storme increaseth, that no remedie but that we must hazzard all to put into the breach over a ledge of rockes. This we did, and no man durst forsake the boat for [fear of] being beaten to pieces against the rocks.'

All night Middleton and his 'blacks' fought to keep the skiff out of danger and when dawn broke they found they had been washed further along the coastline to a shallow bay where they could safely beach her. 'We laid hands on the boat and got her out of the suffe of the sea, and gave God thankes for preserving us from so apparant danger. Being extreme foule weather, with much raine, we could not tell what to doe.'

Middleton sent his men to reconnoitre the bay but they soon returned with grim news:

The Blacks told us that we must goe to sea presently if we meant to save our lives. I asked one of them the reason; who said, it was the canibals countrey, and if they got sight of us they would kill us and eate us, and nothing would ransome a man if they take him; and all Christians that they get, they roast them alive for the wrongs that the Portuguese have done them. And therefore, if we would not goe to sea they would go hide themselves; for the canibals would be at the water side as soon as they can look about to descry if they can discover any fishermen or passengers that by stealth pass by in the night.

This news alarmed Middleton and he put to sea without further ado. But his woes did not end with his escape from the cannibals. An approaching rowing boat brought the unwelcome news that the *Expedition* had broken its anchor and was in danger of being washed onto the rocks. It was imperative that Middleton return to the ship as soon as possible in order to organise a rescue operation, but with the wind blowing a gale the only way back was a twelve-mile hike overland. The English captain and his guides were almost half-way into their walk when they found their path blocked by a great river. The guides made the unhappy discovery that the river was full of alligators, but Middleton was unconcerned by the danger, even when told 'that if I saw any [alligator] I must fight with him or he would kill me'. With this warning ringing in his ears he waded into the water:

I being weary, not having slept in two nights, tooke the water before the Indians, knowing they would bee over before me. The river being broad and with a swift current, which the great raine that had fallen had made, the Indians would have had me turn backe, but being the better halfe way, I was very unwilling.

[While] in the water, one of the Indians that carryed my mandilion had got a great cane (which I knew not of) and strooke me on the side, who feeling the stroke, suspecting it had beene an alligata, dived under water where the current got such a hold on me that before I could come up I was in the sea; and there the sea threw me against the beach and bruised my backe and shoulder till the time that he came and gave me the end of the cane, whereof I got hold and he pulled me out, neere hand drowned, being tossed with the sea, that every suffe washed me into the sea againe.

Headhunters were greatly feared by the English mariners. 'They lay in the rivers on purpose to take off the heads of all they can overcome,' wrote one English factor of the dyak warriors.

Such dangers had a happy ending. Not only was the *Expedition* saved from the rocks but the *Hopewell*, which had now not been seen for a month, suddenly hove into view. She had, it transpired, been blown thirty leagues to the east of the Banda Islands in a terrible storm and it had taken more than a fortnight to bring her back to Ceram.

Middleton's success in buying spices had not escaped the notice of the Dutch. In his own words they were 'starke madde' from the moment he arrived in the Banda Islands, for the local traders had ferried all their available nutmeg over to Ai. This was all the more galling since two of their ships were only half laden with spice and required many more tons before they could sail for Holland.

The Bandanese had been encouraged by Middleton's presence and now rose up against the Dutch, massacring all who had the misfortune to be caught outside the walls of Fort Nassau. And, 'being fleshed with the slaughter of some of the straggling Hollanders which they had murdered, [they] took all the able men to give assault to the Hollander's castles; and determined to fire their ships.'

With the sound of musket fire ricocheting across the harbour, Middleton set sail for Bantam and home. His voyage had been a triumph, for against all the odds he had not only bought a massive quantity of nutmeg but also left the Dutch in an extremely vulnerable position. The Company directors were overjoyed and penned a letter to the Earl of Salisbury, Lord High Treasurer, drawing special attention to Middleton's guile and courage: 'Seeking trade at Banda . . . he was, with many reproachful and insolent speeches, forcibly put from all trading in those parts. What he got [was] with strong hand against their will, from other broken islands near adjoining, with extreme hazard and danger (they devising and oftentimes attempting to

The Dutch-built Fort Nassau on Neira Island. Built against the wishes of the native islanders, its construction led to a massacre of the entire Dutch high command. The Dutch, in return, began 'to execute and practise all revenge possible.'

surprise, consume by fire and cut off by any indirect means both ship, men and goods.)'

With a temporary power vacuum in the Banda Isles, the directors began once again to pore over their maps. It was the island of Run, some ten miles to the west of Great Banda, on which their eyes would eventually settle.

Although the return of Middleton's ship was a cause for great joy, the directors of the East India Company were concerned that their licence would be rescinded by King James I. Courtiers and rival merchants were constantly petitioning the King for their own trading licences arguing, like Edward Michelborne, that one company should not be allowed a total monopoly on trade. Queen Elizabeth I's licence had been for fifteen years and would soon expire. Sir Thomas Smythe, aware of the pressure that certain courtiers were placing on the King, decided that to exclude nobles from their enterprise was no longer advisable. Rallying King James's favourites to his cause, he now petitioned the King for a renewal of the Company's privileges, explaining the absolute necessity of retaining a monopoly on trade with the Indies. King James at length accepted their arguments, agreed to their demands and, instead of limiting his licence to a further fifteen years, he now granted them 'the whole, entire and only trade and traffic to the East Indies . . . forever'. There was just one proviso: if the trade 'should not prove profitable to the realm' the licence could be withdrawn, although even in this extreme situation the King would have to give the merchants three years notice.

Smythe and his directors were overjoyed at this extension of their privileges for it instilled a new-found confidence – and increased investment – in the spice trade. But the nobility, who had played such an important role in convincing the King to grant that extension, were not among those who would pour their money into future voyages. Reticent to sully their hands with trade, they preferred instead to be linked by association to this most fashionable of enterprises. It became de rigueur to be a freeman of the East India Company, a title which involved the participant swearing an absurd and solemn oath forbidding him from revealing 'the secrets and privities of the said Company, which shall be given you in charge by the Governor or his deputie to conceale'. It was a stroke of brilliance on the part of the directors, for aristocrats were soon queuing up to become members of what they excitedly saw as a semi-secret society. Acceptance went quite to the heads of some: the Earl of Southampton was so overjoyed when he heard he had been made a freeman that he sent a brace of bucks to the directors 'to make merry withal in regard to their kindness in accepting him of their Company'. The quick-thinking directors promptly formed a Venison Committee whose sole function was to provide the finest game for banquets at Sir Thomas Smythe's house.

With the King's signature safely on the charter the time was ripe for a new expedition. The Company beadle was sent around London to collect subscriptions and, on his return, it was found he had raised no less than £82,000. With such a vast sum at their disposal, the directors decided to build their own vessel rather than relying upon the inferior ships of previous voyages. At 1,100 tons this new ship was a veritable leviathan, more than double the size of the standard East Indiaman and not exceeded in tonnage until the era of steam. Such a ship could only be launched by the King and so, on 30 December 1609, James I, accompanied by the Queen and Prince Henry, travelled to Deptford for a right royal celebration. The ship was aptly named the *Trades Increase* and was to be accompanied by two smaller vessels – the *Peppercorn* and the *Darling*. The launch was followed by a triumphal banquet served on priceless China-ware and, as desserts were served, the King called Sir Thomas Smythe to his side and slipped 'a greate chaine of golde and a medal about his necke with his own hands'.

This marked the start of a constant flow of gifts between the King and the Company and when the sixth fleet finally set sail it was given instructions to 'carefully keep and reserve for his majesty and the lords all such rare fowles, beasts or other thing as are by you or any of your company brought from those parts'. Mindful, perhaps, of the problems caused by the morose Coree, all three captains studiously ignored these instructions.

The fleet was scheduled to depart London in the spring of 1610 and a rigid timetable was imposed on all involved to ensure it would leave on time. By November the Company was interviewing potential factors and crew, and it is in the list of these new recruits that the name of Nathaniel Courthope first appears. Nothing is known of Courthope's life prior to his joining the East India Company. It is quite possible that he had worked as a trader in London and, like so many of his fellow factors, was lured eastwards by the hope of making his fortune. He certainly made an impression on the sober-minded directors for on 13 November 1609, just five days after petitioning for employment, he was told that his application had been successful. Several of his fellow factors were hired on that same day: 'Benjamin Greene who speaks Spanish, French and Italian [and] Rowland Webb who speaks French and Spanish'. Of Courthope we are told only that the Company 'has an agreement with Nathaniel Courthope for seven years'; two years longer than the other men hired. These extra years were to prove highly significant and would, because of Courthope's bravery, mark a turning point in the history of the Spice Islands.

The fleet sailed in April 1610 under the command of the experienced Sir Henry Middleton with the equally skilful Nicholas Downton in charge of the *Darling*. The governors decided that the two men should head for the Banda Islands and cement the friendship with the native traders. Middleton was also instructed to exploit the anti-Dutch feeling by 'presenting such gifts to the Governor [of Banda] as in your discretion shall seem fitting; and there provide three hundred tons of nutmeg of the best and soundest that may be gotten, freed from dust and rumps ... also twenty tons of mace, the largest and brightest that may be gotten, but none that is dark coloured red maces, which are feminine maces and here little worth'. Having secured his cargo, he was told to leave a large number of factors on the islands – including Nathaniel Courthope – to prepare for the arrival of future fleets.

Sir Henry was also requested to stop at numerous ports en route, not to buy spices but to continue the search for markets for England's 'wollen comodities' in order that 'we may be able to drive a trade without the transportation of money which is the cheefe scope of our desires.' It was this desire that led Sir Henry, after a tiresome journey around the Cape, to nudge his fleet towards the parched port of Aden on the south-western tip of the Arabian Peninsula.

'Wednesday at sun-setting,' wrote Nicholas Downton in his diary, 'on the sudden we descried Aden, which is situated under the foot of an unfruitful mountain, a place I should scarce have looked for a town, but it is set there for strength, where it is very defencible, and not by any enemy easily to be won.' The castle reminded him 'of the Tower of London, which is not by enemies to be in haste ascended'.

Middleton, too, was impressed by Aden's fortifications but was more concerned about the welcome he would receive. This corner of Arabia was under the nominal rule of the Ottoman Sultan, but most of the towns lay in the hands of unscrupulous local governors, whilst the mountainous interior had been carved into private fiefdoms by warring Arab tribesmen. Stopping a local craft, Middleton asked the Arabs on board whether the local Pasha was a good man. Their reply was ominous indeed. The last Pasha was 'very bad', the present was only 'a little better', and the Turks in general were 'stark naught'. Middleton's mind was made up; instructing Downton to anchor the *Darling* off the coast of Aden, he decided to sail to the Red Sea port of Mocha and try his chances there.

It was a decision he would soon come to regret for as he edged the *Trades Increase* towards the town's harbour the enormous ship stuck fast on a sand bank and could not be moved. This put Middleton in a quandary; the only possibility of refloating her was to unload everything on board, but to land goods without an on-shore factory ran contrary to Company policy. Fortunately the local governor, a renegade Greek named Rejib Aga, was most obliging. When Middleton sent a message explaining that he was an English merchant in need of assistance he received answer that 'if we were Englishmen we were heartily welcome, and should not fail of that we look for.'

There was more good news to follow: Laurence Femell, the expedition's amply girthed chief factor, had struggled ashore in a rowing boat and managed to strike a beneficial trading deal with the governor. To celebrate this deal Rejib Aga invited Middleton to an extravagant banquet at which he heaped honour after honour upon the English commander, which an increasingly embarrassed Middleton felt obliged to accept. After being assured of 'good and peaceable trade', Sir Henry might have hoped that this exaggerated display of Oriental politesse was drawing to a close. In fact Rejib Aga had scarcely begun. After offering a waterfront house for the English to use as a base, 'he caused me to stand up, and one of his chiefe men put upon my backe a vest of crimson silke and silver, saying, I needed not to doubt of any evill; for that was the Grand Seignor's protection. After some few complements I took my leave: I was mounted upon a gallant horse with rich furniture, a great man leading my horse; and so in my new coate with the musicke of the towne, conveyed to the English house.'

The next few days passed most pleasantly. The Aga sent daily messages to Middleton 'willing me to be merry' and promising that as soon as Ramadan had come to an end the two men would ride together in his private pleasure gardens. Middleton's initial scepticism as to the Aga's sincerity evaporated with these sugar-coated pleasantries and – foolishly – he took the Aga's words at face value.

On 28 October 1610, he rowed ashore in order to stretch his legs and stroll around the town. It was a glorious evening; the sky had been cloudless all day and Middleton proceeded to the English house in order to watch the desert sun sink slowly into the Red Sea. 'The sunne being set I caused stooles to be set at the doore where my selfe, Master Femell and Master Pemberton sat to take the fresh aire, suspecting nothing of the present ensuing harm that did befalle us.' At eight o'clock a messenger arrived from the governor but because none of the Englishmen present spoke Arabic he was sent away. Soon after he returned with an interpreter who informed Middleton that Rejib Aga's message was simply that the English should make themselves merry. Taking the governor at his word Middleton uncorked a bottle of Madeira and handed it around to his friends, but they had scarcely had time to toast each other before there was a loud bang on the door: 'My man returnes in great feare telling us we were all betrayed: for that the Turkes and my people were by the eares at the backe of the house.' Middleton dashed inside to warn the crew of the danger and to urge them to fortify the house as quickly as possible:

> But whiles I was thus speaking I was strooke upon the head downe to the ground by one which came

behind me. I remained as dead till such time as they had bound my hands behind me, and so straite that the extreame paine thereof brought me to my memorie. As soone as they saw me stirre they lifted me upon my feet, and led me betweene two of them to the Aga, where I found divers of my companie in like taking as I was my selfe. On the way the souldiers pillaged me and tooke from me such money as I had about me, and three gold rings, whereof one was my seale, the other had seven diamonds which were of good worth, and the third a gimmall ring.

This was only the beginning of his misfortune. When all the Englishmen in the town had been captured, including Nathaniel Courthope, they were herded together and clapped in irons; 'my selfe with seven more were chained by the neckes all together: others by their feete, others by their hands.' When this was done, the soldiers left them in the company of two heavily armed guards who 'had compassion for us and eased us of our bands, for the most of us had our hands so straite bound behind us that the blood was readie to burst out at our fingers' end, with pain unsufferable'.

Middleton still had no idea why he had been attacked, but he was soon to learn the scale of the Aga's treachery. Not only had eight of his men been killed in the 'bloudie massacre' and fourteen severely injured, he now heard that a band of one hundred and fifty Turks had put to sea 'in three great boats' with the intention of taking the *Darling* – now anchored off Mocha – by force. The attack caught the *Darling*'s crew completely unawares. Knowing nothing of the treachery ashore they first realised something was amiss when dozens of Turks were seen boarding the ship, their swords unsheathed. The situation quickly became desperate; three Englishmen were killed outright while the rest of the company rushed below deck to gather their weapons. By the time they had armed themselves the ship was almost lost. 'The Turkes were standing very thicke in the waist [of the ship], hollowing and clanging their swords upon the decke.' It was a quick-thinking crew member who saved the day. Realising their plight was helpless he gathered his strength and rolled a huge barrel of gunpowder towards the Turkish attackers, then hurled a firebrand in the same direction. The effect was as dramatic as it was devastating. A large number of Turks were killed instantly while the rest retired to the half-deck in order to regroup. This hesitation cost them their lives for the English had by now loaded their weapons which they 'set off with musket shot, and entertayned [the Turks] with another trayne of powder which put them in such feare that they leaped into the sea, hanging by the ship's side, desiring mercy, which was not there to be found, for that our men killed all they could finde, and the rest were drowned, only one man was saved who hid himselfe till the furie was passed, who yielded and was received to mercie'.

The *Darling* had been saved but Middleton's situation was now even more precarious. Still chained by the neck he was led to the Aga to be told the reason for his arrest. 'He with a frowning (and not his wonted disembling) countenance, asked me how I durst be so bold as to come into this their port of Mocha, so near their holy citie of Mecca.' Middleton remonstrated most strongly, reminding the Aga that it was he who had invited the English to land and persistently invoked them to be merry. The Aga chose to ignore this last remark, telling him that the Pasha in Sana'a had been given orders from the Sultan in Constantinople to arrest all Christians who attempted to

land at any of the Red Sea ports. He also told Sir Henry
that the only way for him to gain his freedom was for him
to send letters to the *Trades Increase* and *Darling* ordering
them to capitulate. Middleton refused, and when the Aga
told him he would starve the ships into submission the
English commander gleefully informed Rejib that they had
enough supplies to last two years. 'He urged me againe to
write to will them to come all ashore and yeeld the ship or
he would cut off my head. I bade him doe so; for therein
he should doe me a great pleasure for I was weary of my
life; but write to that effect I never would.'

This answer did not find favour with the Aga. 'I was
taken out of my chaine and coller and a great paire of
fetters clapt upon my legges, and manacles upon my hands,
and so separated from the rest of my company: they stowed
me all that day in a dirty dogges kennell under a paire of
stairs . . . my lodging was upon the hard ground, and my
pillow a stone, my companions to keepe me waking were
griefe of heart and multitude of rats which, if I chanced to
sleep, would awake me with running over me.'

Sir Henry would soon find himself longing for that
'dogges kennell'. The Aga instructed him to send a letter to
the *Trades Increase* with the message that all the warm
clothing on board should immediately be sent ashore.
Middleton was perplexed and, asking the reason for such a
strange request, was told that the Pasha in Sana'a wanted to
interrogate the men and 'that we should find it very cold
in the mountain country'. Middleton, sweltering in the
heat of Mocha, scoffed at the Aga's talk of frost and snow
and dismissed the request for woollen clothing. And so, on
'the two and twentieth of December, our irons were
knockt off all our legges . . . and my selfe and foure and
thirtie persons more of us were appointed to goe up for

Sana'a, the chief citie of the kingdome where the Pasha is resident.'

One of the men, William Pemberton, managed to give his guards the slip and it was many hours before his absence was noticed. He eventually reached the *Trades Increase* by trekking back to the coast, stealing a canoe and putting to sea. With no food and nothing to drink except his own urine he rowed for several days through choppy waters until a look-out on the flagship spied him in the far distance and sent a pinnace to the rescue. His arrival was invaluable to Downton for it provided him with information about the guards and sentries travelling with Middleton and enabled him to carry on a regular, though clandestine, correspondence with the commander using secret envoys and middlemen. Pemberton twice sent letters to Middleton urging him to plan an escape, suggesting that he could easily pass himself off as an Arab if he disguised himself in Oriental dress, cut the hair from his face, and took to 'besmutting' his skin. He added that he had fully intended to 'besmut' himself but decided that his 'pock-eated' face would have given him away.

The correspondence between Downton and Middleton at times betrays the great stress they were under. When Middleton refused permission for Downton to raid local craft on the grounds that his life would be placed in even graver danger, Downton wrote a strongly worded reply suggesting that he alone could judge what was best in the situation. Sir Henry was most upset at the petulance of his erstwhile friend and replied in what Downton described as 'a very carping and most distasteful letter'. But just as relations between the men seemed in danger of rupturing completely, Downton came to his senses and sent a note with the message that while he was hurt by the tone of

Middleton's letter he would write no more angry words for their mutual enemies to 'cant, construe and cavil at'. In reply, Sir Henry wrote a 'very kind letter' asking forgiveness for his 'melancholie letter' which, he explained, was written while suffering from acute depression.

That depression was soon to get worse as the weather grew ever colder during the enforced march to Sana'a. Middleton now realised his mistake in refusing the woollen gowns, recording that 'I would not beleeve at Mocha, when I was told of the cold we should have upwards, and that made me go but thinly clothed my selfe.' With the little money he still possessed he now bought his men fur gowns, without which they would all have perished. Few can have expected to see a white Christmas in the blistering Arabian Peninsula but as the English prisoners stumbled into the city of Taiz on Christmas Day 1610, the first few flakes of snow began to fall. William Pemberton's 'boy', who had failed to escape with his master, fell sick from cold and was lodged in the governor's house; the rest continued up into the mountains where 'every morning the ground was covered with horie frost, and . . . we had ice a finger thick.'

At last they came to Sana'a, 'a citie somewhat bigger than Bristol,' where their fur gowns were confiscated and they were forced to march barefoot through the city like common criminals. Middleton was in no mood for diplomacy. Dragged by 'two great men' to an audience with the Pasha he gave vent to his fury, accusing Rejib Aga of duplicity, falsehood and murder. The Pasha listened 'with frowning and angry countenance', blamed Sir Henry for causing him numerous problems, then led the Englishmen to a common prison where they were once again 'clapt in waightie irons'.

They had spent almost a month in jail when the Pasha suddenly called Sir Henry into his presence and told him that all the men would be released without delay and were free to return to Mocha. What induced the Pasha's sudden clemency is far from clear but it was rumoured that an influential merchant from Cairo, to whom the Pasha was indebted, had intervened on behalf of the Englishmen. Their release came just in time, for 'many of our people in the meane while fell sicke and weake through griefe, cold, naughtie aire, bad diet, evill lodging, and waightie irons.'

The chameleon-like Pasha now transformed himself into a kindly and avuncular figure, providing the men with a large mansion, suggesting a tour of the city's sights, and even presenting them with six cows on which to feast themselves. Middleton was singled out for special treatment, receiving a purse of 150 gold coins as recompense for his sufferings. In return he was obliged to listen to one of the Pasha's insufferable speeches in which he gave fulsome praise to his own wisdom, insight and mild temper. The English commander was bemused by the turn of events but not altogether surprised; he was fast learning of the inconstancies of these Turkish governors who could flick from friend to foe without even losing their smile.

In mid-February the men at last left Sana'a for the long march back to Mocha. Middleton still had niggling doubts as to the Pasha's sincerity but any fears about returning to Mocha were dispelled when he was told that 'if Rejib Aga wrong you I will pull his skinne over his eares and give you his head.' On their arrival at Taiz, the men hoped to recover Mr Pemberton's boy who had been lodged with the town's governor since collapsing through weakness. But herein lay a problem: 'the governor, Hamet Aga, had forced him to turne Turke, and would by no meanes part with him.' The poor boy had suffered a terrible ordeal during his weeks with the governor: when he refused to convert to Islam, 'some of the Aga's servants [carried] him to a hot-house where they had him naked circumcised perforce.' The governor steadfastly refused to give up his boy and the Englishmen had no option but to continue without him, but Middleton, to his great credit, never forgot the boy and refused to sail from Arabia until he had been released.

On his arrival in Mocha, Middleton was taken straight to the Aga who 'received me after his wonted dissembled shew of love and kindnesse, bidding me and the rest welcome, saying he was glad of our returne safe, and sorrie and ashamed of what was passed, and prayed me to pardon him'. But long before the Englishmen were able to return to their ship they found themselves marched to a 'great strong house' and once again placed under armed guard. Sir Henry's suspicions had proved all too correct and he now knew that escape was his only option. His plan was a simple one: under cover of darkness he sent a letter to the *Trades Increase* asking that a bottle of aqua vitae be smuggled into the prison. With this he planned to get his guards drunk, steal their keys and, aware that his face was well known throughout the town, hide himself in an empty barrel and get his men to roll him down to the beach.

The hour at last arrived. The aqua vitae was successfully smuggled into prison and a boat surreptitiously moored on the southern edge of town. When the guards saw they were being offered alcohol they were unable to refuse and 'fell to drinking hard'. By noon everything was ready: 'the boat being come, and keepers all drunk, and all things fitted . . . I began to put my business in execution.' Unlocking the door to their 'strong house', Sir Henry popped into a barrel as planned and was rolled down to the beach where he clambered into the waiting boat and rowed across to the *Darling* which was riding at anchor.

Not everyone had been so lucky: the ships' armourer, Thomas Eves, was so fearful of being recaptured that he 'took off his shoes and ran through the streets with all the speed he could, whereupon all the towne rise after him'. It was only a matter of minutes before Mocha was crowded with soldiers who, one by one, picked up the sick and wounded. Lawrence Femell soon found himself in difficulty. Unable to run because of his 'unwieldy fatness' he was hounded by a band of troops as he waddled down to the waterfront. He 'discharged a pistoll in the face of one of them that pursued him, and mortally wounded him' but was eventually captured while up to his armpits in water. He later blamed 'the foolish dealing of that idiot and white-livered fellow the coxswain who, we being in the water . . . fell to leeward of us'. The capture of Femell was a set-back, but Middleton was safe and after offering his thanks to God 'for his great mercy towards us' he joined the celebrations on board the English vessels.

He was now in a strong position to gain the freedom of Master Femell, Nathaniel Courthope and the other men, including poor Mr Pemberton's boy who was still incarcerated in Taiz. Sending a letter to Rejib Aga, he bragged of his powerful cannon and threatened that unless all the men were immediately released he would sink every ship that entered the port 'and do my best to batter the towne about his ears'. He also wrote a reassuring letter to Femell repeating the threat and adding that 'if I shoot at the town he saith he will requite me with the like, which he cannot do as you well know for his ordnance is far inferior to mine . . . Though I should fire the town and beat it smooth about their ears, whether it be pleasing or

displeasing to the Grand Seignor I care not, [for] I am out
of reach of his long sword ... let the Pasha and Regib Aga
likewise consider that the King of England will not take
well the betraying, robbing and murdering of his subjects.'

The Aga stalled for time but after his port had been
blockaded for a month he was forced to 'sing a new song'
and all the men were released. Master Femell did not, alas,
enjoy his freedom for long; three days after coming aboard
'at about two of the clock in the morning he ended his life,
as we thought, by poison.' He had bragged once too often
about the power of the English and the enraged Aga,
knowing that the chief factor never turned down a meal,
had dosed his food with delayed-action poison.

With the safe return of Mr Pemberton's boy everyone
still alive was back on board. The sixth fleet of the East
India Company could at long last continue on its voyage to
the Banda Islands.

It was now August 1611, and the fleet which had set sail
with such high expectations some sixteen months
previously had so far accomplished nothing. If the crew
were dispirited by their misfortunes the captains were even
more depressed. A rare insight into this depression has
survived in the form of a private memo that Downton
penned at the height of the troubles; a memo given added
poignancy by the fact that its tone so belies the brave
good-humour that Downton struggled to present to his
crew. In private he was 'environed with swarms of
perplexed thoughts' that now, 'after two years travel [we
find] our victuals spent, our ships, cables and furniture far
worn, men's wages for 24 months already passed, ourselves
deluded and abused in most places we have come . . ..
Whether we wish a languishing end, or a shameful return,

God only direct, for our counsel is weak and our case doubtful.'

Before sailing from Mocha the two captains took stock of the situation. Their overriding duty was to sail to the Banda Islands to buy nutmeg and mace, but their instructions from the Company allowed them to sail first to India to discover how William Hawkins was faring at the court of Jehangir. They chose this latter option and headed for Surat, but when Middleton learned that trade had been denied he once again put to sea, taking Hawkins with him. Fuming at Jehangir's intransigence, the commander decided

The Indian Great Moghul, Jehangir, struck up friendship with English sailor William Hawkins. A capricious alcoholic, he forced Hawkins to watch gruesome gladiator fights.

215

to sail back to the Red Sea and there compel the Indian dhows to sell their cottons to the English. The benefits would be threefold: the Aga in Mocha would be infuriated by the loss of trade, the Indians would be roundly punished and Middleton would acquire the calicoes he so desperately needed to exchange for nutmeg and mace.

It was unfortunate that just as Middleton's ships were setting up their blockade of the Bab-el-Mandeb, the entrance to the Red Sea, John Saris, commander of the East India Company's seventh fleet, was nudging his way towards Mocha. Saris brought with him a letter of recommendation from the Sultan in Constantinople and, ignoring Middleton's warnings about trade with the Arabs, he sailed gaily into the harbour at Mocha. Lavishly entertained by the new Aga – Rejib had since been dismissed – he struck a deal and sent a mission to Sana'a to pay its respects to the Pasha.

When the Aga learned that Middleton was 'rommaging' ships from India he was incensed and immediately annulled the trading deal he had granted to Saris. The English captain protested in the strongest terms and offered repeated assurances that he was not in league with Middleton, but the Aga refused to believe such a story. Saris now turned his fury on Middleton, boarding the *Trades Increase* and berating Sir Henry for his stupidity. He vowed to do everything in his power to break Middleton's blockade, 'wherat Sir Henry swore most deeply that if I did take that course he would sink me and set fire of all such ships as traded with me'. What followed was an explosive row in which the two commanders 'used very grosse speeches not fitting to men of their ranks, and were so crosse the one to the other as if they had been enemies.'

The two men did eventually strike a deal in which they

shared the spoils of the 'rommaging', but Saris's heart was not in the work and he soon set sail for Bantam without paying Middleton the usual compliment of a parting salute. Sir Henry was as angry as he was upset. Realising that his policy of harming the Aga was futile he sailed for Sumatra and Java, finally anchoring in the great harbour at Bantam. Here the East India Company's sixth fleet, which had set out with such high hopes, floundered in the malarial shallows. The *Trades Increase* was discovered to be riddled with teredos (shipworm) and no longer seaworthy, while the crew had fared little better: dozens succumbed to typhoid, dysentery and malaria and died on board their rotting flagship.

'I saluted them with three peeces,' wrote John Jourdain, a merchant on the next English ship to arrive in the Indies, 'but noe awnswere nor signe of English coulours, neither from the shipp nor from the towne.' Suspecting that the ship had been captured by locals, 'I shott annother peece ... with determination nott to go a land untill I had certaine notice from thence.' At length Jourdain 'perceived a prow cominge from the shore, wherein came Edward Langley, Christopher Luther, Nathaniel Courthope, and Thomas Harwood, all of them like ghostes or men fraighted. I demanded for the Generall and the rest of our freindes in particuler; [but] I could not name any man of noate but was dead to the number of 140 persons; and the rest which were remayneinge, as well aland and aboard the Trade, weare all sicke, these four persons beinge the strongest of them, whoe were scarce able to goe on their leggs.'

Most of the men were in the final stages of illness. Middleton himself was dead – some said of a broken heart over the loss of his ship – and the *Trades Increase* had miserably failed to live up to her name. Of her last days a merchant named Peter Floris wrote: 'She was lying on the ground without mast, with three and thirtie men, the greatest part sicke, the ship being sheathed on one side and not on the other. In her had deceased one hundred English and more Chinese which wrought for wages, and eight Dutch by some strange sicknesse.' Her final demise came all too soon; a renegade Spaniard set fire to her timbers and the once-great vessel, pride of the East India Company, was rapidly reduced to ash.

The *Darling* had not fared much better; on arrival at Patani on the Malay Peninsula she was inspected and considered to be in too poor a condition to sail back to England. She would end her days shuttling factors to and from the islands of the East Indies. Only the *Peppercorn* survived the long voyage home, but even she was unable to reach London and Downton suffered the ignominious fate of having to hire a Frenchman to tow her into Waterford in Ireland. There was no triumphal welcome and none of the crowds that had cheered her off three and a half years before. Instead, Downton stepped onto dry land in October 1613, only to find himself arrested and charged with piracy for his part in the Red Sea 'rommaging'. He was eventually released, but it did little to boost his morale and his diary ends in a mood of black despair. 'And so concluded,' he wrote, 'this tedious and out-tyring journey.'

CHAPTER EIGHT

THE BANNER
OF
SAINT GEORGE

FOUR MONTHS BEFORE THE *Trades Increase* had sailed from London, the governor of the East India Company, Sir Thomas Smythe, renewed his acquaintance with Henry Hudson. Smythe was in ebullient mood, for confidence in the spice trade had never been higher and with the successful return of William Keeling, large sums of money were pouring into the East India Company coffers.

He had long been considering financing a new voyage of exploration to the Arctic and, just a few months previously, had reminded his committee 'that three yeares since, this Companie did adventure £300 per annum for three yeares towards the discovery of the North-West Passage' – money that remained unspent. These were not the only funds at his disposal: Sir Thomas was also governor of the Muscovy Company whose merchants were growing increasingly enthusiastic about searching for a northern route to the Indies.

Two other men of importance attended the meeting between Smythe and Hudson. Sir Dudley Digges was a wealthy individual who would shortly write a book entitled *Of the Circumference of the Earth, or a Treatise of the North-West*

Sir Thomas Smythe, the first governor of the East India Company, was instrumental in ensuring the success of James Lancaster's pioneering expedition to the East.

Passage, a turgid piece of prose that led one critic to remark that 'many of his good friends say he had better have given four hundred pounds than have published such a pamphlet.' Nevertheless, Digges harboured a passion for discovery and was in possession of a large enough fortune to indulge that passion. The third man at the meeting was John Wolstenholme, Farmer of Customs, who also had a long record of promoting voyages to unknown lands.

All three had studied Hudson's reports of the area around Manhattan and accepted that the mighty river did not lead through to the Pacific Ocean. But there was one last region of North America that held the possibility of a North-West Passage to the Spice Islands – the mysterious 'furious overfall' described by John Davis. This treacherous passage of water, later known as Hudson Strait, had been attempted by many adventurers (George Weymouth was so confident of reaching China via this route that he carried a preacher equipped for converting the heathen spice traders) and although none had been successful in their quest, most had returned with tales of its certain existence.

With permission from King James sought and gained, Hudson set sail in April 1610 on a mission 'to search and find out a passage by the north-west of America to the sea of Sur, comonly called the South Sea [intending] to advance a trade' to the spice-producing islands of the East Indies. His voyage through the 'furious overfall' was one of the utmost difficulty for spring had yet to arrive and the water was choked with icebergs. Many of the less-experienced crew members began to fear for their lives while the sour-minded Robert Juet, who had accompanied Hudson on his previous voyage, jeered at his hope 'of seeing Bantam by Candlemasse'. The captain was determined to prove Juet wrong and, as he steered the ship into Hudson Bay, pronounced himself 'confidently proud that he had won the passage'. But as the first snows began to fall and the men were forced to winter in desolate James Bay, their enthusiasm plummeted and a handful of conspirators began to whisper of mutiny. 'It was darke,' wrote crew member Abacuk Prickett, 'and they in readinesse to put this deed of darknesse in execution ... Now every man would go to his rest, but wickednesse sleepeth not.'

Stepping out of his cabin, Hudson found himself seized by two men, pinioned with a rope, and cast into the ship's shallop along with seven of his closest supporters. The mutineers then cut the cable and put up the sails, leaving Hudson and his company 'without food, drink, fire, clothing or other necessaries'. As their little boat drifted off into the night, any lingering hopes of discovering a North-West Passage to the Spice Islands seemed to have died and Hudson, one of the great Arctic explorers, was never seen again.

He was destined not to be forgotten, for some seven years after being cast adrift a spirited captain by the name of Thomas Dermer began a detailed study of all the material relating to Hudson's earlier voyages. Dermer had been obsessed since childhood with discovering a quick route to the 'spiceries' and, after scouring the explorer's charts, plans and journals, he confidently declared that the elusive passage did indeed lie in the region around Manhattan. How he reached this decision remains uncertain, but he had sufficient evidence to persuade his financiers and, soon afterwards, he set off on the first of two voyages to the Hudson.

Sailing through Long Island Sound and its ever-narrowing inlet, Dermer passed into Upper Bay where he rowed ashore and got into conversation with a group of

Indians. To his immense satisfaction these men confirmed everything that Dermer had earlier argued. 'In this place,' he wrote excitedly, 'I talked with many savages who told me of two sundry passages to the great sea on the west [coast of America], offered me pilots, and one of them drew me a plot with chalke upon a chest.' The good news was tempered by bad: 'they report one [passage] scarce passable for shoalds, perillous currents; the other no question to be made of.'

Dermer was not prepared to allow their warning to dampen his enthusiasm and, excited about the imminent fulfilment of his life's dream, 'hastened to the place of greatest hope, where I purposed to make triall of God's goodnesse towards us, and use my best endeavour to bring the truth to light'. But no sooner had he reached the 'passage' than the wind whipped up a storm and forced him to turn and flee, 'hardly escaping with our lives'.

Despite this temporary setback, Dermer was thrilled with his discovery and dashed off a letter to Samuel Purchas informing him of the historic news. He even drew a map of the passage, 'yet dare not part with it for feare of danger. Let this [letter] therefore serve for confirmation of your hopes.' Purchas was sufficiently impressed to include the letter in his anthology of exploration, but Dermer's financiers in England were decidedly sceptical about the 'discoveries' of their quixotic adventurer and promptly recalled him to England. Dermer refused, 'resolutely resolving to pursue the ends he aymed at'.

As he sailed towards the mouth of the Hudson on his second attempt, Dermer was surprised to see 'divers ships of Amsterdam and Horna who yearly had there a great and rich trade'. He was even more perturbed to find 'some Hollanders that were settled in a place we call Hudson's River, in trade with the natives'. Curtly informing them that the land belonged to England, Dermer 'forbad them the place, as being by his Majestie appointed to us'. The Dutchmen apologised for their mistake and told him they sincerely hoped 'they had not offended'. Nevertheless, they made no effort to move themselves elsewhere, for the trade in beaver pelts was more profitable here than anywhere else on the coastline.

The news that the Dutch were settling the land around Manhattan aroused considerably more interest in England than had Dermer's supposed discovery of the North-West Passage. King James was already fuming at the belligerence of the Dutch in the 'spiceries' and was determined to prevent them from repeating their successes in America. As far as he was concerned, the American coastline belonged to him by virtue of the discoveries of John and Sebastian Cabot who had sailed in the service of King Henry VII more than a century previously. Although neither one of this intrepid duo had staked England's claim to the land, Queen Elizabeth I had later argued that merely setting foot in America implied sovereignty, a view championed by Richard Hakluyt, author of *The Principall Navigations*.

Despite this, England's merchants had been far too preoccupied with the spice race to show much interest in settling the American seaboard and it was not until 1606 that an ambitious merchant called Sir Ferdinando Gordes petitioned King James for a charter for two new companies, one based in London and one in Plymouth. These were given the right to plant colonies 'in that part of America commonly called Virginia', but were ordered to remain one hundred miles apart, a fatal decision, for it was into this gap – in the Hudson River region – that the Dutch had neatly staked their claim.

When the King learned of the Dutch settlements he

granted Sir Ferdinando a much larger swathe of land which made him the proprietor of a huge region that stretched from the Hudson to the St Lawrence. Although forbidden from seizing any land already belonging to any Christian prince, the charter noted that King James was of the opinion that no prince was in possession of this stretch of land 'by any authority from their sovereigns, lords, or princes'.

With Manhattan and the Hudson River now safely placed under English jurisdiction – on paper at least – King James wrote to his ambassador in Holland, Sir Dudley Carleton, asking him to investigate whether or not the Hollanders had indeed planted colonies and were in the process of sending vessels to supply them. Sir Dudley, who had spent years arguing with the Dutch over their claims to the Spice Islands, wrote back with the alarming news that the Amsterdam merchants did indeed have a regular trade with the land around Manhattan and 'kept factors there continually resident'. But he added that stories of a Dutch colony had been somewhat overblown and rejected claims that one had been 'either already planted or so much as intended'. The King nevertheless insisted that Sir Dudley register a formal complaint to the effect that, 'the King's government has lately been informed that the Hollanders have planted a colony in these regions, and renamed the ports and harbours, as is their fashion'.

The King was, in fact, wrong to draw a parallel between the traders in Manhattan and those in the 'spiceries', an ironic mistake given the future destiny of these islands. Although a handful of Dutchmen were indeed living in wooden shacks in the Hudson River area – they had arrived in 1611, soon after Hudson's report of a rich and fertile land reached their ears – they would hardly have labelled themselves colonists for they only remained on land for as

long as it took to barter their trinkets for the beaver pelts
that were in such plentiful supply. Like nutmeg and mace,
these pelts fetched astronomical prices on the open market
and had been eagerly sought after in northern Europe for
centuries, particularly in Germany and Russia where 'they
are used for mantle linings; [and] whoever has the costliest
fur trimmings is esteemed the greatest.' They retained their
value even when they had been worn for years by the
Indians and were 'foul with sweat and grease'; indeed, worn
skins were often the most highly prized of all for 'unless the
beaver ... is greasy and dirty it will not felt properly.'

The spectacular success of the Dutch in the East Indies drove
King James to be ever more vociferous in his claims to the
land around Manhattan. But the hard work of his ambassador, Sir Dudley, proved to be of no avail for in June 1621,
less than three years after Dermer had encountered Dutch
vessels in the Hudson, the States General bestowed their
charter upon the Dutch West India Company, an organisation modelled on its eastern counterpart. The Company
was granted exclusive rights to trade with both the east and
west coasts of America and was permitted to conclude
treaties with native princes, build castles and settle provinces.

It was not long before the first settlers began to arrive in
what was now known as New Netherland. In the spring of
1623, the appropriately named *New Netherland* slipped out
of the Texel carrying a handful of families, 'all of the
Reformed religion,' on the long journey across the
Atlantic. Their departure did not go unnoticed by the crew
of the *Bonnie Bess*, an English vessel which had only
recently been commissioned by 'high authorities' to sail to
Manhattan, conduct a search of the area and, 'if we there
find any strangers, as Hollanders or others, we are to give

them fight and spoil or sink them down into the sea.'

In the event the *Bonnie Bess* never got to execute these orders and the colonists on board the *New Netherland* arrived safely at their destination after a trouble-free voyage. Only one of the settlers' names is known, Caterina Trico, who wrote her memoirs some six decades after arriving in America. Although she muddles dates and names, she remembers 'that four women came along with her in the same ship ... which four women were married at sea'. She is equally forgetful about the voyage itself and it is only from maritime records that we learn the *New Netherland* sailed first to the Canary Islands and the 'Wild Coast' (Guiana) before heading towards the mouth of the Hudson. Later settlers would not forget the trials of the long sea voyage quite so easily as Madame Trico. As with the ships that sailed to the East Indies, there were only a handful of cabins reserved for those who could afford the substantial fare of one guilder a day and everyone else was crammed into the stinking and claustrophobic confines between decks. For two months in summer, and many more in winter, scores of passengers lived, unwashed, in total squalor, sharing their floor space with the filth of pigs, sheep and chickens. Dysentery and fevers were rife and although most settlers carried their own medicine chests, the homespun pills and unguents they contained were useless against life-threatening disease. It is hardly surprising that many went into raptures when they at last spied the eastern coastline of America. 'There came the smell of the shore,' wrote one early traveller, 'like the smell of a garden.' It was as if they had arrived at the Spice Islands.

The natural beauty of Manhattan also made a deep impression after the long sea voyage. 'We were much gratified on arriving in this country,' reads one account.

'Here we found beautiful rivers, bubbling fountains flowing into the valleys, basins of running waters in the flatlands, agreeable fruits in the woods. There is considerable fish in the rivers, good tillage land; here is, especially, free coming and going, without fear of the naked natives of the country.'

The settlers spread themselves over a wide area of land. According to Caterina Trico, two families and eight men went to Delaware, six to the mouth of the Connecticut River and the rest – totalling eighteen – sailed up the Hudson to Fort Orange, close to the site of present-day Albany. Only eight, all men, were left behind on Manhattan 'to take possession' of their new home. Unlike their fellow colonists in Bantam and Banda who were generally drunkards and 'wholly unsuitable for the plantation of colonies', the settlers despatched to the Hudson were honest and hard-working. They were reliant upon their own labour for food and shelter, but their work paid handsome dividends and it was not long before they were 'bravely advanced' and the grain they had planted was 'nearly as high as a man'. They did have one complaint: 'Had we cows, hogs, and other cattle for food (which we daily expect by the first ships) we would not wish to return to Holland, for whatever we desire in the paradise of Holland is here to be found.' In fact, the cows, hogs and other cattle were on their way. In a meticulously planned operation, a relief expedition set sail carrying more than one hundred horses, cows and sheep on three vessels imaginatively named the *Horse*, the *Cow* and the *Sheep*.

It is not easy to picture the Manhattan of those first settlers. The terrain of the island in those days was hilly and rugged and at its southern end, close to the present-day site of the World Trade Center, were a series of low wooded hills dotted with freshwater ponds. It was here that work started on the much-needed Fort New Amsterdam. Engineer Cryn Fredericks and a number of builders had been sent out with 'special instructions' outlining the precise dimensions of the fort. A carbon copy of the impregnable Fort Belgica on Neira Island in the Bandas, it was shaped like a pentangle and stretched more than a thousand feet in circumference. For additional security, the entire structure was surrounded by a wide moat. The outlines of the fort can still be traced today. Beaver Street, Broad Street, Pearl Street and Whitehall Street in Lower Manhattan all follow engineer Fredericks's original ground plan, as do Broadway, Park Row and Fourth Avenue.

It was while work on the fort was in progress that Peter Minuit, the first governor-general of New Netherland, arrived on the island. One of his first acts was to purchase Manhattan from the native Indians, a transaction that the merchants in Amsterdam had been urging for some time. 'In case there should be any Indians living on the aforesaid island or claiming any title to it,' they wrote, '... they must not be expelled with violence or threats, but be persuaded with kind words (to let us settle there), or otherwise should be given something for it to placate them or be allowed to live amongst us, and a contract should be made of such an agreement to be signed by them in their manner'.

Minuit obliged by purchasing the island from the native Indians, paying them to the value of sixty guilders in trinkets. A copy of this transaction, was sent to The Hague and records that 'here arrived yesterday, the ship Arms of Amsterdam ... they report that our people [on Manhattan] are of good cheer and live peaceably. Their wives have also borne children there. They have bought the island Manhattes from the savages for the value of sixty guilders. It is 11,000 morgens in extent. They had all their grain sown by the middle of May and harvested by the middle of August. They send small samples of summer grain, such as wheat, rye, barley, oats, buckwheat, canary seed, beans and flax'.

By the time this letter arrived in Holland, the fledgling settlement in Manhattan had survived its first difficult years. But although the population soon began to grow, New Amsterdam was never really considered to be a colony by the directors. As with the settlements in the Banda Islands, in Bantam and elsewhere in the East Indies, it was nurtured not for its own sake but for the sake of a profitable trading company. What Amsterdam's merchants could never have imagined is that in seizing Manhattan from the English they had gained themselves a bargaining chip of immense value.

Nathaniel Courthope was one of the sickly few who survived Sir Henry Middleton's disastrous 1610 expedition to the East Indies. His contract still had five years to run when the *Trades Increase* ran aground in Bantam harbour and he would soon find himself despatched in the near-rotten *Darling* to search for potential trading partners in the lesser-known Spice Islands. In the meantime he and his fellow survivors recuperated from their trials in the Javanese port of Bantam.

Bantam was the hub of English activity in the East Indies and the first port of call for most of the Company's vessels. Although the city was almost a thousand miles from the 'spiceries,' it was nevertheless from Bantam that ships sailed, factors were despatched and trade organised; and it would eventually be the men living in the port upon whom Courthope's fate was to rest. It had gained the unenviable reputation of being the least hygienic place in the East Indies – 'that stinking stew,' wrote Nicholas Downton, after watching most of his men die in the town. Few disagreed with such a conclusion: 'Bantam is not a place to recover men that are sick,' wrote one, 'but rather to kill men that come thither in health.'

The annals of the East India Company are filled with notices of plagues, sicknesses and deaths that occurred in Bantam but only one journal, written by Edmund Scott, charts the full horror of life in this rotting, disease-ridden port. For more than two years Scott held the post of chief factor to the dozen-strong English community: a period of unremitting hardship in which he witnessed his two superiors die in rapid succession and his men succumb to typhoid and cholera. Malaria, too, was rife, for the oozing mud flats and tidal swamplands that surrounded Bantam provided a fertile breeding ground for swarms of mosquitoes.

Scott's men lived in constant fear of attack and scarcely a day passed without one of their number being assaulted by thieves or bandits. For almost two years their flimsy wooden warehouse, surrounded by a palisade of sharpened stakes, was under a state of siege and 'these continuall alarames and greevous outcryes of men, women, and children grew so rife in oure eares,' wrote Scott, 'that our men in their sleepe would dreame that they were pursuing the Javans and suddainely would leape out of their beddes and ketch their weapons.'

The English looked in vain for any support from the native government for the King was but a child and real power lay in the hands of an unscrupulous Protector who was forever haranguing the foreign traders in the town. Business could only be transacted after proffering large bribes to native officials, yet the bustling commercial life of Bantam continued to attract rival traders from all over the region and within its fly-blown alleys lived a mêlée of residents whose mutual animosities created endless troubles. Chinese, Indians, Christians and Muslims all lived within a stone's throw of each other and were equally loathed by the quarrelsome Javanese who only tolerated these foreigners because they depended upon their trade. A more worrying threat to the English was the town's unscrupulous head-hunters who faced a constant shortage of heads. 'There were some Javan women that would cut off their husbands' heads in the night and sell them to these people,' records Scott. 'They did linger much about our house; and surely, if we had not kept good watch, they would have attempted the cutting of our throates, if not our heades.' Such was the shortage of heads in the town that 'many times they would digge up such as were new buried at Bantam and cut off their heads.'

There was an unrelenting rivalry between the English and Dutch in all matters pertaining to business. Fuelled by the heat and insufferable humidity, disagreements frequently boiled over into violence and it was only when faced with serious trouble from the natives that the two nations presented a united front. Indeed, it was Dutch support in times of strife that saved the small English factory from extinction. 'Though we were mortall enemies in oure trade,' penned Scott in one of his more conciliatory moments, 'yet in other matters we were friendes and would have lived and died for one another.' Even this occasional amicability vanished in later years. 'The Flemings thunder it most terribly in these parts,' wrote an English factor a decade later. 'Their untruths are daily more discovered, and they are rather feared than respected by their brutal carriage.'

An additional problem that faced the English in Bantam

was the frequent fires that threatened to ravage their warehouse. It was a favourite ploy of would-be thieves to light a fire to the windward of the English warehouse and, in the ensuing confusion, raid the premises and carry off the spices. 'Oh this worde fire!' writes Scott. 'Had it been spoken neere mee, either in English, Mallayes, Javanese or Chynese, although I had been sound asleepe, yet I should have leaped out of my bedde; the which I have done sometimes when our men in their watch have but whispered one to another of fire; insomuch that I was forced to warne them not to talk of fire at night.'

One night, the threat of fire became all too real. At around ten o'clock, as the second watch took over from the first, the men noticed the acrid smell of smoke filtering out from the warehouse. Summoning Scott, they made a thorough search of the premises yet were unable to locate its source. 'Then one of them remembered a hole which a rat had made behind a trunk, that went through the ceiling down into the cloth warehouse.' Heaving the trunk away from the wall, they saw that the smoke was indeed coming from this hole and that the little-used lower warehouse was on fire. There was no time to lose, for two huge jars of gunpowder were stored in the same room 'which caused us greatly to fear blowing up'.

The Englishmen tried again and again to extinguish the flames but the fire had by now taken hold and the smoke was so thick that they were continually forced back outside. The situation was desperate for there was more than a thousand pounds of gold stored in the upstairs room which would soon be lost. There was no alternative but to call for help from the 'damned Chinese' who lived next to the English warehouse and who agreed to empty the building in return for a large share of that gold.

'When the fire was all out,' wrote Scott, 'I stood musing alone by myselfe how this fire could come, being verie much grieved in minde.' What disquieted him was the fact that the fire appeared to have started underground and had only spread so rapidly because it had already taken hold in the joists beneath the floorboards. His suspicions of treachery were confirmed when he wrenched up a short length of the floor and discovered a tunnel leading in the direction of the house opposite. Vowing to have his revenge, Scott stormed around to this building, seized two men and marched them back to the warehouse where he had them clapped in irons.

He was keen that everyone involved in the plot should be punished and with the judicious application of a branding iron soon had a list of all the guilty men. One of these, handed over by the authorities, refused to admit his part in the affair even though he had openly bragged about his involvement around town. 'Wherefore,' wrote Scott in a matter-of-fact entry in his journal, 'I thought I would burne him a little (for we were now in the heate of our anger.)'

What follows is a clinical account of the torture, a barbarous affair which makes for painful reading even when one allows for the fact that the employment of torture to extract confessions was standard procedure in the English judicial system:

> First, I caused him to be burned under the nayles of his thumbes, fingers, and toes with sharpe hotte iron, and the nayles to be torne off. And because he never blemished at that, we thought that his handes and legges had beene nummed with tying; wherefore we burned him in the arms, shoulders, and necke. But all was one with him. Then we burned him quite

thorow the handes, and with rasps of iron tore out
the flesh and sinewes. After that, I caused them to
knocke the edges of his shinne bones with hotte
searing irons. Then I caused colde screws of irone to
be screwed into the bones of his armes and sodenly
to be snatched out. After that all the bones of his
fingers and toes to be broken with pincers. Yet for all
this he never shed a teare; no, nor once turned his
head aside, nor stirred hand or foot, but when we
demaunded any question, he would put his tongue
betweene his teeth and strike his chynne upon his
knees to bite it off. When all the extremity we could
use was but in vaine, I caused him to be put fast in
irons againe; where the emmets [white ants] (which
do greatly abound there) got into his wounds and
tormented him worse than we had done, as we
might well see by his gesture.

The King's officers desired me he might be shott
to death ... wherefore, they being verie importunate,
in the evening we led him into the fields and made
him fast to a stake. The first shott caried away a peece
of his arme bone, and all the next shot struck him
thorough the breast, up neare to the shoulder. Then
he, holding down his head, looked upon the wound.
The third shott that was made, one of our men had
cut a bullet in three partes, which strooke upon his
breast in a tryangle; whereat he fell down as low as
the stake would give him leave. But betweene our
men and the Hollanders, they shot him almost to
peeces before they left him.

Power was commensurate with brutality in Bantam but
despite the horrific barbarity inflicted on the instigators of

the fire, life got no easier for the English. The stresses of living cooped up in a confined space, coupled with the lack of sleep caused by round-the-clock watches, began to tell on the men. 'What with overwatching and with suddaine waking out of our sleepe (we beeing continually in feare of our lives) some of our men were distract of their witts; especially one, who sometimes in the night would fall into such a franticke rage that two or three of his fellowes could hardly keepe him in his bed.' On more than one occasion the men began fighting among themselves and could only be brought to their senses by being clapped in irons.

Scott soon realised that one of the main reasons why they faced the constant threat of violence was that the native Javanese were unable to distinguish between the English and Dutch. The Hollanders, who lived in Bantam in considerable numbers, paid scant regard to the sensitivities of the local population and thought nothing of staggering home through the streets of this staunchly Muslim town after a lengthy drinking bout. Their behaviour led to 'much falling out betweene the Hollanders and the countrey people, by means of the rude behaviour of some of their marriners; and many of them were stabbed in the eveninges'. The situation was made worse by the fact that some of the Dutch would pretend they were English if they thought it would be to their advantage when buying spices. It was Scott's subordinate, Gabriel Towerson, who dreamed up a clever way to draw a distinction between the two nations. Realising that the anniversary of Queen Elizabeth I's coronation was drawing near – 'for at that time we knew no other but that Queene Elizabeth was lyving' – he suggested they celebrate the event in the most extravagant manner possible. Then, when quizzed about the pageantry, they could explain to the natives that they, unlike the other rabble, were commemorating their monarch.

Scott listened to Towerson's plan but was initially sceptical. 'I stood in doubt many times whether I should put this in practise or not,' he wrote, 'for feare of being counted fantasticall when it should be knowne in England.' In the end he relented and ordered the small English community to dress themselves in white silk, don scarves of red and white taffeta, make 'a flagge with the redde crosse thorow the middle', and dust down their military drums.

'Our day beeing come, we set up our banner of Sainct George upon the top of our house, and with our drumme and shott we marched up and downe within our owne grounde; being but fourteene in number, wherefore we could march but single, one after the other, plying our shotte.' The performance had the desired effect. Hundreds of curious locals, including many of the most important personages of the town, flocked to the English factory to enquire the reason for the celebration. 'We told them that that day sixe and fortie yeares our Queene was crowned; wherefore all Englishmen, in what country soever they were, did triumph on that day. He [a local dignitary] greatly commended us for having our prince in reverence in so farre a countrey.'

Others were bewildered by the behaviour of the English and asked why the other Englishmen in the town were not celebrating the Queen's anniversary. It was exactly the question Scott had hoped they would ask and, with a distinct note of pride, 'told them they were no Englishmen, but Hollanders, and that they had no king, but their land was ruled by governours'. Some were sceptical when they heard this explanation and told him that these so-called

Hollanders had persistently called themselves English. 'But we told them againe that they were of another countrey, neere England, and spake another language; and that, if they did talke with them now, they should heare they were of another nation.'

The day ended in triumph. As a constant stream of shot was fired in celebration from the English factory a procession of children wound through the streets shouting ' "*Oran Enggrees bayck, orak Hollanda jahad*," which is: "the Englishmen are good, the Hollanders are naught." '

Scott was fast learning that when dealing with the native Javanese, style was every bit as important as substance. Now, with a feast day to celebrate the king's circumcision just weeks away, he prepared to lay on a gift that, while less costly than that of the Dutch, would be guaranteed to leave a deep impression. 'Amongst all others,' he wrote, 'we were to make a show, the best we could.' While the local chieftains, princes and Dutch merchants were buying gifts of gold and jewellery, the English 'bought a very faire pomegranate tree, being full of fruite growing on it ... which we set in a frame beeing made of rattan or carrack-rushes, somewhat like a bird's cage, but very wyde. At the roote of this tree we placed earth, and upon that greene turfe, so that it stood as if it had been still growing. Uppon these turfes we put three silver-headed conies [rabbits] which our Vice-Admirall had given me; and at the top, and round about upon the boughs, we with thread made fast a number of smalle birds which would ever be cherping. Soe that tree was ... full of faire fruite, and birdes merily singing on the top.'

The men spent some days on their handicraft and Scott was delighted with the end result. He would have liked to deliver it to the King accompanied by a troupe of English damsels but, 'we had no women; wherefore we borrowed thirty of the prettiest boys we could get.' Once again Gabriel Towerson proved his usefulness. 'Master Towerson had a very pretty boye,' writes Scott, 'a Chinese, [who] we attyred as gallant as the King, whom we sent to present these thinges and to make a speach to him.' The procession was led by a trumpeter and followed by ten musketeers, all dressed in the red and white colours of England. Next came the pikemen, all Chinese, and finally the 'pretty boye' who had a canopy held over him to screen the sun.

The King was overjoyed with the gift, the more so when he learned that the English entourage had filled their pockets with fireworks which they proceeded to light for his amusement. The day came to a climax with a tiger parade, a circus act and, unhappily for the King, his circumcision. Whether he made immediate use of his favourite present, a 'fair quilted bed with twelve bolsters and pillows of silk', is not recorded.

When Scott finally came to leave Bantam he expressed amazement that he had survived his ordeal: throughout his years in the city he had dug many a grave for his fellow countrymen and been a witness to (and participant in) unprecedented brutality. Yet the harsh treatment he received had done nothing to dent his pride in being English, and his dogged determination to defend his country's flag became the inspiration for the factors who followed – men like Nathaniel Courthope for whom patriotism and devotion to duty were more important even than trade.

'And here it is not fit I should omit one thing,' writes Scott in the final pages of his journal, 'and yet to make relation of it, some may thinke I do it of a vaineglorie to myselfe and those that were with me ... It was a common talke among all straungers and others how we stoode at defiance with those that hated us, [and] it will be a thing generallye talked of, in all parts of the worlde, what different carriage we have beene of, when it is likely there will be no English [left in Bantam].'

His prophetic words would in time be fulfilled, but the English presence in the East still had more than a decade to run. Although Sir Henry Middleton's second expedition had ended in disaster, the East India Company directors remained in buoyant mood and were considering expanding their trade in the East. By the time Courthope arrived in Bantam in 1611, they had factors dotted all over the region searching for markets for English goods, and the Company records are filled with letters from obscure backwaters reporting on the feasibility of trade. These missions often ended in disaster: in Macassar the factor was forced to flee for his life after 'a pitiful tragedy' caused by the Dutch who 'murdered the King's most dearly loved nephew more like cannibals than Christians'. In Johor it was the English who made a bad impression; so bad, indeed, that the King of Johor sent a letter to a neighbouring king warning him to steer clear of what he described as 'a vile people, drunkards and thieves'. Even China, which had once been viewed as a most promising market, was henceforth out of bounds. The King of Cochin attacked an English trading vessel and overturned it, and 'both English, Dutch and Japans, their followers, [were] cut to pieces and killed in the water with harping irons like fishes.'

The London merchants proved incredibly resilient to the continued bad news and resolved not only to search for trade 'at other places' but to appoint a far greater number of factors. Yet for all their enthusiasm, most English factories were never more than temporary bases which lasted for only as long as the factor stayed in good health – usually little more than a few months. For if life was unremittingly hard in Bantam, it was often far worse on the island outposts to which Courthope would find himself posted. The steady trickle of letters from the Company's factors contain a litany of complaints and grievances for, notwithstanding the constant threat of sickness and disease, most found themselves afflicted with homesickness and extreme loneliness. For some the loneliness quite addled their minds, as is revealed in an extraordinary letter written by one William Nealson, factor in Firando. Full of riddles, puns and strange allusions it begins: 'Morrow, bully; morrow morrow. To recover my health, I forgot not, fasting, a pot of blue burning ale with a fiery flaming toast and after (for recreation's sake) provided a long staff with a pike in the end of it to jump over joined stools with. Hem.'

Others retained their sanity only to complain bitterly at the treatment they received from their employers. 'At home men are famous for doing nothing;' wrote one disgruntled factor, 'here they are infamous for their honest endeavour. At home is respect and reward; abroad disrespect and heartbreaking. At home is augmentation of wages; abroad no more than the third of wages. At home is content; abroad nothing so much as griefs, cares and displeasure. At home is safety; abroad no security. At home is liberty; abroad the best is bondage. And, in a word, at home all things are as a man may wish, and here nothing answerable to merit.'

The complaint that wages had gone unpaid is frequently heard and one that grieved factors greatly since most had only been lured eastwards by the prospect of making money. More frightening was the ever-present spectre of the grim reaper who demanded a high price from those

who settled in the East. The average life expectancy for
factors was no more than three years and it is little wonder
that many followed the example of William Hawkins in
India who brazenly admitted to using his time to 'feather
my nest'. Nathaniel Courthope was no exception: in a
letter sent from Bantam to London in the winter of 1613
he, along with a number of other factors, was accused of
'purloining the Company's goods, deceiving private men,
insolent behaviour, and vanity in wearing buckles of gold
in their girdles'. Furthermore, the Company's attention is
drawn to 'the great wealth they have gathered suddenly,
being worth £500 or £600 each', and the fact that 'they
are false and unjust to their masters.'

With the threat of his 'great wealth' being confiscated by
the next vessel to arrive in the East – and doubtless
concerned that he would be left penniless and without
prospects in these distant lands – Courthope repented of
his misdemeanours and wrote 'a voluntary confession' of
his wrong-doings. It was a shrewd move for he soon found
himself back in favour and, in the spring of 1614, was
instructed to sail to Sukadana, a port on the south-west
coast of Borneo where, it was rumoured, 'the best
diamonds in the world [are] to be procured'.

Sukadana was already home to one of the Company's
more flamboyant factors, a professional sailor called
Sophony Cozucke. Known as 'Sophony the Russe', but
more probably Sophonias the Kazak, he had established a
base at the only place in the East where diamonds were
indeed in plentiful supply. With the help of Courthope, 'of
whom there is great hopes that he shall do your Worships
good service,' the two men set about expanding this
lucrative trade and investigating what goods were of
greatest value for barter.

The hardships they faced in Sukadana were similar to those facing all factors in such remote spots. As they were totally dependent on English vessels for food and money, it only took one supply ship to be blown off course for a factory to be plunged from prosperity to near-starvation. When the *Darling* re-entered the harbour at Sukadana after a lengthy absence, its captain was alarmed to find the factory 'indebted to the Hollanders, and in a poor, beggarly state, because the junk that was despatched from Bantam first touched at Macassar'. Although in good health, Courthope and Sophony were 'altogether unfurnished with money [and] report that they had in consequence been obliged to refuse 1,000 carats of diamonds'.

Once Courthope had turned Sukadana into a going concern, buying gemstones on the cheap and exporting them to Bantam for re-sale, he was keen to expand his trade. Learning that Borneo was rich in gold, diamonds and bezoar stones, a concretion taken from the stomach of animals which was believed to be an antidote, he despatched Sophony to the island on a reconnaissance mission. His instructions, a copy of which he forwarded to Bantam, ordered 'the Russe' to 'proceed to Landak and confer with the governors of those parts upon what security the English may settle a factory there'. In addition he was 'to learn privately whether they stand in fear of the Sukadanians or not, for if so, I see not how our people can be safely with them'. With characteristic cynicism – a cynicism that would become more pronounced during his long years in the Banda Islands – he ended with a caution: 'Above all, be not flattered with fruitless hopes, but if possible, bring firmans [written confirmation] for what they say or promise.'

The mission was not a success, largely because of the

'savageness of the people ... who lie in the rivers on purpose to take off the heads of all they can overcome'. Sophony and his two companions were attacked by a mob of a thousand men and 'escaped a miraculous danger', only surviving the onslaught when they discovered the natives were 'not used to powder and shot [and] were fain to run ashore'. A second, heavily armed expedition had more success, largely because of the English muskets. 'The force of the whole country,' wrote Sophony, 'was not able to withstand nine men.'

In the summer of 1616, Courthope relinquished his lonely job as chief factor in Sukadana and returned to Bantam. The energy he had put into his work had not passed unnoticed and it was with regret that the Company allowed him to leave. Within months of his departure the diamond trade was 'in hugger mugger', there was much 'stealing and griping' and Sukadana became a haven for 'heavy and unprofitable hangers-on that have meat, drink and money to do harm'. Those in responsibility called for Courthope's return, 'for it is fitting that it be a man that hath experience here'.

The request went unheeded for Courthope was needed for a mission of far greater importance. A new chief factor had arrived in Bantam, a man by the name of John Jourdain who had considerable experience of life in the East Indies and who brought with him an unbounded enthusiasm for the task ahead. He was determined to stake his country's claim to the Banda Islands and, in Nathaniel Courthope, he had just the man for the job.

CONFLICT BETWEEN GENTLEMEN

JOHN JOURDAIN TRAVELLED TO London in the winter of 1607 to seek employment as a chief factor with the East India Company. It is unclear what drove him to this decision for he was involved in a profitable shipping concern in the Dorset port of Lyme Regis and, as son of the town's mayor, was able to involve himself in many overseas business ventures. Perhaps he was lured to the East India Company by the hope of getting rich quick, but a more compelling reason is that relations with his wife were strained and he chose self-imposed exile in preference to a life of domestic unhappiness. By the time he came to write his will, the marital breakdown was complete and he totally excluded her from the management of his estate, leaving her a paltry sum of money. The poor woman's final years were spent 'begging from door to door' and writing endless letters to the East India Company asking for 'some competent yearly means proportionable to her birth and breeding'.

The directors responded by despatching the occasional gift to Dorset – the least they could do for a widow whose husband was to prove the greatest of all the Company factors. Jourdain had long held that the future of the spice trade lay in the Banda Islands and he did everything in his power to promote English interests in the region. Returning home after a stint of more than five years in the East he penned a persuasive document in which he argued the importance of strengthening trading links with these remote islands. He sent this document directly to Sir Thomas Smythe who declared himself most impressed with what he read and called a special meeting in order to make public 'his [Jourdain's] opinion concerninge the contynueinge and prosecutinge of trade in the Indies'. After discussing its contents the committee summoned Jourdain to the Company headquarters and listened attentively as he set out the weaknesses of the English in the region and argued that it was essential to 'saufeguards their buysines at Bantam and attempt trade at Banda'. When a number of members protested that this would surely bring them into conflict with the Dutch, Jourdain assured them 'that the Flemings neither dare not or will not sett upon the English'. It was a disingenuous answer for Jourdain had already concluded that future trade in the Spice Islands would inevitably involve coming to blows with the Dutch, a conclusion that had been more than reinforced by his previous trip to the East. Sailing from Bantam in the winter of 1613 he had headed for Amboyna, a clove-rich island under the firm control of the Dutch. Jourdain was only too aware of their presence on Amboyna: graciously introducing himself to the Dutch captain at Hitu, a village on the north of the island, he suggested that instead of buying cloves from the natives, thereby driving up prices, he should buy them from the Dutch at a little over cost price. The captain expressed interest in this proposition but said he would have to clear the matter with his superiors, a response that irritated Jourdain who 'awnswered that this country did nott belonge to the Dutch'.

When he was at last handed the official reply to his

246

proposition, Jourdain was stunned by its strong language. In a 'skoffing' two page letter, the governor 'marvelled that we would presume to thrust ourselves into a countrye where they had made a contracte with the people for all the cloves growinge upon the iland', and strongly advised Jourdain 'nott to deale with the contrye people for any cloves; which if we did they would seek their uttermost to prevent us'. They proved all too willing to carry out this last threat, for no sooner had native chieftains started to offer the English small quantities of spice than the Dutch sent a warning that 'they would build a castle at Hitu and burn their town.' This was enough to panic the natives who were 'made soe fearfull that they durst not give us any enterteynement'.

When Jourdain finally met the Dutch governor he could scarcely contain his rage, accusing him of deceit, arrogance and lies. The helplessness of his situation was a cause of great amusement to the governor who goaded Jourdain about his failure to buy any spices and made a number of cruel jokes about the diminutive size of the *Darling*. These proved too much for Jourdain, who told the governor that the Dutch followed the English 'as the Jews did Christ' and added, in a threat that would pass into legend at the East India Company, that they would one day answer for their arrogance 'betwixt Dover and Calais'. Still smarting from the insults, he then put to sea and headed to the neighbouring island of Ceram where David Middleton had successfully set up his temporary base.

He stepped ashore only to find himself face to face with Jan Coen, the youthful captain of one of the Dutch vessels and a man destined to become the most ruthless of all of Holland's governor-generals in the East. The first meeting between these headstrong men developed, appropriately enough, into a scrap with both men accusing and abusing each other. Coen upbraided the English captain 'in a chollericke manner'; whilst Jourdain employed character-istically insulting language, the product of many years in the company of mariners. Asked to show his commission, 'I replyed that I wondred much that he should be soe well acquainted with my comission; but seeinge he knewe it so well, his long beard (for he had none att all) could not teach me to followe my comission.' This jest, he knew, would wound Coen's pride for the smooth-faced Dutchman was just twenty-six years old and acutely conscious of his youth. Indeed, he never forgave Jourdain the insult and would spend the next six years plotting his bloody revenge. Coen also took the trouble to send an account of his meeting with Jourdain to his superiors in Amsterdam; an account which praised his opponent in order to boost his own standing. 'Jourdain gave us much trouble,' he wrote, 'and I had many disputes with him; for he is a clever fellow and left no means untried which would in any way serve his designs ... We on our side did everything to frustrate his endeavours, for it would have been all up with us there had he succeeded.'

It was not long before Jourdain found his chance to humiliate the Dutchman for a second time: when Coen boasted that the natives hated the English, Jourdain summoned a great council of local chieftains and, cajoling Coen into attendance, asked them to publicly declare whom they preferred as trading partners. 'In awnswere of which they all with one accord stoode up, sayinge: Our onelie desire is to deale with the English, but we are daylie threatned by the Hollanders ... so we dare not almost to speake with you for fear of their forces which are neere.' The council gave Jourdain the moral victory and even provided him with a little spice, for the natives were emboldened by his presence and began to sell him cloves 'oute of sight of the Hollanders'. When continued Dutch threats caused them to abandon their trade, a disillusioned Jourdain set sail for Bantam.

Here the news could hardly have been worse. The last survivors of Sir Henry Middleton's expedition were on their deathbeds and trade had ground to a virtual standstill because of animosities between rival factors. As Jourdain stepped ashore and probed the trusty Nathaniel Courthope for news it became apparent that discipline had broken down completely. The two groups of merchants in the town, those of the sixth and eighth voyages, were engaged in bitter in-fighting and neither was happy at the arrival of Jourdain who had been named as chief factor by Middleton shortly before his death. Jourdain was aware that 'they did not greatly care for my coming aland, and that they were determined not to receive me as principal merchant' but he did not realise that his presence would create such hostility. 'Not knowing of any civil wars,' he made the mistake of visiting the factors who lived in the lower town before proceeding to those in the upper. The latter group treated this as a snub and greeted Jourdain with open hostility. A headstrong mariner called Robert Larkin, 'though not able hardly to stand on his legs,' proclaimed himself chief factor and consented to speak with Jourdain only if he returned later in the day. Jourdain duly obliged, only to find Larkin 'haveinge lost his paine and sicknes, came runninge forth like a madman, askinge for the bilboes, threatninge that if I would not begone out of his house (as he tearmed itt) he would sett me into them'.

Characteristically, Jourdain took the threats in his stride. 'I laughed to see the world soe much altered,' he noted in his diary, perhaps because he realised that in this total breakdown of authority lay his strongest chance of recovering his position. But when he returned the following morning to demand the keys and accounts, 'they, beeinge armed with guns, halberts and swordes, came out against me as in defiannce, sayinge that they knewe me not for cheife factour, neither should I have any thinge to doe in thatt buysines.' Thoroughly disheartened, Jourdain told them that 'I would not staie in Bantam to trouble them; and I, as much desirous to be rid of their companie, made as much haste as might be to fitt our shipp.' True to his word, the *Darling* was made ready and put to sea within a few days.

Six weeks later an unforeseen event brought Jourdain back to Bantam. As he sailed along the coast of Sumatra, he caught sight of two English vessels which, he discovered, were under the captainship of Thomas Best, commander of the East India Company's tenth fleet. Best was an 'ungratefull, covetous and prowde' man whose rumbustious personality was not always appreciated by his crew. When he learned that the *Darling* was laden with half a cargo of cloves he was struck by the brilliant idea of buying this cargo, thereby saving himself the trouble of sailing to either Amboyna or the Banda Islands. Jourdain was most unhappy about this and suggested a number of other solutions but 'all this could not satisfie the Generall [Best], the cloves smellinge so sweete that we must retourne for Bantam in his companie; and seeinge no remedy, I was content.' Best had, in fact, struck an agreement whereby he would use his authority to reinstate Jourdain as chief factor in return for the cloves on board the *Darling*.

No sooner had the men arrived in Bantam than Best put his plan into action. Summoning the English factors to a general meeting 'he propounded that he understoode of some disorders and controversie that there was betwixt the factors of the sixth and eighth voyages, as alsoe of other voyages formerlie.' To much nodding of heads, he now turned on the factors, haranguing them for 'the greate disgrace it was to our nation and the Honourable Companie, our employars, to have so many houses in one place, seperated both in qualitie and friendshippe, beeing all as it were for one Companie; which was a greate scandall to our nation'.

In speaking these words Best had got to the heart of the problem. Although the men in Bantam were all employed by the East India Company, each voyage sought its own profit and not the general profit of the Company. In forcing Jourdain to sell his cloves, Best was behaving no more honourably than the men he was chastising but he did at least have the foresight to realise that the English community in Bantam could only survive if there was some central authority which could override the claims of individual voyages. 'It was fittinge,' he concluded, 'there should be but one head in the countrye.'

Who that 'one head' might be was never in doubt. 'After perswations of the Generall and them all,' writes Jourdain modestly, 'I was content (though against my will) to take the place.' At last Bantam had a chief factor, and one who had a vision for the future of trade in the East Indies.

Jourdain was convinced that the English should now concentrate their activities on the Banda Islands and sent word to the native chieftains that his merchants would shortly be arriving in far greater numbers. But despite his title and influence Jourdain was powerless to decide the final destinations of vessels arriving at Bantam. It was up to expedition commanders to choose which islands they would visit, and Jourdain's authority only extended over a handful of pinnaces based in the Javanese port. It angered him that for more than a year he was unable to send a single ship to the Bandas and he scribbled a strongly worded letter to London complaining that '[because] there is not any ship gone this year they [the natives] will be out of hope; for that they did depend much upon the English this year, which now they will be frustrate of their hopes and hold the Hollanders' words to be true, who tells them that they shall never see any English ship there but once in four years, and then some small ship which can do them no good.'

A small English vessel did touch at Great Banda in the spring of 1614 and its captain, Richard Welden, wrote to Jourdain to inform him of his visit and urge him to send a ship – any ship – to the islands. 'For the Bandanese do much marvel that in so long a time there have come no English shipping there, protesting if they come they will live and die with the English, for now all the Bandanese hath open wars with the Hollanders and have slain many of them.' Welden added that trade in Banda was more profitable than in previous years and that he was resolved to sail there again 'at the first of the next monsoon'.

His letter arrived at a fortuitous time, for Jourdain had recently found himself with two small ships at his disposal. Fitting out the *Concord*, together with a pinnace called the *Speedwell*, he despatched two factors, George Ball and George Cokayne, to explore the possibilities of increased trade with Banda. Ball was instructed to 'confer with the country people concerning the estate of their business; and if you perceive them to be willing of trade … you may leave there Mr Sophony Cozucke and Richard Hunt, with one English more, and some black that is willing to serve them.' This was a significant development – the first time that someone of influence had proposed a permanent English presence in the Banda Islands.

The news from Banda was not good. Gerald Reynst, the

Dutch governor-general had recently arrived in the islands bringing with him a fleet of eleven ships, an army of a thousand soldiers, and orders to impose his unchallengeable control over the Banda Islands. As he sailed into Neira harbour the volcano, Gunung Api, erupted in spectacular fashion, convincing the superstitious islanders that something portentous was about to occur.

The two Georges, Ball and Cokayne, arrived soon after, sailing straight to Neira and anchoring before the Dutch castle. The Hollander vessels caused them a moment's anxiety but they saluted them with a couple of cannon shots and prepared to visit Reynst the following morning. They used the intervening hours wisely. Both men rowed over to Great Banda and made contact with the native chieftains, enquiring about the possibility of building a fortified English factory. The sight of the Englishmen caused the natives to pour out their feelings and one of the headmen, 'pointing to the Fleming castle, [said] that it makes old men to weep, and will the child that is unborn, saying as God hath given them a country to them and their, so He hath sent the Hollanders as a plague unto them, making wars upon them and by unjust proceedings seeking to take their country from them'.

So far the English vessels had been untroubled by the Dutch, but as the men returned to their ships a Dutch pinnace crowded with soldiers stopped them and ordered them to a meeting with the governor-general. After a brief stand-off the soldiers opened fire and Ball, realising the futility of resistance, sent Cokayne ashore as his messenger.

Reynst had been fuming ever since he watched the English ships sail into his harbour. Now, with the Englishman standing in front of him, he demanded to see Cokayne's East India Company papers. Cokayne's refusal sent Reynst into an apoplexy of rage. 'He then standing up, fluttering his papers at my face, saying we were rogues and rascals, not having anything but from Thomas Smythe of London, most vilely railing of our Honourable Company.' He added that King James I had recently declared that the Dutch 'had all the right that might be, and no others, to these places of Banda'. After a few further words of abuse Reynst finished by saying 'that we came to steal more voyages from them as others had done before, naming Keeling and Middleton'.

It was clear that the English were not going to have much luck trading at Neira or Great Banda and the following morning they hoisted their sails and headed for Ai, five miles to the west of the main islands. Reynst immediately ordered a squadron of Dutch ships to follow them but these were shaken off in a gale and Cokayne slipped ashore unhindered, the islanders 'much rejoicing of our coming'. Reynst's control over this small, nutmeg-rich island was almost non-existent but Ai's chieftains were nonetheless nervous about the thousand soldiers barracked on Neira and, fearing attack, provided the English with a warm welcome. They knew from the antics of Keeling and Middleton that the English were united in their hatred of the Dutch and, when they learned of their desire to settle a permanent factory on the island, consented immediately. An agreement was struck, a factory built, and Ball and Cokayne sailed away laden with nutmeg, leaving Sophony Cozucke and a few men to guard the island. One of these, a trader called John Skinner, felt so confident of their impregnable position that he wrote to a friend: 'Truly I durst lay all that I ever shall be worth whilst I live that the Hollanders never get the islands of Banda, for all the Bandanese will lose their lives before they will be under the Hollanders.' What gave him even greater satisfaction was that Gunung Api, the volcano, was now erupting with such force that huge boulders were raining down on the Dutch castle on Neira. Skinner claimed that the soldiers had 'begun to make way to leave the castle' and believed that were it not for the choleric Reynst they would have fled the islands altogether.

The Dutch governor-general soon knocked the waverers into shape, informing them not only that they were here to stay, but that they were about to launch a massive offensive against Ai. Many were only too keen to escape the dangers posed by the volcano, unaware that Ai's awkward geography made an invasion extremely hazardous. 'The sea shoare is so steepe that it seemeth nature meant to reserve this iland particularly to herselfe,' wrote one observer. 'There is but one place about the whole iland for a ship to anchor in; and that so dangerous that he that letteth fall his anchor seldome seeth the weighing of it againe; besides he incurreth the imminent dangers of his ship.' The invasion was scheduled for the morning of 14 May 1615, and Reynst – who dismissed the difficulties – declared himself confident that it would be in Dutch hands within a matter of hours. He was taking no chances; almost a thousand Dutch and Japanese soldiers were pitched against Ai's five-hundred-strong fighting force and the Hollanders were armed to the teeth with muskets and cannon. But from the moment they launched their attack the Dutch troops were surprised by the resistance they encountered. The native marksmanship was far more accurate than anything they had experienced on Neira or Great Banda and the island strongholds were particularly well designed. These fortifications snaked upwards from the shoreline to the hills so that even when the Dutch captured long sections of wall they found to their annoyance that they were open to attack from defenders higher up the hillside.

The English on Ai had spent time and effort preparing themselves for the invasion. Not only had they planned a detailed defence of the island, they had also trained the natives to use muskets and taught them how to hold their positions. Had they not been faced with such an over-whelmingly larger force, the men of Ai might well have saved the island from capture. But successive waves of Dutch attackers gradually disheartened the defenders and by night-fall their army had succeeded in overrunning most of the island, leaving only one remote fort still controlled by the Bandanese. As the sun went down the Dutch celebrated their victory, then went to sleep in the knowledge that tomorrow the whole island would be theirs.

It was a fatal mistake, for in the early hours the Bandanese crept out of their fort and launched a savage counter-attack. The Dutch soldiers, heavy with sleep and in unfamiliar surroundings, were sitting ducks. Twenty-seven were killed outright and dozens more wounded as they fought their way back to their ships. Two Dutchmen, convinced that all was lost, suddenly switched over to the enemy. One of them clambered into a tree and killed two of his erstwhile comrades with a single shot. The Dutch humiliation was complete. As the ships limped back to Neira, the scale of their defeat gradually became apparent. In one day's fighting they had lost thirty-six soldiers, with two hundred wounded and two defections. Reynst was devastated, never recovered from the humiliation and died a few months later.

The role of the English in this debacle did not pass unrecorded by Jan Coen who sent two letters to the Seventeen in Amsterdam. In the first he informed them that the English 'want to reap what we have sowed, and they brag that they are free to do so because their king has authority over the Netherlands nation.' In the second he

*The crumbling entrance to Dutch-built Fort Revenge on Ai. Dozens
of Englishmen were imprisoned in its dungeons and complained
bitterly about their harsh treatment. 'They pissed and **** upon our
heads,' wrote one, 'untill such time as we were broken out from top to
toe like lepers.'*

was more forthright. 'You can be assured,' he wrote, 'that if
you do not send a large capital at the earliest opportunity
... the whole Indies trade is liable to come to nothing.'

The Seventeen, in fact, had every intention of continuing their war against the island of Ai and in the spring of 1616 they despatched Admiral Jan Dirkz Lam to the Banda Islands with one simple order: Ai was to be brought under Dutch control. The natives on Ai knew that the Dutch would return to punish them and were equally certain that they would be unable to withstand a second attack. They therefore asked Sophony Cozucke to sail one of their chieftains to Bantam so that he could personally deliver a letter to John Jourdain.

'We have all heard even from farr countryes of the greate love and peace that the Kinge of England has with all the world ...' it read, 'and hath done no hurt to any of our religion, or doth seeke to overthrowe our lawe, and doth not by force attempt to overcome any man's kingdome, but only peace and frindshipp doth seeke trade without violence.'

> Therefore we all desire to come to an agrement with the Kinge of England, because that nowe the Hollanders do practize by all meanes possible to conquer our country and destroy our religion, by reason whereof all of us of the Islands of Banda do utterly hate the very sight of theis Hollanders, sonnes of Whores, because they exceed in lying and villainy and desire to overcome all men's country by trechery. These are the occasions whie we soe extreamely hate them. We have nowe therefore with one general consent, resolved never hereafter to trade with them, but allwayes to esteeme them our utter enimyes, wherefore we all thought good to send this lettre ... that if so be the kinge of England out of his love towards us will have a care of our cuntry and religion and will help us with artillary powder and shott and

help us to recover the castle of Neira, whereby we
may be able to make warrs with the Hollanders, by
God's helpe all the spice that all our island's shall
yeald, we will onely sell to the King of England, and
to no other nation in the world.

There was only one proviso attached to the agreement:
'that [if] in small matters the Bandanezers should give
occasion of discontent to the English, or the English doe
that which might be distastful to the Bandanezars, that then
with mutuall consent like frinds they would beare with
each others errors; onely we all desire that you doe not
seeke to overthrowe our religion, and that you do not
comitt offence with our weomen, because theis twoe onely
we are not able to endure'.

Such words were music to the ears of Jourdain who was
already dreaming of expanding the English factory in Ai.
Now was the time to act and, in December 1615, he
assembled a squadron of three ships, the *Thomas*, the *Concord*
and the *Speedwell*, and instructed them to sail for Banda
without further ado. But just as they were about to leave
Bantam Jourdain received a note from Jan Coen warning
him that henceforth all English shipping was banned from
the Banda Islands and that any vessel contravening this order
would be expelled by force and 'if any slaughter of men
happened ... they would not be culpable.'

The arrival of two new English ships under the
command of Samuel Castleton strengthened Jourdain's
resolve. Castleton had always intended to sail to the Banda
Islands and had no intention of being deflected from his
mission by an arrogant letter from Jan Coen. He suggested
that all the ships sail together in a mini-armada, and set off
in January 1616 on what was to prove one of the most

bizarre English expeditions ever to reach the Banda Islands. This was largely due to the eccentricities of its commander whose behaviour left the Dutch both puzzled and bemused. Castleton had already caused raised eyebrows among the Company directors in London after trumpeting his unorthodox methods for preserving the health of his sailors. These included the daily baking of fresh bread on board his ships, the manual grinding of corn which he considered 'an exercise fit to preserve men in health' and the distilling of fresh water from salt by means of an elaborate system of stills and furnaces. Had this worked, he intended that each of his vessels would have its own mobile desalination plant. Unfortunately it proved a complete failure, his crew still died, and Castleton concluded that it was their own fault since they were all confirmed alcoholics.

By the time his fleet arrived off Ai Island a new Dutch armada under the command of Admiral Lam had anchored in the shadow of Fort Nassau. Lam had come in even greater numbers than his predecessor: a fleet of twelve ships and more than a thousand soldiers who were shortly joined by a second fleet and military reinforcements. For a few days they watched the English ships lurking around Ai and Run Islands before Lam realised that both islands were being fortified and that on Run the English were building some sort of castle. He immediately ordered his men to prepare for a full-scale invasion of Ai, but scarcely had their squadron of ships set sail from Neira than they discovered they had a fight on their hands. Castleton had manoeuvred his five vessels into the deep channel separating the two islands, blocking access to Ai. A few shots were fired and the men were about to do battle when a curious incident brought the fighting to an abrupt halt. Castleton, it seems, had only just learned the name of the Dutch commander and, despatching a rowing boat over to Lam's ship, he offered his compliments to the commander and explained that he, an Englishman, was so deeply grateful for a service Lam had once rendered him that he was unable to bring himself to continue with the battle. To an astonished Lam he added that he was ordering his vessels to withdraw and apologised for any offence he might have caused.

Castleton did indeed have good cause to thank Lam. Some three years previously he had been watering at the Atlantic island of St Helena when he was surprised by two Portuguese carracks and forced to put to sea, leaving half his men on the island. Two Dutch vessels commanded by Lam had just left the island; vessels which Castleton chased after and begged for assistance. Lam agreed to attack the Portuguese, an action which saved the English sailors but cost him dear for he lost one of his ships in the fight.

Now, in very different circumstances, Castleton wished to repay Lam's former kindness. Invited over to the Dutch commander's ship, Castleton found himself heartily welcomed by Lam who was only too happy to strike a gentleman's agreement in which the Englishman would withdraw his fleet and provide intelligence about Ai's defences in return for freedom of trade with Ai once the Dutch had occupied the island. The two men shook hands and Castleton, perhaps a little ashamed at the way he had just abandoned the islanders of Ai, sailed to Ceram while Lam conquered the island. His last act was to instruct Richard Hunt, the resident English factor on Ai, to observe a strict neutrality throughout the forthcoming battle.

The island elders watched in despair as the English vessels sailed away. A council was convened at which they pinned their last hopes on Hunt, formerly surrendering Ai and Run to him and dutifully raising the flag of St George from the island's battlements. There was little else to do but await the Dutch onslaught.

Despite their overwhelming superiority the Dutch found their second battle for Ai no less challenging than the first. Once again a huge force of Dutch and Japanese soldiers were landed and they fought their way from stronghold to stronghold, surprised by the tenacity of their Bandanese foes. By nightfall they had taken most key positions but still the island was not under control. Fearful of a repeat of the previous year's catastrophe the men remained on their guard all night and in the morning a large band of reinforcements were landed. Violent rainstorms hindered the Dutch and it was a further two days before the island was finally brought under their control. By this time the Bandanese had run out of ammunition and most escaped to Run Island where they could continue their resistance to the Dutch.

Lam took no chances once he had conquered Ai. He built a sturdy fort close to the shoreline, provided it with a permanent garrison and gave it the appropriate name Fort Revenge. 'It is a regular pentagon, well fortified, and furnished with all manner of provisions and souldiers, and is held to bee the strongest castle the Dutch have in the Indies.' It stands to this day, its neglected ramparts overgrown with climbing ivy and its parade ground home to a family of goats. But the battlements are in a fine state of repair and a rusting cannon still points towards Run, the letters VOC – Vereenigde Oost-Indische Compagnie – embossed on the barrel.

Lam drew up a formal agreement with the conquered Bandanese and took the opportunity to confirm Dutch authority over most of the Banda Islands. Great Banda and Neira reluctantly signed up to the Dutch monopoly; tiny

Rozengain soon followed suit. Ai got the worst deal of all for Lam fixed the price of nutmeg at 20 per cent less than on the other islands. Of all the Bandas, Run now stood alone – the only island that remained unoccupied by Dutch troops and was party to no agreement with the Dutch East India Company.

It was to Run that Richard Hunt now fled 'in fear of his life, the Hollanders having sworne to hang him, and did offer great sums of money for his person'. He eventually arrived back in Bantam where news of his clandestine activities had spread far and wide and where he had the misfortune to become a walking symbol of the Dutch hatred for the English. In the words of John Jourdain, 'Richard Hunt, passinge in a very narrowe streete, mette with two of the Dutch marchannts, which came abrest towards him and would nott give him way to passe by. Soe Hunt put one of them aside to make waye, whereupon they fell to blowes. The Dutch beeinge neere their backe dore called for their slaves who presentlie came, to the number of 20 persons, and fell upon him and beate him very sore, and halled him through the durte by the haire of the head to their owne howse.' Vowing to make him suffer before they killed him they 'sett him in the boults at their gate in the hott sunne, without hatt'. All this was done very publicly in order to demonstrate to the townspeople that the Dutch were a force to be reckoned with. Jourdain realised this and decided to meet force with force, threatening to seize 'the best of their marchannts', clap them in irons, and put them on display outside the English gates. But Hunt was unexpectedly released before he had a chance to carry out his threat, and a new English fleet arrived in the bay of Bantam. Its commander, the experienced William Keeling, urged restraint and although annoyed by the treatment of Hunt, was 'was willing to wink at it, and so the matter rested'. Individuals continued to fight in the streets, and even to kill one another, but on an official level the two nations remained at peace.

Peace was something that the office-bound directors of both the English and Dutch East India Companies recognised as essential if the spice trade was to continue to be profitable. Yet the peace had always been an uneasy one and, in the remoter islands of the East Indies, had all too often spilled over into a virtual state of war. As early as 1611 the English directors had felt the need to complain about the warlike stance taken by some of the Dutch commanders. Enraged by persistent reports of violence shown to their employees, and 'having long and patiently endured sundry notorious wrongs and injurious courses at the hand of the Hollanders', they were 'enforced at last to break silence'. In a lengthy letter to the Lord High Treasurer of England they set out their woes and requested help in their desire to enter into dialogue with the States General. King James approved the idea and instructed his minister in The Hague to set the ball rolling. Although the Dutch disputed most of the English complaints they agreed to meet in 1613 'in order to promote friendly feeling and good neighbourly relations'.

The Dutch negotiating team was a distinguished one, led by the noted jurist Hugo Grotius who had published his celebrated *Mare Librum* in the previous year. Grotius, whose book had the significant subtitle, *A Discourse concerning the right which the Hollanders claim of trade to India*, argued, as had the Dutch in Manhattan, that as soon as a nation erected a building on a piece of land, the land automatically became the property of that nation. He added that the Dutch, unlike the English, had spent vast sums of money fighting the natives in the East Indies and, in view of that, it was totally unfair of the English to dispute their rights to trade with these islands. The English East India Company disagreed, maintaining its right to trade with the Spice Islands by virtue of the fact that it got there first. 'Before these regions were known to you,' announced the directors grandly, 'we stood legally approved by their leaders and peoples, in pacts and agreements, as we can easily prove.' The conference ended with no formal agreement, but it had achieved the useful result of bringing the two sides together and many felt that it would be foolish not to continue the dialogue. It was therefore agreed that the teams should meet again within two years.

This second conference, which took place against a backdrop of much bloodshed in the Banda Islands, was to prove one of the more extraordinary events in the saga of the two companies. The conference began in a similar manner to its predecessor with each side retreading the same old ground. But after a few days the English contingent were invited to a meeting with the Attorney-General of Holland who made the startling suggestion that the two companies unite to form one unbeatable organisation. Chief negotiator Sir Henry Wooten immediately wrote to the directors in London pointing out the benefits: 'If we joined with them to beat the Spaniards out of the East Indies we shall make them as profitable unto us as the West Indies should be unto them.'

Although the English directors remained extremely sceptical, a detailed proposal concerning the merger was prepared and plans were formulated for the finance of the giant company. The benefits were deemed to be enormous: each year more than £600,000 of spices could be shipped from the East, the maximum that western Europe could consume annually. Spain would quickly be forced out of the region, native chiefs would be compelled to reduce duties paid at Bantam and trade with China would be vigorously pursued. Even discipline among sailors would be improved since there would no longer be any rivalry between the two nations.

So keen were the Dutch to prove conciliatory that shortly before the suggestion was mooted the Seventeen wrote to the hot-headed Jan Coen ordering him to avoid any conflict or 'maltreatment' of the English. Coen was stung by this letter and immediately penned a sarcastic reply: 'If by night and day proud thieves broke into your house, who were not ashamed of any robbery or other offense, how would you defend your property against them without having recourse to "maltreatment?" This is what the English are doing against you in the Moluccas. Consequently, we are surprised to receive instructions not to do them bodily harm. If the English have this privilege above all other nations, it must be nice to be an Englishman.'

In the event the negotiations in The Hague broke down and the English, who had presented their own list of propositions, found they were rejected by the Dutch. After all the excitement and many months of discussions, both parties found themselves back at the drawing board. By late spring 1615 the English commissioners realised there was nothing left to discuss and they returned to London.

It was during the years in which these negotiations were taking place that Jan Pieterszoon Coen began his spectacular climb to the top. He had first sailed east in 1607, a most unfortunate introduction to the spice trade for it was while he was stationed in the Banda Islands that Verhoef and his lieutenants were massacred. Coen was in

Ten pounds of nutmeg cost one penny in the East Indies yet sold in London for fifty shillings. Apothecaries reaped vast profits from their pomanders, particularly during the plague. 'I confesse they are costly,' wrote one, 'but cheape medicines are as dear as death.'

no doubt that the English had played a significant role in planning the ambush and much of his hatred seems to have stemmed from this belief.

In 1612 he sailed to the Spice Islands for a second time and it was on this occasion, while serving as chief merchant, that he engaged in his first scrap with John Jourdain. The men shared the similar aim of capturing the entire Bandanese spice trade but Coen was willing to employ far bloodier methods to pursue his goal. He wanted to conquer islands, subjugate the natives and plant Dutch colonies as a balance to the English presence in the region. Although the Seventeen had already sent out a handful of settlers they were hardly what Coen had in mind; a motley crew much given to 'drinking and whoring'. In later years Coen would persistently call for a better class of settler, particularly those with manual skills. 'Even if they come naked as a jaybird,' he wrote, 'we can still use them.'

A portrait of Coen hangs in the Rijksmuseum in Amsterdam. Painted in Bantam, it depicts a tall, upright figure with a long and narrow face and deep-set eyes. His lips are thin, his nose aquiline and his cheeks hollow and pale. It is by no means a flattering portrait but it does suggest that Coen was a man in total control of his destiny. The few contemporary descriptions of Coen are far from complimentary. One of his colleagues describes him as 'full of Italian tricks' whilst others refer to his bony hands and pointed fingers. His nickname was De Schraale, which means 'thin and lanky' but also refers to his grim character.

His numerous letters give a greater insight into his character. Coen was a reserved man who was preoccupied with what he considered to be his duty and who did not suffer fools gladly. He never hesitated to speak his mind, frequently admonishing his superiors for what he believed to be their stupidity and short-sightedness. He was a practical man, a great mathematician, who, as a strict Calvinist, was devoid of any frivolities. As for a sense of humour, he had none.

His rise through the ranks was rapid. A year after proving himself a successful chief merchant he was promoted to the important post of book-keeper general and, after a further twelve months, was made a member of the influential Council of the Indies. He might have hoped that when Gerald Reynst died shortly after his abortive attack on Ai he would be promoted to the position of governor-general. As it turned out, the Seventeen in Amsterdam elected Laurens Reael, an effete aristocrat who appears to have spent much of his time concerned with his dress. Coen, not surprisingly, could not stand the man and argued vehemently against his tactics in dealing with the English. Reael responded by countermanding Coen's instructions forbidding the English from sailing to the Banda Islands, ordering him that 'no harsh measures were to be used to disperse the English by force, fearing that this might not only lead to war in these quarters but might spread to Europe as well.'

Coen studiously ignored these instructions and continued his attacks on English shipping. 'If I did wrong,' he wrote in a letter to Amsterdam, '(which I do not believe) please tell me and I will act accordingly. The English threaten to hang me in effigy on the highest gallows in England and to pickle my heart ... Reael cannot decide to deal firmly with the English, demanding more pertinent orders. I hope that your latest orders will satisfy him and change his attitude.'

The Seventeen had initially expressed concern about their bellicose servant in the East, but as his detailed letters, documents and balance sheets poured into their headquarters in Amsterdam they were convinced that they were dealing with someone of remarkable talent. Despite the shortage of capital he continued to send back huge cargoes of spice, and the directors, hinting that he might one day be considered a suitable candidate for the top job, raised his salary and promised it would keep rising if Coen continued the good work. The directors got no thanks from their industrious servant. 'I thought my services were more valuable to you than what you offer,' he wrote in his characteristically sneering style, referring to the fact that others received far more than him 'and accomplish little'. This barbed comment was directed at Reael who was also deeply dissatisfied with his pay rise. Determined to force the directors into reconsidering their offer, Reael upped the stakes considerably by resigning from his position as governor-general. He then dropped heavy hints to the effect that he would be only too willing to resume his post when his pay rise had been satisfactorily sorted. 'It being human nature to change one's mind ...' he wrote, 'I might be induced to stay longer if the situation, and especially a good salary, would warrant it.' In resigning, Reael had seriously misjudged his employers. The Seventeen had long been considering removing him from his post and he had now presented them with the perfect opportunity. Writing a polite letter accepting his resignation, they promptly installed Jan Coen, just thirty-one years old, in his place.

The time for being conciliatory was over: in a letter to Coen they instructed him that 'something on a large scale must be done against the enemies; the inhabitants of Banda must be subjugated, their leaders must be killed or driven out of the land, and if necessary the country must be turned into a desert by uprooting the trees and shrubs.'

Coen was only too keen to carry out these wishes. Courthope was determined to stop him.

CHAPTER TEN

RAISING THE
BLOOD-FLAG

NATHANIEL COURTHOPE was appointed commander of two ships, the *Swan* and the *Defence,* in October 1616. He was given the post by John Jourdain who had long recognised Courthope's abilities and was now sending his friend on a mission of the utmost importance. Courthope was to sail his ships to Macassar in order to buy rice and provisions, then proceed directly to Run where it was hoped that the natives 'expected him and would be ready to receive him.' It was critical that he should be successful in taking control of the island for of the six principal Bandas, only Run still lay outside the grasp of the Dutch. If they seized this island, as they had seized Ai, they would control the world's entire supply of nutmeg. They would also have completed their stranglehold on the Spice Islands, leaving the English without a single base from which to launch future attacks.

Jourdain was only too aware of the consequences of failure and provided Courthope with detailed instructions about his mission. He was to gather together the chieftains of Run and Ai and confirm whether or not they stood by their former surrender to Richard Hunt, the factor on Ai Island, to whom they had proclaimed their allegiance to King James I. If they did, Courthope was to get this confirmed in writing; if not he was to coerce them into submission. Jourdain added that if the Dutch 'offered violence, to the utmost of his power, even to the loss of lives and goods, to make the good the same'. Little could he have imagined how thoroughly Courthope would fulfil this last command.

The *Swan* and the *Defence* sailed on the last day of October and, helped by a freshening breeze, arrived before Run Island on 23 December 1616. The ever-cautious Jourdain had warned his friend to be wary of treachery on the part of the natives: 'At your arrival at Run,' he said, 'show yourself courteous and affable, for they are a peevish, perverse, diffident and perfidious people and apt to take disgust upon small occasions, and are, being moved, more cumbersome than wasps.' Fearing a hostile reception, Courthope anchored in the bay and 'sent my skiff ashore to understand the state of the islanders'. It became immediately apparent that far from planning treachery the natives were overjoyed at the sight of the English ships for they had been worn down by their constant struggles with the Dutch and many were in a pitiful state having fled to Run as refugees from Ai. Since then, the island had been under a virtual blockade and much of the population was on the verge of starvation.

Courthope records with great precision the formal surrender of the island; a wise precaution, for it was his documentation that was later used as incontrovertible proof of England's sovereignty over Run. Inviting the chief orang-kayas aboard the *Swan*, he asked them 'whether they had made any contract with the Hollanders, and given them any surrender; they all replied, they had not, nor never would; but held them as mortal enemies'. Indeed the island's headmen surpassed themselves in their protestations of loyalty to England, repeatedly assuring Courthope that their former submission still held.

When asked to record their surrender in writing, the orang-kayas obliged by producing an agreement which made over the island of Run to the English Crown 'forever'. 'And whereas King James by the grace of God is King of England, Scotland, France and Ireland, is also now by the mercy of God King of Pooloway [Ai] and Poolaroone [Run].' It was a title that King James would come to cherish, and with good reason. On reading these lines one of Courthope's men wryly remarked that these two islands would prove a great deal more profitable than Scotland ever had.

The document continued: 'Moreover, we doe all of us make an agreement that the commodities in the two foresaid ilands, namely mace and nutmegs, we cannot nor will sell to any other nation, but only to the King of England his subjects ... And whereas all the orankayas of the foresaid ilands have made this agreement, let it be credited that it was not made in madnesse or loosely as the breathing of the wind, but because it was concluded upon in their hearts, they cannot revolt from or swerve from the same againe.'

There was one condition attached to the treaty: 'that we doe desire of his Majestie that such things as are not fitting in our religion, as unreverent usage of women, mayntayn-ing of swine in our countrey, forceable taking away of men's goods, misse-using of our men, or any such like... that they be not put in practice, being out of our use and custome.' The document was duly signed by eleven of the islands' headmen and the two sides shook hands. There was one last ceremonial which was to prove, above all else, that the chieftains stood by their pledge. A nutmeg seedling wrapped in the unique soil of the country was handed to

Courthope as a gesture of loyalty, an act that was more than mere symbolism for it demonstrated that they placed all their trust in his leadership. The colourful little ceremony that followed, which threw a carnival-like atmosphere over the proceedings, was undertaken with great sincerity on the part of both the orang-kayas and Nathaniel Courthope. As the English fired all their cannon in celebration of the island's 'capture', the village elders reciprocated by raising the flag of St George and the next two days were spent in friendly festivities.

It is unfortunate that there is no record of what the local headmen made of this strangely attired Englishman – nor has any portrait of Courthope survived – but letters in the East India Company archives testify to his impressive stature and

In Elizabethan times, the nutmeg tree only grew in the Banda Islands. Its fruit was believed to cure the 'sweating sickness' – the plague – that accompanied the 'pestiferous time of the pestilence'.

he appears to have engendered an instant respect both from his fellow men and from the native Bandanese. He was honest, straight-talking and scrupulously fair, and his sense of justice and strict morals were in striking contrast to those of the Dutch commanders so despised by Run's islanders.

The festivities presided over by 'the captain' were brought to an abrupt halt on Christmas Day when a Dutch ship was spied approaching from the west. A hastily convened council agreed that the island should be urgently fortified and, to this end, three of the largest cannon were landed and heaved up to a makeshift platform atop Run's highest cliff. This proved to be a wise precaution for three days later the vessel sent its pinnace into the bay 'within shot of our fort'. A tense stand-off followed before the Dutch ship raised the blood-flag to signify the start of hostilities, then hastily sailed for Neira. This gesture ended Courthope's fading hope that his stay on Run would be a short one. It was clear that the Dutch had no intention of allowing the English to remain on the island and were prepared to use force in order to evict them.

Yet Courthope was not unduly worried by threats of Dutch aggression for he knew that Run's natural defences would make it extremely hard for any enemy to capture the island. Its southern coastline consists of a long bank of precipitous cliffs which are virtually impossible to scale without ropes. The sea here is a boiling fury for the strong current hurls the waves against the black rock with tremendous force. Any vessel attempting to land would almost certainly be dashed to pieces on the rocks or wrecked on the reef that lies just below the surface. The island's northern shore, where the *Swan* and *Defence* lay at anchor, presented Courthope with more of a problem. Its small harbour was accessible to ships arriving from either east or west and, once anchored in the bay, they would have few difficulties in targeting Run's only settlement. But here, too, Courthope had geography on his side. The western end of the harbour is overlooked by a high cliff that commands a splendid view of the bay: by fortifying this bluff of rock the English could effectively bar enemy ships sailing from Java from coming within shot of the village.

The harbour's eastern entrance was the most difficult part of the island to defend – a long coral reef linking Run with the tiny islet of Nailaka, a low-lying atoll of powdery beaches and palm-trees. This islet was of great importance to the islanders because its surrounding shallow waters provided rich pickings for fishermen. It was essential that in times of siege Nailaka remained in their hands. As Courthope made a study of the little island he realised that if he set cannon pointing eastwards he could attack any ship sailing from Neira long before it got within shot of Run harbour. By placing a second battery facing west he would have virtual command over all shipping sailing from Bantam.

His men began work on the fortifications shortly after Christmas. One bastion was christened Fort Defence, the other Fort Swan, and each was armed with three stout cannon. Scarcely were these guns in place than a small fleet of Dutch ships took advantage of the stiff easterly wind and sailed over from Neira, catching the English unawares. Before Courthope had even primed his cannon, the ships had sailed into Run harbour and moored alongside the *Swan* and the *Defence*, cutting off any assistance from the shore.

Courthope's immediate task was to inform the Dutch that Run had surrendered to England. He therefore sent a

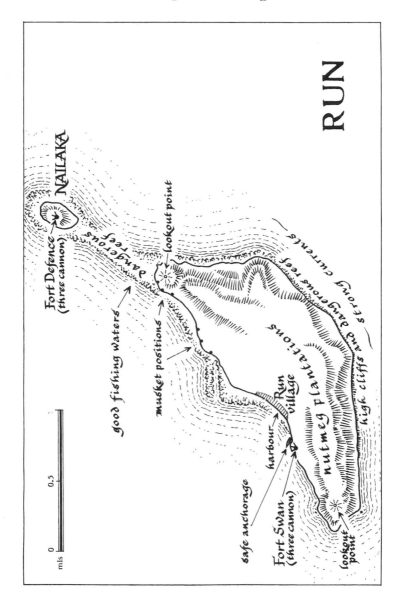

RUN

NAILAKA

Fort Defence
(three cannon)

dangerous reef

lookout point

good fishing waters

musket positions

high cliffs and dangerous currents

nutmeg plantations

Run village

harbour

safe anchorage

Fort Swan
(three cannon)

lookout point

0   0.5
mls

277

messenger across to the Dutch flagship to warn the commander, Cornelis Dedel, that the island was now English, and that he should 'depart the road before six glasses were run, for that the islanders ... would have shot unto them from the shore'. Dedel was intrigued by this news and played for time, asking to meet Courthope aboard the *Swan*. The English captain agreed 'and shewed him the surrender of Polaroone, and our right and possession there for his Majesty of England, which we would hold and maintain to our utmost power'. Dedel seemed impressed with the document and, according to the English account of the event, took it in his hands and, 'perusing it, he said with these words: "This is a true surrender." '

Yet he refused to leave the harbour. Although 'the glass was running in the Great Cabin' he wished to learn more about the English commander and probed him for information about the forces at his disposal. Courthope repeatedly reminded Dedel that he had hidden cannon trained on the Dutch vessels and that the natives would open fire when the sixth glass had run. Having gauged his man, Dedel at last took this threat at face value and, outmatched and outgunned, sullenly retreated to Neira. The English later learned that he had come with instructions to attack the island but had not reckoned with the batteries that Courthope had erected on the shore.

Less than a week later a Dutch pinnace was observed taking soundings around the island of Nailaka. This caused Courthope serious concern and he instructed his men to let fly with their muskets, forcing the pinnace to put hastily to sea. This event was later used by the Dutch as evidence that the English had been the first to open hostilities.

Although Run's defences made a Dutch assault unlikely,

The narrow channel separating the central group of Banda Islands provided safe anchorage for English and Dutch vessels. Although the English were banned from mooring here, most captains treated Dutch threats to their shipping with derision.

at least in the short term, Courthope realised that the island was extremely vulnerable to a sea blockade, a situation aggravated by the fact that he had landed on Run with scarcely any provisions. His two ships had been loaded with only a few chickens and a small quantity of rice and arak, most of which had been consumed on the journey to Run. Unable to restock en route, the Englishmen arrived to find that the island offered little in the way of food. Although nutmeg grew in abundance, there was not enough fresh fruit or vegetables to feed the native islanders and the only other plant that thrived was the sago palm whose pithy trunk could be boiled down into a glutinous, porridge-like starch. The inhabitants of Run had always depended on their neighbouring islands for their supplies, but all of these were now firmly under Dutch control. Their only hope of replenishing stocks lay in the occasional junk or trading craft that happened to put into the island's natural harbour.

More serious was the shortage of water. Run had no water reserves and the islanders had traditionally survived by collecting the monsoon rains in 'jarres and cisternes' and using the water sparingly during the dry season. But Courthope's men brought an increased demand and water soon began to run low. A group of them offered to sail across to Neira or Great Banda to replenish supplies but Courthope considered such a move far too dangerous and ordered them to survive on reduced rations. But his authority over one group of rebellious spirits, never strong, was now weakened by dissension between the ships' companies. Many of the professional sailors were horrified at the prospect of spending many months on this remote island and, led by John Davis, the master of the *Swan*, they announced their intention of sailing to Ceram to fill the water casks. Unrelated to his more famous namesake, Davis was nevertheless a sailor of ripe experience who had taken part in no fewer than five voyages to and from the East Indies. But his abilities as a leader of men were not so obvious. His quarrelsome disposition upset many of his own crew while his deep attachment to the bottle frequently clouded his judgement.

Courthope, 'very sick,' pleaded with him to rethink but Davis had already tired of Run and refused to stay on land, 'obstinately contrarying my command'. He was about to set sail when a native pinnace arrived from Great Banda with some surprising news. The elders of one of the villages on that island, hearing of events on Run, had held a meeting at which it was decided to surrender themselves 'unto his Majestie'. The island of Rozengain, four miles farther to the east, had followed suit and also asked for English protection.

Since Davis was adamant about putting to sea, Courthope ordered him to call first at Great Banda and then at Rozengain in order to receive the islanders' formal submission. He also suggested that Sophony Cozucke and three other merchants should hoist the flag of St George on the latter island and establish a factory there. Davis carried out these instructions but was unable to persuade Cozucke to step ashore at Rozengain. As soon as the village elders had surrendered their islands to the English king, the men set sail for a watering hole on the coast of Ceram.

The casks were soon filled and Davis shaped his course for Run, but scarcely had he put to sea than the *Swan* found itself in difficulty. The wily Dutch commander, Cornelis Dedel, had been spying on the English from his ship the *Morgensterre* and now decided to attack. The *Swan* was of a similar size to the Dutch vessel and at one time a 'very warlike ship,' but its crew were sick and hungry and most its guns were ashore on Run. Sensing his vulnerability, Davis tried to outsail the *Morgensterre* but 'they did shoote at me twice before I began, although I was in the sea eight leagues off when they chased me.' Aided by the wind, Dedel managed to manoeuvre his ship alongside the *Swan*, enabling his men to hurl grappling irons onto the decks of the English vessel. The Dutch then boarded the ship and, swords drawn, began a bloody hand-to-hand battle. 'We fought almost boord and boord for the space of one houre and a halfe,' recalled Davis, 'untill they had killed five men, maymed three and hurt eight. And when we began we had not thirtie men able to doe anything, nor no wind to worke withall.' Those who hid inside the ship were flushed out with musket fire; those on deck were cut down with swords. One of the dead was the adventurous Sophony Cozuke, 'torne in pieces with a great shot,' while those who were 'maimed' were unlikely to live, 'having lost legs and arms, and almost all hope of life, if not dead already'.

After the *Swan* had been ransacked, her cabins smashed to pieces and all the trunks thrown into the sea, she was towed in triumph to Neira, the Hollanders 'much glorying in their victory, and showing the Bandanese their exploit, in the great disgrace of the English ... saying that the King of England might not compare with their great King of Holland, and that one Holland ship would take ten of the English ships, and that Saint George is now turned child'. It was three weeks before Courthope learned for certain of the *Swan's* capture – the news being brought to him by a local merchant who described how she was lying crippled and rifled under the guns of Neira Castle. One of Courthope's most trusted men, Robert Hayes, was despatched to Neira under a flag of truce to demand the restitution of both the ship and her crew. Not surprisingly the Dutch refused, boasting that it would only be a matter of weeks before they had captured the *Defence* as well. They also warned Courthope that unless he submitted without a fight, 'there will be much slaughter about it.'

The loss of the *Swan* was a terrible blow for the Englishmen left on Run for they were totally reliant on their ships, both for supplies and for escaping in an emergency. Although the *Defence* was still seaworthy, Courthope desperately needed her cannon to make his island fortress secure. Since disarming her would render the ship unserviceable, his only option was to draw her up onto the beach where she would be protected by the on-shore gun batteries. This would maroon him on Run, a precariously exposed position which left him unable to replenish his supplies.

He was soon struck by further misfortune: long before he had a chance to land the *Defence's* weaponry, the ship mysteriously drifted from her anchorage and floated out to sea. Courthope initially thought this had happened through carelessness but it soon became apparent that the cable had been deliberately cut by 'a plot of knaves' whose long months on Run had proved more than they could endure. The ship was sailed to Neira where her crew surrendered to the Dutch and proceeded to hand over detailed plans of all the defences on Run and Nailaka. They were, remarked one of Courthope's more loyal companions, 'a company of treacherous villains who have deserved hanging better than wages'.

It was shortly after this unfortunate event that the Dutch governor-general, Laurens Reael, arrived in the Banda Islands to take over the handling of the crisis. Informed of the hopelessness of Courthope's position, Reael decided to bring to an end the English stand on Run by negotiation rather than force, inviting Courthope to Neira for discussions. But although the Dutch governor-general held the upper hand, his position was an awkward one for he could scarcely ignore Courthope's treaty, nor could he claim any authority over Run. Instead, he took the line that the islanders had pledged to sell their spices to the Dutch after the 1609 murder of Verhoef – which was not true – and argued that this pledge still held.

Courthope agreed to meet with Reael as long as suitable hostages were sent to Run as a sign of good faith. These duly arrived bearing a letter from John Davis who languished in Neira prison. 'If I lose any more men by your arrogance,' he warned Courthope, 'as I have here lost by sicknesse already, their lives and blouds shall rest upon your heads ... and this I will write with dying hand.' Courthope ignored the note and rowed across to the Dutch castle on Neira to discuss the future of the Banda Islands. Reael was the first to lay his bargaining chips on the table, offering to return the captured ships and men, pay compensation for everything that had been rifled and assist the English in leaving Run with a full cargo of nutmeg. In return he demanded that England sign away forever her rights to the island. Courthope flatly refused to countenance such an offer, answering that 'I could not, unlesse I should turne traitor unto my King and Countrey, in giving up that right which I am able to hold; and also betray the countrey people, who had surrendered up their land to our King's Majestie.'

It was the sort of answer he might have expected from the Englishman, but Reael had naively assumed his offer would be accepted and, infuriated by such defiance, 'threw his hat on the ground and pulled his beard for anger'. Courthope now placed his chips on the table, informing Reael that he would leave Run immediately if the Dutchman would agree to the question of sovereignty being settled in Bantam or Europe. This time it was Reael's turn to refuse and the two men parted with the island's fate unresolved. It was clear that the issue could only be settled by war, and the Dutch governor-general curtly informed Courthope that within three days he 'would bring all his forces and take us perforce'.

These forces were not inconsiderable. In addition to his bases on Neira, Great Banda and Ai, Reael had more than a dozen ships at his disposal as well as a thousand soldiers. He had a total mastery of the sea, leaving Courthope with no option but to sit tight, knowing that Reael could stop any supply ships from reaching the island of Run.

Courthope had taken an enormous risk in declining Reael's offer but he remained confident that the Dutch would find it almost impossible to mount a frontal assault on Run, even with their overwhelmingly superior forces. The battery on Nailaka was virtually impregnable and Courthope had a brave and highly competent network of spies at his disposal – local men – who rowed backwards and forwards between Run and the other islands keeping him informed of every development.

In the spring of 1617 he took a gamble, despatching six men to Bantam in a hired vessel, a small native pinnace, in order to urgently request reinforcements and aid. The man in charge of this perilous journey was Thomas Spurway, one of Courthope's most trusty lieutenants who, after numerous mishaps, pitched up in Bantam to plead Courthope's case. To his dismay, he discovered that John Jourdain had left for England some months earlier and instead found himself dealing with George Ball who had visited Run the previous year and must have understood the precariousness of Courthope's position. But Ball's promotion had quite gone to his head and he spent much of his time tending to his extensive and lucrative private ventures. A man of inordinate pride and vanity he maintained a personal guard of fifty negro slaves and was preoccupied with continual quarrels with other factors, caring little for the Company's concerns. Indeed, for an entire year not a single ship was laden for England, even though there were six vessels in Bantam harbour and plenty of money in the coffers. Despite continued pleas from Spurway, Ball refused to send a ship to relieve Courthope.

Reael, too, had returned to Bantam, determined to bring to a satisfactory conclusion the tiresome business in the Banda Islands. He wrote to Ball ordering the immediate evacuation of Run and declaring that any ships found in the Banda Islands, or anywhere else in the Moluccas, would be sunk. 'If you refuse,' he fulminated, 'we shall have to help ourselves with all means time and opportunity will give us, believing ourselves to be guiltless before God and the world.' Ball scoffed at this threat and stood defiant, so infuriating Jan Coen that he posted a declaration of war on the gates of the Dutch compound, 'threatening to put them [the English] to the edge of the sword'. Hostilities between the English and Dutch now became so serious that even the local ruler became alarmed. When he asked to see a copy of the Dutch declaration of war, the English ran back to the Dutch compound 'and when they were unable to detach the paper, they tore down the gate and brought it to him (document and all)'.

Ball now decided it was time to act. In a letter to Reael he wrote: 'for your threats, I respect them not, having God and a just cause for my comfort, and you a foul and horrid and shameful matter ... Hitherto I have shed no blood willingly; and if blood must be shed, it shall not be my fault, it being lawful in defence of myself.'

That Ball had shed no blood was hotly disputed by the Dutch. Fifteen of their compatriots had recently been massacred in Macassar, an atrocity they ascribed to the machinations of the English factor. Worse still, a number of Spanish and Portuguese prisoners had escaped from a Dutch ship in Bantam harbour and the English had promptly given them asylum. This last event tipped the balance from hatred into warfare and every day there were skirmishes on the streets of Bantam as rival sailors attacked each other with knives and cutlasses. The East India Company archives are littered with accusations of Dutch brutality; a steward named

William Clarke, for example, claims to have been wandering through the marketplace when set upon by a gang of Dutch sailors, stripped naked, and whipped across his bare back. They 'cruelly cut his flesh, and then washed him with salt and vinegar, and laid him again in irons'.

The seas around Bantam had become equally dangerous. In November 1617, the English pinnace *Speedwell* was met by three Dutch vessels carrying a Dutch dignitary from Bantam to Jakarta. She was ordered to lower her flag and submit to a search by Dutch troops but before she had a chance to comply (according to the English report) she was 'shot through and through, and lastly entered and taken, having one man wounded and one killed'. Her crew were manacled and the vessel towed towards Bantam in triumph, 'and it was verily thought they [the English and Dutch] would have fought together in the Road, for the General of the Hollanders had brought thither fourteen great ships ready to fight, where the English had nine, which they fitted for defence; but they fought not, for the Governor of Bantam forbade them to fight in his Road, and threatened them that if they did fight, contrary to his command, he would cut the throats of all their men that he should find upon the land.'

The English, still fuming over the seizure of the *Swan* and the *Defence*, now had the *Speedwell* to add to their list of grievances. They sought all possible means to recover the ships, as Coen recounted in a gleeful letter to Amsterdam. 'It caused a great to-do,' he wrote. 'One day they threaten to sail to Banda in force and take revenge, and the next they say they will attack our ships at sea. They expect to get even by reprisals in the Channel at home and they are going to break our heads. Daily they come up with new threats which clearly shows that they are quite confused.'

All the time that these arguments were raging in Bantam, Courthope had been maintaining his dogged stand on Run. Although he and his men were plagued by a constant lack of supplies, the occasional junk broke through the Dutch blockade and landed rice and arak on the island, to everyone's great relief. Many were suffering from malnutrition and dysentery – a result of their bland diet and the putrid and infected water. But after more than fifteen months of hardship, 'the captain' learned from a passing trader that help was on its way. In the spring of 1618, three English ships were despatched to Run with orders to relieve Courthope and develop trade with the rest of the islands. The crew were bullish and ready to fight, believing their force sufficient to scatter any Dutch ships sent to intercept them.

As one of the ships, the *Solomon*, neared the Banda Islands a cheer went up from the little force of besieged Englishmen on Run. It was a moment of great excitement and they scrambled up Run's cliffs for a better view of the vessel. She was 'some five leagues from Polaroon [Run],' wrote Courthope in his journal, 'comming from the westwards with the very last of the westerly windes'. She was a large ship and was heavily laden with hundreds of tons of rice, fish and 'six hundred jarres of arack'. With the wind blowing a stiff westerly they confidently predicted that she would make the harbour in less than an hour.

Four Dutch vessels had been despatched from Neira to monitor the *Solomon*'s progress but these were unable to reach Run due to the wind, a cause of much mirth to Courthope's men. But their jeering was brought to an abrupt halt when the wind suddenly changed direction and the sails of the Dutch ships 'were taken with an easterly'. The Hollanders were now able to give chase and the

Englishmen watched in horror as the unequal forces prepared to do battle.

'The fight was in sight of Polaroon [Run],' recorded a nervous Courthope, 'some three leagues off.' Stuck on his island prison, he could only hope that the *Solomon* would score an early success and send the Dutch ships scurrying back to Neira. But almost from the beginning the English found themselves at a massive disadvantage for the *Solomon* was so deeply laden with supplies that she was unable to use her lower tier of ordnance, dramatically reducing her ability to fight. The crew put up a valiant resistance, answering 'shot for shot all that afternoone, but our powder was naught, and could not carrie the shot home'. The Dutch, meanwhile, 'plyed their great ordnance upon us, killing three men and hurt thirteene or fourteene others'.

For almost seven hours the ships did battle, peppering each other with shot until they were 'almost board and board' and the rival soldiers were engaged in hand-to-hand combat. The English captain, Cassarian David, soon found himself within shouting distance of the Dutch commander who ordered him to take in his colours, strike his sails, and come aboard to negotiate. Perceiving his situation to be hopeless the Englishman agreed, descending into the commander's cabin for discussions. When several hours had passed and Cassarian did not return the crew assumed that he had been taken prisoner.

It was during this lull in the fighting that a party of warlike Bandanese had rowed out to the *Solomon*. To them, surrender was both shameful and unthinkable and the English feared that if these fighters learned that their captain was negotiating a truce they would go on the rampage, killing everyone irrespective of nationality. Muttering vaguely about a cease-fire they disarmed the

Bandanese of their weapons, taking special care to relieve them of their deadly *kris* daggers. It was a wise precaution for when the Dutch finally came to take possession of the ship, eight Bandanese who had managed to conceal their daggers hurled themselves at the invaders. 'They played their parts excellently,' wrote one of the crew, 'for they drove the Flemings overboord, by fortie at once; some up into the foure shrouds, some one way, and some another, that they had scoured the deckes of them all. I thinke that if the Bandanese had had them upon plaine ground, they would have put the Flemmings to the sword, every man of them.' After wreaking havoc on the Dutch, the Bandanese were overpowered and all but seven were killed.

Courthope was exasperated as he watched these events from the cliffs of Run. In a letter to the directors in London he informed their worships that rather than yielding in the disgraceful way that the *Solomon*'s captain had done he 'would have sunke downe right in the sea first'. It was a characteristically defiant attitude and doubtless Courthope meant every word. He was bitterly disappointed by his continued misfortune and speaks of 'the hard fortune fallen to our ships bound thither this year.' He placed much of the blame on the authorities in Bantam who sent the ships so close to the monsoon that they invariably did not even get within sight of Run.

> I much marvel you sent this year with so weak forces, you seeing they use all the means possible they can to bar us of all trade in these parts ... Therefore, if you mean the Company to have any trade with these islands, or the Moluccas, it must not be deferred any longer, but to send such forces the next westerly monsoon to maintain that we have, or

Run seen from neighbouring Nailaka. Nathaniel Courthope built a bastion on this low-lying atoll which was to prove critical to Run's defence. When ordered by the Dutch commander to surrender his stronghold, he vowed to fight to the last man. 'And if they win it,' he wrote, 'by God's help I make no doubt but they shall pay full dearly for it with effusion of much blood.'

else all is gone, and not to be expected hereafter any more trade this way.

This year I have withheld it from them with much difficulty, without any relief or aid ... not so much as one letter from you to advise me what course you intend to take in this business, I having but 38 men to withstand their force and tyranny, which is a very weak strength to withstand their unruly odds of forces. Our wants are extreme; neither have we any victuals or drink, but only rice and water, which had not God sent in four or five junks to have relieved us with rice I must have been fain to have given up our

King's and Company's right for want of relief, which relief is weak. Therefore I pray you consider well of these affairs, and suffer us not to be forced to yield ourselves into such tyrants hands ... I am determined to hold it out until the next westerly monsoon, in despite of them, or else we are determined all to die in defence of it. At present they have eight ships here, and two gallies, and to my knowledge all fitted and ready to come against us; so I look daily and hourly, and if they win it, by God's help I make no doubt but they shall pay full dearly for it with effusion of much blood.

Courthope's position had never been weaker. His small force had been decimated by sickness and his supplies were almost non-existent. With just a couple of sacks of rice left in their storehouse, his beleaguered garrison was now forced to subsist on the revolting sago porridge, supplementing their diet with the occasional fish caught in the waters surrounding Nailaka. 'Had not foure of five Java[nese] junkes come in,' he wrote in his diary, 'for want of victuals we must have given up; and still [we] live on rice only, with a little fish, which in foule weather is not to be found.' Worse still, they were 'daily expecting an assault from the Hollanders' and had to keep a constant watch from the battlements. Such threatened attacks rarely materialised, but the fear of assault wearied the men who were already suffering the effects of prolonged hardship and starvation. Yet Courthope continued to exert a powerful influence over both his own men and the local islanders and when the Dutch attempted a landing on Run some weeks after the *Solomon's* capture, the invading force was crushed by a group of Bandanese warriors.

Courthope managed to stay in close contact with the English prisoners; both those from the *Swan* and the *Defence*, and also the survivors from the *Solomon*. Under the cover of darkness, his Bandanese troops repeatedly put to sea and smuggled letters to and from the English held on Ai Island and Neira. One of the first replies he received was from Cassarian David whose decision to surrender the *Solomon* had earned him good treatment at the hands of the Dutch. Ignorant of Courthope's anger about the manner in which he submitted, he wrote to the English commander gleefully explaining that 'my selfe with one English boy to attend me remayne on Pooloway, where the Generall and his Councill doe abide, at whose hands I doe daily find much favour and kind usage.'

The same could not be said of the other English prisoners. Most had been incarcerated in Fort Revenge on Ai Island from whose dungeons there was no hope of escape. Chained together by the neck and with nowhere to relieve themselves, conditions soon became intolerable. The Dutch made life even less bearable by their routine humiliation of their captives. 'They pissed and **** upon our heads,' wrote Bartholomew Churchman, 'and in this manner we lay, untill such time as we were broken out from top to toe like lepers, having nothing to eat but durtie rice, and stinking rainewater.' That they were still alive at all, he writes, is thanks to a Dutch woman 'named Mistris Cane, and some poore blackes, that brought us a little fruit'.

Others had similar complaints. 'We were very hardly and inhumanely used,' wrote one, 'being fettered and shackelled in the day time, and close locked up at nights.' 'They keep many of us fast bound and fettered in irons,' recorded another, 'in most loathsome and darke stinking dungeons,

and give us no sustenance, but a little durtie rice to eat ...
many have dyed, who were fetcht out of the dungeons and
so basely buried, more like dogges than Christians.' Those
that dared to complain were given an even harsher regime.
Churchman found himself 'clapt in irons and [placed] in
the raine and the cold stormes of the night, and in the day
time where the hot sunne shone upon him, and scorched
him, without any shelter at all'. All this was because he
berated a Dutchman for insulting King James I's wife.
Others would be set in the sun until they were blistered
with sunburn, then chained below the sewers 'where their
ordures and pisse fell upon them in the night'.

Courthope was even more horrified to learn that the
English prisoners were being used as pawns in a nasty
game of propaganda played out by the Dutch governor-
general. 'Lawrence Reael ... caused grates and cages to be
made in their ship, and did put us therein, and carryed us
in them bound in irons from port to port amongst the
Indians, and thus in scornfull and deriding manner and
sort spake unto the Indians as followeth: "Behold and see,
heere is the people of that Nation, whose King you care
so much for." '

After many months of such treatment the English
prisoners could endure no more and wrote to the Dutch
governor-general pleading for mercy. But to their dismay
they found that Reael had been replaced by an even less
compromising individual, a man they knew as John Peter
Sacone but whose real name was Jan Pieterzoon Coen.
They begged him to 'consider of our extreame wants
and miseries, and help us to some better sustenance'.
Unfortunately they could not have picked a worse man to
ask for clemency for Coen 'most wickedly replied with
base speeches, and bade us be gone, and trouble him no

more; for if we did, he would cause us all to be hanged speedily'. Courthope wrote frequent letters to the prisoners urging them to bear their trials with fortitude: 'For make no question but this year to be all set free ... [and] what extremity the Dutch useth unto you,' he told them, 'they shall have their measure full and abounding either in gentleness or rigour; and whereas they have heretofore protested fire and sword, fire and sword they shall have repaid unto their bosoms.' The English prisoners never forgot their grievances, reserving particular hatred for Coen, and long after the Run saga had drawn to a conclusion the survivors continued to complain of their hardships and demand compensation from the Dutch government.

Courthope's had ceased to count the passing weeks and months. Each new day brought boredom and fear, punctuated by lengthy watch duties from the battlements and an endless battle against hunger. The little pinnace that Courthope had managed to acquire from a passing junk proved to be of little use. After a single journey to the island of Ceram, from which she returned laden with yet more sago, she was 'so full of leakes ... that we haled her on shoare and found her so rotten that we saved what we could and set fire on the rest'. When the rains failed to materialise in the autumn of 1618, the island's water reserves became precariously low and were soon so teeming with tropical parasites and worms that the men had to drink through clenched teeth to sieve out the fauna. At one point a group of them could stand their hardships no longer and threatened Courthope with mutiny. For a while the situation looked desperate but Courthope's 'mild carriage and earnest protestations' won them back and the men eventually repented.

It was not until January 1619, more than two years after they had arrived on Run, that the English had an inkling of good news. A local junk which managed to sail undetected into the harbour brought a letter arrived from Bantam, a letter written by Sir Thomas Dale who had sailed from England with a huge armada. 'Master Courthope,' began Sir Thomas's letter, 'as unknown I remember my love, which I will always be ready to express in respect of your worthy service for the honour of our country and the benefit of our honourable employers.' His mission was to expel the Dutch from Java and when that had been accomplished he intended to race eastwards to relieve Courthope's brave band of men. Attached to his letter was a note from John Jourdain who had returned to the Indies with Dale's fleet to take up his new position as 'President of the English' living in the East. Jourdain promised that as soon as the Dutch had been defeated, 'we determine to proceed for Banda ... hoping in God that we shall be able to lay some part of their insolent pride.'

Courthope was most pleased to learn that the English fleet was under the command of Sir Thomas Dale. Dale was a man of great experience, a 'heroike lion', who had excelled in a number of different capacities. Previous to his employment with the East India Company he had been selected by the Virginia Company in London to serve as governor of their fledgling colony in America, 'the hardest task he ever undertook,' but one he carried out with such aplomb that he left the colony 'in great prosperity and peace'. When he arrived back in England in 1616, he did so in style, bringing with him the celebrated Indian princess Pocahontas. Soon after his return, Dale was called to a meeting with the East India Company and was offered the job of chief commander of a critical expedition to the

East. He accepted and was given the command of five ships and an annual salary of £480.

The outward journey was not without its incidents. At the Cape both Dale and Jourdain almost drowned when a little skiff capsized, whilst a few weeks later the aged and corpulent Captain Parker, vice admiral of the fleet, dropped dead. Far more serious was an accident at Java when Dale's magnificent flagship, the *Sun*, was wrecked on the island of Engano. The heavy loss of life troubled Dale less than the fact that he had lost his possessions and he bemoaned in a letter to London that 'the *Sun* was cast away, wherein I lost all that I had in that ship to my shirt.' He later returned to the site of the wreck to see if he could recover his goods but was disappointed to find nothing of value. Although a number of his crew had managed to swim ashore, not a single one was left alive and the only trace of their existence was a pile of eighteen skulls lying on the beach. As revenge for this apparent act of cannibalism Dale shot two natives, burned their houses and cut down all their trees. Such a response was typical of this pugnacious commander who was ruthless in his revenge. Punctilious in official matters and slow to give praise, he was feared rather than loved by his men. 'It was always "I will and require" ', wrote one of his juniors, ' "this must be done," and "this shall be done," and yet in the end we must signe what he says.' All too often he allowed his temper to overrule his judgement, a fault which would prove dangerous when pitched against the calm detachment of Jan Coen.

The loss of the *Sun* sharpened Dale's resolve and he determined to revenge himself on the Dutch. As he sailed towards the Javanese coast he spied a richly laden Dutch ship called the *Black Lion* sailing through the straits. He promptly set upon her and the ship was soon captured.

Continuing towards Bantam he was delighted to see a large number of other English vessels at anchor, bringing his total fleet to no less than fifteen ships – 'the bay was not large enough to harbour them all.'

The Dutch were now seriously alarmed and Coen immediately sent a letter of protest to Dale demanding the release of the *Black Lion*. When Dale was handed this letter he 'only scolded, stamped on the ground, swore, cursed [and asked] why the letter was written in Dutch and not in French, Spanish or any other language'. He finally sent the messenger on his way, 'swearing and cursing that he would take all he could get.'

Dale was driven by revenge, as he admitted in his letter to Courthope: 'My stay [in Bantam] is to revenge the abuses received from them [the Dutch], having now an opportunity by a difference between them and the King of Jakarta.' Jakarta, a small port that lay fifty miles to the east of Bantam, had become increasingly important to the Dutch: Coen found life in Bantam intolerable and petitioned the King of Jakarta for permission to build a fort in his town, intending to make it the future centre of Dutch activities. A few weeks later he learned that the English were also in the process of erecting a fortified factory, presumably to stop the Dutch from gaining the upper hand. In the ensuing game of cat and mouse the Dutch retaliated for the capture of the *Black Lion* by burning this factory to the ground.

Dale toyed with the idea of destroying the Dutch factory in Bantam but was soon struck by an altogether more destructive plan. With a large fleet at his disposal and the Hollanders in the middle of moving to Jakarta, he made a pact with the native ruler and vowed to wipe them out altogether. Coen panicked: 'I am sitting here in a cage,' he wrote, 'surrounded by various bulwarks and batteries, the river closed with piles, and a very strong battery at the place of the English.' Realising that an attack was imminent and defeat a certainty, he convened an emergency council and, after much deliberation, it was decided to withdraw most of the men to the ships and contest the issue at sea.

On the morning of 30 December 1618, the English fleet gathered within sight of Jakarta. Dale had eleven ships at his disposal, with four more left to protect Bantam, while Coen had just seven ships, many of them in a deplorable state. He was outnumbered and outgunned and had a total fighting force of just seventy men. Yet Dale seemed in no hurry to press the attack and spent the day sailing to and fro, hoping that the sight of his vastly superior fleet would weaken the Dutch resolve. In the afternoon he sent a messenger to Coen demanding that his entire fleet surrender. Coen refused, only to be informed that the English admiral intended to sink each and every ship. When Coen shrugged off this threat a battle became a certainty and the two sides spent that night, New Year's Eve, in a state of nervous excitement. Yet it was not until 2 January, after another day's stand-off, that the battle finally began. The two fleets fought all day, 'a cruel bloody fight,' according to Sir Thomas, 'with 3,000 great shot between both the fleets, many men maimed and slain on both sides, but they had (as we are given to understand) four times as many men slain and maimed as we'. The English should have trounced the Dutch; as it was, they appeared hesitant and defensive, the unfortunate consequence of Dale's armada consisting of three separate ventures, each with its own commander who refused to risk his own ships for the common good. As night closed the battle still hung in the balance.

Coen called a council of war to decide what to do. The

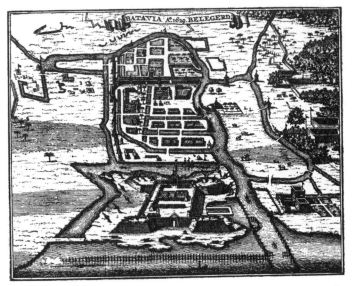

Jan Coen built his new capital at Batavia in Java (now Jacarta). After 'a cruel bloody fight,' the English came close to capturing the city in 1619, but snatched defeat from the jaws of victory.

Dutch were now in a perilous position for their ammunition had run low, they had numerous wounded and their vessels were scarcely seaworthy. Some argued in favour of retreat, others wanted to continue the fight, but 'all glumly looked at each other, not being able to come up with the answer.'

It was the English who made up their minds. As dawn broke, Dale's fleet was joined by another three ships (those from Bantam) and he prepared to renew the battle. Coen immediately ordered his men to hoist the sails and head for the Banda Islands. The indomitable Dutch were in retreat.

It was now that Dale made his greatest mistake. He should have chased after Coen with his overwhelmingly superior force and pressed the battle to its inevitable conclusion. Instead, he chose to remain where he was, arguing that Coen's flight would enable him to capture their Dutch headquarters. Yet a letter to London reveals that he was doubtful about his strategy and wondered if he had made the wrong decision: 'Their fleet [sailed] away eastward for Banda,' he wrote, '... and so by this means we lost them which troubled me very much.'

Coen also wrote home, castigating the Seventeen for their lack of support and for not listening to his warnings. 'And now see what has happened,' he said, informing them that the Company is faced with 'a thousand perils ... even if the Almighty wills us his best'. He ended the letter with a stark warning: 'If your Lordships have no intention to send me yearly large numbers of ships, people, and other necessities, I pray once more that you release me at the soonest, because without such means I cannot execute your wishes.'

In the event, the Dutch were saved by Dale's hesitancy. Had he defeated Coen at sea he would have been able to return to Jakarta, seize their headquarters, then sail to the Banda Islands and relieve Courthope and his men. Instead, he allowed the Dutch fleet to escape intact and even bungled the storming of their fort, snatching defeat from the jaws of victory. Dale now lost heart completely. Rankled by the feeling that he failed where he should have been victorious, he ordered his fleet to sail for India's Coromandel Coast. The voyage was a tiresome one for his officers were close to mutiny and more than eighty of his crew died at sea. Soon after arriving at Masulipatam, Dale became grievously ill and, for the next twenty days, he fought his illness, talking contemptuously of death and testifying to his good Christianity. On 19 July 1619, he 'departed this life in peace' and his body was 'enclosed and housed in form of a tomb, which is almost finished'.

Coen was overjoyed when he heard of Dale's death but was soon to learn of even better news. His old adversary, John Jourdain, had taken charge of two ships and, concerned about his friend Nathaniel Courthope, set sail for the East. But no sooner had he reached a sheltered harbour on the Malay Peninsula than he realised he was being tailed by three Dutch vessels. These blocked the harbour's entrance and attacked the English while they were at anchor. Jourdain fought fiercely but when almost fifty men had been killed he raised the flag of truce and prepared to negotiate. 'He showed himself aboard the Sampson before the main mast ... where the Flemings espying him, most treacherously shot at him with a musket, and shot him into the body near the heart, of which wound he died within half an hour after.' His death caused a scandal, particularly when everyone questioned confirmed that he was in the midst of negotiating a surrender. 'Our noble minded President was slain in parley with Henrie Johnson [the Dutch commander],' wrote one crew member. 'The President had sounded a parley and in talking with Hendrike Johnson received his death wound with a musket,' recorded another. Others claimed that Coen himself had ordered Jourdain's death. 'General John Peter Sacone [Coen] gave Hendrike Jansen a gold chain worth 1,400 guilders, putting it himself about his neck. He also gave 100 reals to the man who actually shot the President.'

The directors of the Dutch East India Company were embarrassed by the incident and took the unusual step of issuing an official statement of what had happened:

Your President and our Commander came above the

hatches and began to confer (while the two ships were alongside). Our other ships could not be advertised of the aforesaid parley by reason of shortness of time. The Morning Star coming up fired in ignorance of what before had passed between the chiefs of both fleets. A musket shot hit your President in the belly, without any special aim, but the mishap might as well have befallen our own Commander because a cannon ball (from the Morning Star) went through his own ship.

Whether true or not, Coen's position was considerably strengthened by the deaths of Dale and Jourdain. He now had just one thorn in his side, Nathaniel Courthope, who was as resolute as ever about the defence of his island fortress.

The dreadful news about Sir Thomas Dale's fleet took time to reach Run. On 13 February 1619, more than a month after the sea battle, Courthope spied three Dutch ships heading for Neira, 'one whereof had her beak-head shot off, and shot through in forty places'. His spies informed him that Coen was at Amboyna, busily assembling a huge fleet with which to launch a massive attack against Jakarta. Soon after, Courthope learned to his dismay that the bulk of Dale's fleet had sailed for India. 'This was cold comfort to me,' he wrote in his journal, 'which had neither direction nor stocks.' The news soon got worse. Courthope was informed of Jourdain's death in a letter from his old friend George Muschamp, himself on the verge of death. 'I [am] in miserable torture with the losse of my right legge (shot off with a canon) for want of medicines to apply to it … I doe not much value my life, and have every day lesse comfort and courage to remain in these parts.' His letter ends with the news that Courthope's defiance has spread far and wide: 'and I make no question [that] our honourable Masters will truly value your deserts'. Indeed they did: with glowing reports of Courthope's defiance filtering back to London the directors voted that he be awarded a gift of £100 a year for services to King and Company.

When Courthope learned that he and his men had been abandoned to their fate his most sensible course would have been to surrender to the Dutch. His heroic stand had been way beyond the call of duty and he could have retired with honour intact. But to submit now, after more than three years of hardship, was not in Courthope's nature. He was to choose a far more glorious path, vowing to fight to the bitter end in defence of his island stronghold. He no longer had any money and was reduced to bartering his men's remaining possessions for essential supplies, but there was never enough food for everyone and the sick began to die, often from dysentery contracted from the foul water. 'We have rubbed off the skinne alreadie,' he writes, referring to their destitution, 'and if we rub any longer, shall rub to the bone.' Each day Courthope would rally his malnourished men, urging them to stand resolute in the face of Dutch brutality. And each day his men would vow to stand by 'the captain', greeting his words with noisy acclaim. They manned their defences, primed their cannon, and awaited the imminent Dutch onslaught.

On 18 October 1620, Courthope was heartened by some good news. The men of Great Banda had risen up against the Dutch and plunged the island into turmoil. It was rumoured that they now wished to join Courthope's men in a full-scale attack on the hated Hollanders. For Courthope, this news came not a moment too soon and he immediately decided to visit Great Banda and instil in the natives the same sense of resolution that he had brought to his band of Englishmen. But these men, reliant for so long on their captain, were most unhappy about him sailing to Great Banda — even under the cover of darkness — and petitioned him to think again. 'I prayed him to stay,' wrote Robert Hayes, his number two, 'but hee refused.'

'Thus went he over that night with his Boy William, wel fitted with muskets and weapons; promising to returne in five dayes.' But unbeknown to anyone there had been a traitor lurking on Run. A lone Hollander, who had passed himself off as a deserter, had sent message of Courthope's movements to the Dutch governor-general in Neira. The governor-general could scarcely believe his good fortune and acted immediately, equipping a heavily armed pinnace and despatching it to sea with one simple order: kill the troublesome Englishman. Nothing was left to chance; the assassins planned precisely where they would attack Courthope, in a treacherous channel of water where the current and tides would leave him no manoeuvrability.

The Dutch soldiers put to sea as night fell and lay in wait some two miles off Ai's coastline. For hours they saw nothing but the dim outline of the island, but at 'about two or three a clocke in the morning' a lantern came into view — Courthope's boat. In the pitch darkness they waited until he was almost upon them, trapped and surrounded, before suddenly opening fire with their muskets. In a flash Courthope was firing back, his weapon ready loaded in preparation for just such an attack. But right from the outset it was an uneven battle. Although Courthope momentarily silenced the Dutch guns, he noticed a second boat approaching, armed with 'some fortie small shot'. Undeterred, he returned shot for shot until his 'piece being choked', he could fire no more. Hurling his gun into the water, he was now a sitting duck – an unarmed and defenceless target for more than fifty Dutch soldiers. His final end was not long in coming. 'Receiving a shot on the brest [he] sate downe … then leapt over-board in his clothes.' It was the last time he was seen alive.

News that Courthope had been 'slain by Hollanders' filtered slowly across the Banda Islands and it was not until 27 October 1620, more than a week after his death, that the Englishmen on Run learned of the treachery that had killed their captain. They were devastated by what they were told. For four years they had been led by the inspired Courthope and had suffered the greatest of hardships in withstanding a force hundreds of times stronger than their own. Now, 'the captain' was dead and their future as bleak as it was uncertain. After allowing the men to recover from the initial shock, Courthope's second-in-command, Robert Hayes, summoned a council and asked them if they would accept him as their leader. There was not a moment's hesitation. With a tremendous cry, 'they all promised that as they had been ruled by the captaine, so now they would be ruled by Robert Hayes.'

It was a brave show but with Courthope's death the men had lost their defiance and their heroic stand on Run was nearing its tragic end. With the loss of more men to sickness, the long nightly watches broke the spirit of these half-starved survivors, particularly as there was no longer 'the captain' to rouse them. Their last day came soon enough. The Dutch governor-general sent twenty-five ships and a huge army to Run with the intention of leading a massive frontal assault on the island, 'whereupon the blacks came to Mr Hayes and asked him whether he would defend them, and told him if he would then they would fight it out to the last man. But Mr Hayes answered that he was not able, nor could not.'

So the Dutch 'landed unopposed' and harangued the 'poor miserable people of the island'. Knowing that the tiny band of Englishmen were finished, the Dutch reserved all their anger for the natives. 'They forced the country people to dismount the ordnance from the two English forts on the great island, and threw them down on the rocks; four were broken, the rest remained on the sands altogether unservicable.' Next they ordered the natives to demolish the island's defences 'with their own hands ... so that before night there was not one stone left upon another; and ranging the whole island, caused all the walls, little and great, to be made even with the ground, not so much as sparing the monuments of the dead'. Once this was complete they took all the chieftains prisoner, publicly humiliating them by compelling each and every one to submit to the Dutch 'by presenting them with a nutmeg tree in a basin, as is the custom of these parts'. Their last act before sailing away was to rip down the flag of St George that was still flying in the village. It was replaced by the Dutch colours, signifying the end of a siege that had lasted 1,540 days.

The English were no less humiliated. Forced to watch their island fortress being dismantled, they were then summoned to the Dutch commander who contemptuously informed them that they could keep Nailaka, the sandy atoll adjoining Run. With no nutmeg trees it was useless to the Dutch; with cannon trained upon it from Run, it was equally useless to the English. Hayes and his men stayed on the island only long enough to catch a passing boat and escape to Amboyna.

'Thus was Pooloroon lost,' wrote Captain Sir Humphrey

Fitzherbert, the newly arrived captain of an English fleet, 'which in Mr Courthope's time by his good resolution with a few men maintained itself to their [the Dutch] disgrace, and now by the fearfulness of Mr Hayes and his irresolution is fearfully lost'. Such words are unfair on Hayes and do not sit easily with Captain Fitzherbert's own actions. When he arrived in the area in charge of a heavily armed vessel, the only shots he fired were a brief salvo nervously to celebrate the Dutch victory.

Courthope's defiance would ultimately pay handsome dividends, but his cruel death passed quietly into English history and we look in vain for any tomb or epitaph commemorating this very English hero. Even his final resting place remains a mystery: 'And what became of him I know not,' wrote Hayes at the time, 'but the blacks said surely he there sunke, by reason of his wounds and his clothes all about him.'

Yet he later received information, brought by a Dutchman, that suggested the English captain had been buried with full honours and given a tomb befitting to his heroism. 'The Captaine Nathaniel is killed in the prow,' said this Dutchman, 'for which God knoweth I was heartily sorie. We have buried him so stately and honestly as ever we could fitting for such a man.'

CHAPTER ELEVEN

TRIAL BY
FIRE AND WATER

NATHANIEL COURTHOPE'S MURDER left Coen in a seemingly invincible position. For almost four years this stubborn Englishman had been a thorn in his side, thwarting his ambitions of total dominance in the Spice Islands. Now he was dead, leaving the Dutchman with unchallenged control of the Banda Islands.

During the long years of siege, Coen had concentrated his efforts in other parts of the East Indies. He had wasted no time in regrouping his forces after his flight from Sir Thomas Dale. Heading for Amboyna, he had trained his men for battle, then led them back to Jakarta where he vowed to flatten every building in the town. He attacked within two days of arriving, leading his thousand-strong force from the front. Although the local population outnumbered the Dutch by more than three to one, they soon lost heart and their defences crumbled. True to his word, Coen had the towers and fortifications destroyed and the rest of the town burned to the ground. By the end of the day Jakarta had ceased to exist. When it rose again from the ashes it was built to Coen's specifications as befitted the 'capital' of the Dutch East Indies. It was given the new name Batavia in honour of the first tribes who had settled in the Netherlands.

*Jan Pieterszoon Coen, circa 1626, when Governor-General of the
Dutch East Indies. Ruthless in crushing opposition, he sold most of
the Bandanese population into slavery. 'They are indolent people,' he
wrote, 'of whom little good can be expected.*

Coen immediately informed Amsterdam of his triumph: 'It is certain that this victory and the fleeing of the English will create quite a furore throughout the Indies,' he wrote. 'This will enhance the honour and the reputation of the Dutch nation. Now everyone will want to be our friend.'

Within a week of his arrival in Java, Coen had reversed the balance of power. His next plan was nothing less than the total annihilation of the English fleet whose ships were scattered over a wide area of ocean. But scarcely had he given the order to sink every vessel east of Arabia than a messenger arrived at Batavia bearing wholly unexpected news. To Coen's astonishment he was informed that in July 1619, the Dutch East India Company, together with its English counterpart, had signed an agreement whereby all fighting between the two companies must cease at once. The document, known as the Treaty of Defence, was the fruit of the third Anglo-Dutch conference which had been summoned to discuss the deteriorating situation in the East. After much argument the two sides decided that all grievances should be 'forgiven and forgotten'. Captured ships were to be returned, prisoners released and employers, 'both high and low, should henceforth live and converse as trusted friends'. The most important clause of the treaty stated that the English were to be granted one third of all trade in the Spice Islands. In return, the English agreed to take active steps to defend the region from the Spanish and Portuguese.

Coen was stunned when he read the terms of the treaty. 'The English owe you a debt of gratitude,' he wrote to his employers, 'because after they have worked themselves out of the Indies, your Lordships put them right back again ... it is incomprehensible that the English should be allowed one third of the cloves, nutmegs and mace [since] they cannot lay claim to a single grain of sand in the Moluccas,

Amboyna, or Banda.' With the stroke of a pen all his hard work had come undone.

Had the Dutch directors known the true picture in the East Indies it is doubtful that they would have signed the treaty. But with their signatures duly attached Coen was left with just two options: to abide by its terms or to wreck it. Given his hatred of the English it is scarcely surprising that he chose the latter option, playing his hand with characteristic skill.

The treaty had called for the establishment of a joint Fleet of Defence in which the English would supply one third of the men, money and ships and the Dutch would supply the rest. This fleet was to complete the expulsion of the Spanish and Portuguese from the East Indies, destroying their remaining bases in the Malay Peninsula, China, and the Philippines, and to act as a naval patrol force to guard the monopoly on spices. Coen was well aware that the English had few ships at their disposal and with this in mind proposed long and time-consuming expeditions across huge expanses of ocean. Within months the English were struggling to meet their side of the deal.

Coen now saw his chance. He had always vowed to crush the Banda Islands but had hesitated in recent months because any military expedition would have to include English ships. Knowing that these were all currently at sea, Coen now proposed a massive expedition and when the English argued that they lacked resources he accused them of reneging on the deal and haughtily informed them that he would proceed without them.

His fleet arrived at Neira Island in the spring of 1621, anchoring under the guns of Fort Nassau. Here he gathered his forces, assembling a fleet of 13 large ships, 36 barges and 3 messenger boats, as well as an army of 1,600 men and 80

Japanese mercenaries, most of them experts in the art of execution. It was the largest force ever seen in the Bandas and it was augmented by a band of freed slaves, Dutch townspeople and the 250-strong garrison of Fort Nassau.

Despite the humiliating capitulation of Run, a handful of English were still living on the Banda Islands. Great Banda was home to an English merchant, two helpers and eight Chinese guards, while a couple of men continued to stage a token resistance to the Dutch on the tiny atoll of Nailaka. To these hardy survivors Coen now sent a message inviting them to take part in the forthcoming invasion of Great Banda. All declined his offer – a response that came as no surprise to Coen who had been informed that there were many other English secretly training Bandanese soldiers.

The forthcoming invasion placed the English merchant, Robert Randall, in something of a quandary. Many of the village elders stood by their former submission to the English king and, claiming that Great Banda was technically English soil, reminded Randall that any attack on the island would effectively be an attack on His Majesty. Desperate to delay the invasion, Randall wrote a strongly worded letter to Coen advising him 'not to attempt any violence'. Needless to say Coen was most displeased to receive such a letter and 'threw [it] from him in a great rage, scarce vouchsafing to reade it over, and caused the messenger to be thrust out of doores'. As the poor man picked himself up from the dirt, Coen warned him to escape while he could, 'for whomsoever he should find [on Great Banda] he would take them as his utter enemies, and they should fare no better than the inhabitants'.

Prior to his attack Coen sent his yacht, the *Hert*, to circle its coastline. The boat came under sustained and extremely accurate musket fire which cost the lives of two crew members and injured ten others. The *Hert's* commander reported that he had identified no less than a dozen forts close to the shore. Furthermore, all the island's ridges were heavily fortified, and he had sighted numerous English gunners.

Great Banda had long been a magnet for thousands of disaffected Bandanese who had taken refuge in its wild and inaccessible mountain range. It was, according to one English visitor, 'the greatest and richest iland of all the iles of Banda; strong and almost inaccessible, as it were a castle'. The village of Lonthor on the island's northern coastline was an almost impregnable stronghold 'situate on the brow of a sharpe hill, the ascent as difficult as by a ladder'. It had three lines of fortifications and each of these was lined with cannons and muskets which could be trained on passing ships with devastating effect. Coen's men knew the risks of attacking the island and lost heart before the fight had even begun. To rally his troops the Dutch governor-general made an impassioned speech about glory and destiny, urging his men to fight with honour and courage. Then, hoping to confuse the enemy, he landed them at a number of different points on Great Banda. The Dutch fought with considerable daring, scaling the sea cliffs and crawling along ledges and promontories in order to capture key positions. It was an uneven struggle and the invaders were repulsed on numerous occasions because 'one man above was worth twenty below', but by the end of the first day they had most of the lowlands under their control. In this they were helped by the treachery of the Bandanese. At the strategic position of Lakoy, a native guided the attackers through a hidden rear entrance in return for two hundred and fifty pieces-of-eight, while at Orantatta small purses of gold were awarded to any Bandanese who would betray his fellow fighters. With the use of bribes, treachery and daring Great Banda was eventually brought under control and the great defences of Lonthor fell into Dutch hands after a tough struggle on the evening of the second day. The Dutch lost just six men in the attack with a further twenty-seven injured.

The leading orang-kayas now visited Coen aboard his vessel, bringing with them gifts of gold and copper and offering to sue for peace. Coen's terms were harsh; they were to destroy all fortifications, hand in all weapons, vow never again to resist the Dutch, and present their sons as hostages. They were also ordered to sell exclusively to the Dutch East India Company and recognise Dutch sovereignty. This last clause was significant for any future uprising would not be considered as an act of war but an act of treason, and treason in Holland was punishable by death. The chieftains duly signed the agreement – they had little alternative – but Coen was in no doubt that they would renege on it. When they did he vowed to crush them completely.

Robert Randall had wisely kept a low profile throughout the invasion. He and his colleagues had locked themselves into the English warehouse and 'kept themselves within doores' until the island had fallen. His neutrality did little to endear him to the Dutch soldiers who 'sacked our house, tooke away all our goods, murthered three of our Chinese servants, bound the rest (as well English as Chinezes) hand and foote, and threatned them to cut their throats'. The Japanese mercenaries took particular delight in tormenting their prisoners: having decapitated the Chinese, they rolled the severed heads around the feet of the English captives, laughing at the panic they were causing. Then, 'with their weapons readie drawne out, [they] did put a halter on our principall factor's necke, drawing up his head, and stretching out his necke, readie to put him to death'. But they stopped short of executing Randall. Instead, 'as they were bound hand and foot (as foresaid) [they] tumbled them downe over the rocks like dogges, and like to have broken their neckes, and thus bound, carried them aboord their shippes, and kept them prisoners in irons.' Randall was convinced that the Dutch had ordered his execution but that the Japanese had failed to understand the command.

Coen was correct in his belief that the Bandanese had no intention of honouring his treaty. The weapons they handed in were rusty and quite useless whilst the fortifications they demolished were soon replaced by new battlements. Worse still, most of the native population had fled into Great Banda's mountainous hinterland where they staged irregular attacks on stray Dutch troops. On one occasion they ambushed a large group of soldiers, killing nine and leaving twenty-five others with serious injuries.

Coen still had forty-five orang-kayas aboard his ship and these were now interrogated. After a judicious application of burning irons they confessed that the Bandanese never had any intention of abiding by the terms of the surrender and that they planned to launch a counter-offensive against the Dutch within a few weeks. On hearing this the Dutch council condemned the hostages to death – an execution that left at least one Dutch eyewitness horrified and disgusted:

> The forty-four prisoners [one had committed suicide] were brought within the castle, the eight foremost orang-kaya – those, who it was said had 'belled the cat' – being kept apart, the others being herded together like sheep. A round enclosure was built of bamboo just outside the castle, and into it were brought the prisoners, well bound with cords

and surrounded by guards. Their sentence was read out to them for having conspired against the life of the Heer Generael and having broken the terms of the peace. Before the reading of the sentence it was forbidden on pain of death for anyone else to enter the enclosure except only fathers and mothers.

The condemned victims being brought within the enclosure, six Japanese soliders were also ordered inside, and with their sharp swords they beheaded and quartered the eight chief orang-kaya and then beheaded and quartered the thirty-six others. This execution was awful to see. The orang-kaya died silently without uttering any sound except that one of them, speaking in the Dutch tongue, said, 'Sirs, have you then no mercy' but indeed nothing availed.

All that happened was so dreadful as to leave us stunned. The heads and quarters of those who had been executed were impaled upon bamboos and so displayed. Thus did it happen: God knows who is right.

All of us, as professing Christians, were filled with dismay at the way this affair was brought to a conclusion, and we took no pleasure in such dealings.

Coen's conscience was untroubled by the deaths of so many Bandanese: 'They are indolent people,' he wrote, 'of whom little good can be expected.' But the directors in Amsterdam found his brutality distasteful and wrote: 'We had wished that it could have been accomplished by more moderate means.' Coen could rightly feel indignant at such criticism since it was the directors themselves who had originally recommended that 'the Bandanese should be overpowered, the chiefs exterminated and chased away, and the land repopulated.'

Repopulation had long been on Coen's mind and he now prepared the way by rounding up whole communities of Bandanese and shipping them to Batavia to be sold as slaves. The total number transported from the islands remains unknown, but one ship alone was registered as carrying nearly nine hundred people of whom a quarter died en route.

The conquest of the Banda Islands was almost complete. The natives who remained were totally at Coen's mercy for their leaders were dead and their defences in ruins. The English, too, were no longer a threat. All who had survived the siege of Run were now either imprisoned on Ai or in chains on board one or other of the Dutch ships. With little possibility of further trouble, Coen now set sail for Batavia and Holland. On the way he took the opportunity to stop at Amboyna and warn the governor, Herman van Speult, to be on the look-out for any suspicious activities. He was convinced that the English would try to strike back at the Dutch, either in Amboyna or in the Banda Islands and told van Speult to nip any conspiracy in the bud. 'We hope to direct things according to your orders,' replied van Speult, 'and if we hear of any conspiracies ... we shall with your sanction do justice to them without delay.'

Carrying out Coen's command to the letter, van Speult employed a large network of agents to inform him of any suspicious activity in town. The events that followed, which would become known across Europe as the Massacre of Amboyna, destroyed any hope that England might have had of recovering ground in the Spice Islands. They also brought England and Holland to the brink of war.

The island of Amboyna was of great importance to the Dutch, both strategically and in terms of the spices it produced. Not only was it the principal port for ships setting sail for the Banda Islands, it was also rich in cloves with much of its 280 square miles given over to clove plantations. 'Amboyna sitteth as Queene between the Iles of Banda and the Molucas,' wrote Captain Humphrey Fitzherbert in his *Pithy Description of the Chiefe Ilands of Banda and Moluccas*. 'Shee is beautfied with the fruits of severall factories and clearly beloved of the Dutch.' Coen had chosen the town of Amboyna as his principal headquarters in the Spice Islands and ordered the building of a 'very stronge castle' from which he could keep an eye on all shipping heading towards the Banda Islands.

One side of Amboyna Castle was washed by the sea while the rest of the building was divided from the town by a moat five fathoms wide which was filled with sea water. The walls and ramparts were strongly fortified with each corner boasting a tower upon which were mounted 'six great pieces of ordnance'. The garrison comprised two hundred Dutch soldiers and a company of free burghers. In addition there were four hundred *mardikers*, or free natives, who could be summoned to defend the castle at a moment's notice. In the harbour eight Dutch vessels lay at anchor as a further line of defence.

That the English could have launched any sustained campaign against the Dutch is most unlikely. By the time Coen sailed for Amsterdam the small band of Englishmen still living in the East Indies were struggling to make ends meet. They received little support from London and the factories they guarded were for the most part broken and half derelict. All were on the brink of insolvency and had virtually abandoned the trade in spices. Indeed the question of closing down these factories had been discussed in the winter of 1622 and the final decision postponed only when it was agreed that advice was needed from London.

The small English factory on Amboyna was in the principal town, also called Amboyna. Here there were a dozen or so men. On the same island, at the villages of Hitu and Larica, resided a handful of other factors bringing the total number of Englishmen to eighteen – a motley band of merchants, sailors, a tailor and a barber who doubled as a surgeon. Between them, these men could muster a total arsenal of three swords and two muskets. Their chief factor was Gabriel Towerson, a veteran merchant who had married William Hawkins' widow, the regal Armenian lady, and chosen to settle in the East. He was a formidable survivor who had outlived all of his contemporaries by many years, and his letters reveal that he was quick to adapt to unfamiliar surroundings and had a shrewd understanding of eastern customs. He was indolent yet reliable, fond of pomp yet intensely practical. When he pitched up at Ahmedabad in India, the new English ambassador Sir Thomas Roe complained that Towerson 'is here arrived with many servants, a trumpet, and more show than I use' – a clear sign that Towerson knew how to win influence at the Moghul court. He held the Dutch in deep distrust, of that there can be no doubt, but he bore no malice against the Dutch governor of Amboyna, Herman van Speult, who had helped him to secure lodgings for the English factors. Indeed even as Van Speult was worrying himself about conspiracies, the Englishman was writing to his superiors in Bantam asking that they send a letter of thanks to the Dutch governor 'together with some beer or a case of strong waters, which will be acceptable to him'. Towerson and his men were frequent guests at the castle and had been given virtually free access to the place, coming and going as they pleased. Towerson himself often dined with the Dutch governor and always came away charmed by his 'courtesies' and 'love'.

Trial by Fire and Water

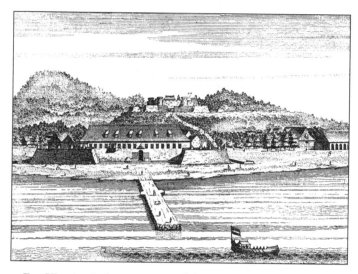

Fort Victoria, Amboyna – scene of the torture and execution of the entire English population of the island. Dutch claims that the English wished to seize the castle were unsubstantiated.

He would soon learn how hollow those courtesies were to prove. On the night of 10 February 1623, a Dutch sentinel patrolling the walls of the castle stumbled across one of the Japanese mercenaries regularly employed by the castle authorities. There were about thirty Japanese serving the castle but they were looked upon with suspicion by the regular garrison and, for this reason, they were lodged in a house in the town. The sentinel grew suspicious of the line of questioning pursued by the Japanese and at the end of his watch declared to his colleagues that there was a spy staking out the castle. This news soon reached the ears of the governor who arrested the Japanese and questioned him more closely. The man admitted that he had asked questions concerning the strength of the castle but said they were prompted by mere curiosity and 'without any malicious intentions'. It was a common practice among soldiers, he said, to learn the strength of a watch 'so that they might know how many hours they might stand'.

Such a reply would have satisfied most men, but van Speult confessed himself to be totally unconvinced by this answer and ordered the man to be tortured. He 'endured pretty long', according to the official Dutch report, but eventually the torture had the desired effect and the poor man 'confessed' that the Japanese had organised a plot to seize the castle by force. That such a plot existed was unbelievable, preposterous even, but the Dutch were so terrified by what they heard that the rest of the Japanese were arrested and similarly tortured. All this time 'the English men went to and from the castle upon their businesse, saw the prisoners, heard of their tortures and of the crime laid to their charge.' After fifty-six hours the Dutch interrogators got the answer they had been looking for all along. The Japanese, mangled and burned, confessed that they were conspiring together with the English and that it was Towerson and his men who had instigated the plot to storm the castle.

There was at this time an English surgeon called Abel Price in solitary confinement in the castle dungeon. Price was a drunkard who had got himself into trouble by threatening to set a Dutchman's house on fire after a particularly debauched evening. It was now decided to bring Price to the torture chamber to see what he knew about the conspiracy. It was dawn when he was brought to face the fiscal, the Dutch legal official, and his head was still swimming with drink. Told of the Japanese confessions and shown their wounds, the Dutch inquisitors scarcely had to heat the torture irons before Price confessed 'whatever they asked him'. In fact, they asked him very little; all they required was for him to agree to their version of events. Price duly obliged, confessing, according to the Dutch records, that 'on New Yeares Day, Captain Towerson had called them together, viz. the English merchants and the other officers, and first had had them take their oathe of secrecy and faithfulness on their Bible. After this he pointed out to them that their nation was greatly troubled by us and treated unjustly, and was very little respected; for which he thought to revenge himself. If they would helpe him and assist him faithfully, he knew how to render himself master of the castle, to which some of them had objections, saying their power was too small. On which the said Captain Towerson replied that he had already persuaded the Japanese and others and they were willing to assist him. He would not (he said) have want of people for all of them were willing.'

Price went on to give details of the attack. The Japanese, he said, were to be the first into the castle and it was their job to murder the guard and governor. Once this was accomplished the rest of the men would storm the gates and murder all the Dutchmen who refused to capitulate. The money and merchandise would then be divided among the victors.

'I was extremely surprised when I heard of this conspiracy,' said van Speult when told of the confession, and well he might have been for the English were in no position to capture a heavily fortified castle. Even if they had incited a rebellion throughout Amboyna, with just three swords and two muskets such a plan would certainly have failed, while to attempt such an attack without an escape ship waiting off-shore would have been little short of suicide. But Coen had warned van Speult that this was exactly the sort of conspiracy to expect and the governor decided it was his duty to investigate the matter more closely.

On the pretext of wishing to discuss some important business matters he sent word to the English house asking that they come to the castle immediately. All answered the summons save one who was left to guard the house. No sooner had they been brought to van Speult than they were accused of conspiracy and told they would be held as prisoners 'until further notice'. Towerson was locked inside the English factory with a guard of Dutch soldiers while Emanuel Thomson was kept in the castle. The rest of the men, John Beomont, Edward Collings, William Webber, Ephraim Ramsey, Timothy Johnson, John Fardo and Robert Brown, were manacled together and cast into confinement aboard a Dutch vessel at anchor. Afterwards Samuel Coulson, John Clarke and George Sharrocks who lived at Hitu, and William Griggs and John Sadler, who were at Larica, were brought to Amboyna. Lastly, John Powle, John Wetherall and Thomas Ladbrook, who were based at Cambello, were arrested and imprisoned. The English house was then ransacked and all the merchandise seized, along with chests, boxes, books and letters.

The men were still oblivious to the charges laid against them and faced their imprisonment with little anxiety. They had always maintained good relations with van Speult and felt sure that the misunderstanding would soon be clarified and they would be set free. In this they were mistaken, for even before the last prisoners had arrived from Cambello the first tortures were under way.

An account of the proceedings was published in a 1624 pamphlet entitled *A True Relation of the Unjust, Cruel and Barbarous Proceedings against the English at Amboyna*. With no detail of the tortures left to the imagination, this grisly account became a bestseller in England and ran into dozens of editions, with reprints still being made forty years after the event. Such was its effect on the English public that many clamoured for war against the Dutch. Even in Holland the account caused a stir and the States General professed itself horrified by its details.

John Beomont and Timothy Johnson were the first to be called before the fiscal. While Johnson was led into the torture chamber, the trembling Beomont was left standing outside, guarded by soldiers. This refinement of cruelty allowed him to hear his friend being tortured before being cast into the chamber himself. He did not have to wait long before the fiscal set to work upon Johnson. Beomont heard him 'cry out very pitifully, then to bee quiet for a little while, and then loud again'. After a 'taste of the torture,' Johnson was released for a moment while Abel Price was wheeled in and forced to accuse him. 'But Johnson not yet confessing anything,' runs the report, 'Price was quickly carried out and Johnson brought again to the torture where Beomont heard him sometime cry aloud, then quiet again, then roare afresh. At last, after he had been an houre in this second examination, hee was brought forth wailing and lamenting, all wet, and cruelly burnt in diverse parts of his body.' He was thrown into a corner 'with a soldier to watch him that he should speak with nobody'.

Next into the chamber was Emanuel Thomson. At fifty-one years old he was an old man but his age did nothing to save him from the hideous interrogation. For more than one and a half hours he endured the torture, although he was heard 'to roare most lamentably and many times'.

At last the fiscal called for the trembling Beomont who had been outside the torture chamber all this time. He was repeatedly questioned and accused, 'all of which hee denied with deep oaths and protestations'. His denials were to no avail for he was strung up against the wall with a cloth bound tightly around his neck, and the bloody instruments of torture displayed to him. But before they could be used the Governor suddenly halted Beomont's torture and declared that 'hee would spare him a day or two because he was an old man'.

The following day was a Sunday. After a longer than usual service at the castle chapel attended by van Speult and his gang of interrogators the tortures continued. First into the chamber was Robert Brown, a tailor, who broke down and confessed before the fiscal had a chance to torture him. Collins, the next in line, caused them more of a problem. Informed of the accusations laid against him, he denied everything 'with great oathes and execrations'. This angered the fiscal who ordered his henchmen to 'make his hands and feete fast to the rocke [and] bound a cloth about his throate'. When Collins saw what he would have to endure he begged to be taken down, promising to confess everything. But no sooner had he been released than he once again denied any knowledge of the plot, stating that since they were determined to use torture, 'to make him confesse any thing, though never so false, they should do him a great favour, to tell him what they would have him say, and hee would speake it to avoid the torture'.

'The fiscal hereupon said: "What? Do you mocke us" and bade, "Up with him again," and so gave him the torment of water which he not being able to endure prayed to be let down again to his confession. Then he devised a little with himself and told them that about two months and a half before himself, Thomson, Johnson, Brown and Fardo had plotted with the help of the Japans to surprise the castle.'

'Here he was interrupted by the fiscal and asked whether

Towerson were not of the conspiracy. He answered, "No."

‘ "You lie," said the fiscal. "Did he not call you to him and tell you that those daily abuses of the Dutch had caused him to think of a plot and that he wanted nothing but your consent and service?"

‘ "Yes," interjected a Dutch merchant – one John Joost – that sat by: "Did you not swear upon the Bible to be secret to him?"

‘Collins answered with great oaths that he knew nothing of any such matter. Then they made him fast again. Whereupon he then said all was true that they had spoken. Then the fiscal asked him whether the English in the rest of the factories were not consenting to this plot. He answered "No." The fiscal then asked him whether the president of the English at Jakarta or M Welden in Banda were not plotters or privie to the business. Againe he answered "No." ’

The fiscal now asked Collins how the Japanese planned to carry out their attack, at which poor Collins ‘staggering and devising of some probable fiction’, at length turned to the fiscal and silently shook his head. The fiscal was only too willing to help, supplying him with the story that was wanted: ‘Should not the Japaners have gone to each point of the castle, and two to the Governors chamber doore; and when the hurly-burly had been without, and the Governor coming to see what was the matter, the Japaners to have killed him?’

Even the torturers were shocked when they heard the fiscal put such leading words into Collins' mouth and ‘one that stood by said to the fiscal, "Do not tell him what he should say but let him speak for himself." ’ After further torments, Collins agreed to everything that was asked of him and was sent away in chains, ‘very glad to come clear of his torture though with certain belief that he should die for his confession'.

Next in line was Samuel Coulson, factor at Hitu, who was so distraught when he saw Collins, 'his eyes almost blowne out of his head,' that he chose to confess everything, 'and so was dismissed, comming out weeping, lamenting, and protesting his innocency'.

John Clarke, also from Hitu, proved the most resilient of all, refusing to confess to a single crime. 'They tortured him with water and fire' for two hours but still he protested his innocence. Like the others he was subjected to the horrific 'torment of water' which left the person grotesquely deformed. 'First they hoisted him up by the hands with a cord on a large dore, where they made him fast upon two staples of iron, fixd on both sides at the top of the doreposts, haling his hands one from the other as wide as they could stretch. Being thus made fast, his feete hung some two foot from the ground, which also they stretched asunder as far as they would reach and made them fast.' This being done they bound a thick piece of canvas about his neck and face leaving an opening at the top. Then, 'they poured the water softly upon his head untill the cloth was full, up to the mouth and nostrils, and somewhat higher, so that he could not draw breath but he must suck in all the water.'

This was continued for hours until water 'came out of his nose, eares and eyes; and often as it were stifling and choking him, at length took away his breath and brought him to a swoune or fainting'. At this point the torturers had to act quickly. Releasing the cloth from his face and neck 'they made him vomit up the water' and as soon as he was breathing again 'they triced him up.'

Clarke endured this terrible torment four times in succession, 'till his body was swollen twice or thrice as bigge as before, his cheekes like great bladders, and his eyes staring and strutting out beyond his forhead'. Still he refused to confess, at which point the fiscal and torturers grew worried, 'saying that he was a Devill, and no man, or surely was a witch; at least had some charme about him, or was enchanted, that he could bear so much. Whereupon they cut off his haire very short, as supposing he had some witchcraft hidden therein.'

There was a brief discussion as to whether they should continue the torture. All agreed that it was necessary, whereupon 'they hoisted him up againe as before, and then burnt him with lighted candles in the bottome of his feete, untill the fat dropt out the candles; yet then applyed they fresh lights unto him. They burnt him also under the elbowes, and in the palmes of the hands, likewise under the arme-pits, until his inwards might evidently be seene.'

At last he was taken down and, 'being thus wearied and overcome by the torment, he answered yea to whatsoever they asked.' With the confession down on paper and, 'having martyred this poor man, they sent him out by foure blacks who carried him between them to a dungeon, where he lay five or six daies without any surgeon to dress him until (his flesh being putrified) great maggots dropped and crept from him in a most loathsome and noisesome manner.' With the torturers now exhausted after their ordeal, 'they thus finished their Sabbath day's work.'

Over the next week the rest of the English were individually brought into the torture chamber. All endured various degrees of disfiguration before being thrown back into the castle dungeon burned and bleeding, their sores and wounds infected and putrefied. Griggs confessed early on, saving himself from being burned, Fardo endured the water torture before breaking, and then Beomont, the aged invalid, was carried in for the second time. Several of his tortured colleagues were brought in to denounce him but Beomont denied all the charges 'with great earnestness and deep oaths'. The fiscal soon tired of waiting for a confession and the stubborn prisoner was 'triced up and drenched with water till his innards were ready to crack'. After an hour or so of endurance, 'he answered affirmatively to all the fiscal's interrogatories' and 'had a great iron bolt and two shackles riveted to his legs and then was carried back to prison.'

Desperate to avoid torture George Sharrocks was the most inventive in his story. Seated before a water butt and surrounded by candles he was told that unless he confess he would be tortured to death then 'drawne by the heels to the gallows and there hanged up'. This was too much for the poor man and he began a rambling tale of conspiracies against the Dutch. Since the prisoners were forbidden from talking to each other, his story bore little resemblance to the others that the fiscal had been told. Sharrocks continually denied that Towerson had ever spoken to him on the subject and said that he had not seen his fellow countrymen for four months – long before the so-called conspiracy was hatched – since he lived on the north of the island. Despite these protests his confession was prepared and read out and Sharrocks was asked if it was true. ' "No," said Sharrocks. "Why then," said the fiscal, "did you confess it?" "For fear of torment," replied Sharrocks.' At this, 'the fiscal and the rest in a great rage told him he lied; his mouth had spoken it, and it was true, and therefore he should subscribe it.'

At long last Gabriel Towerson was brought to the examination chamber 'deeply protesting his innocence'. The fiscal told him that all the others had accused him of conspiracy, then ordered three of them into the room to reaffirm in Towerson's presence the crimes they had accused him of perpetrating. Coulson was the first brought in: pale and trembling he stood silent, his head hung in shame. At length he was told he would be tortured again if he did not speak, at which point Coulson 'coldly re-affirmed' his confession. Next Griggs and Fardo were led in and stood before Towerson. A dramatic scene then followed, for Towerson 'seriously charged them, that as they would answer it at the dreadful day of judgement, they should speak nothing but the truth. Both of them instantly fell down upon their knees before him, praying him for God's sake to forgive them, and saying further openly before them all, that whatsoever they had formerly confesed was most false and spoken only to avoid torment.' On hearing this the fiscal exploded and threatened them with more torture, 'which they would not endure, but then affirmed their former confessions to be true'.

Towerson bowed his head silently, realising now that his situation was hopeless. Neither Griggs nor Fardo could stand further torture and both assented to sign a declaration of guilt. When Griggs signed his confession he asked the fiscal 'upon whose head he thought the sinne would lie; whether upon his that was constrained to confesse what was false, or upon the constrainers?' At this the fiscal left the room to confer with van Speult before returning and ordering Coulson to sign.' "Well," quoth he, "you make me to accuse myself and others of that which is as false as God is true: for God is my witness, I am as innocent as the child new borne." '

What happened to Towerson after the signing of these confessions remains uncertain. There is no doubt that the most brutal treatment was reserved for him yet he withstood the torture to the very end. The two survivors later recorded that van Speult's henchmen used even more brutal methods, such as 'the splitting of the toes and lancing of the breast and putting in gunpowder, and the firing the same, whereby the body is not left entire, either for innocency or execution'. The stench of burned flesh was said to be so pungent in the castle dungeon 'that no one was able to endure the smell'.

There was a two day respite from the torture before the prisoners were assembled in the great hall of the castle to learn their fate. A handful, believing their sufferings would entitle them to compassion, were certain that they would be banished rather than murdered. But van Speult was not a man noted for his clemency. Seated at a massive table and flanked by his officers he gravely 'stated his suit and drew his conclusions'. All the men had confessed their guilt – all except Towerson whose continued protestations of innocence had so incensed the fiscal. As the men waited to hear the judgement read out, Towerson was once again 'brought up into the place of examination, and two great jarrs of water carried after him'. What he suffered during the hours he was interrogated will never be known for he was next seen at the scaffold, his features blenched and drawn.

Before the fiscal read the sentence, 'prayers were said to the Lord that He might govern their [the Council's] hearts in this gloomy consultation and that He might inspire them only with equity and justice.' With this done the fiscal called the room to order. Towerson was condemned to be decapitated and quartered and his head to be suspended from a post as a warning to others. The rest of the men were to be spared the quartering; they would simply be decapitated, along with their Japanese conspirators. As the men listened in horror a whisper arose among the Dutch officers. It was realised that by executing all of the men they would leave themselves with the burden of having to

administer the affairs of the English factory. It was therefore
decided to reprieve two of the men to look after the
Company's interests. Beomont was one of the men spared;
he was fortunate enough to have a Dutch merchant friend
who argued for his release. To choose the second man it
was decided that Coulson, Thomson and Collins should
draw lots. They knelt on the cold flagstones and joined
hands in communal prayer, and this being done they each
delved their hands into the lottery box. Collins drew the
right paper and was duly set free. The others resigned
themselves to their deaths.

They were led back to their prison cells for their last
night before execution. The men were visited by Dutch
ministers who 'telling them how short a time they had to
live, admonished and exhorted them to make their true
confessions; for it was a dangerous and desperate thing to
dissemble at such a time'. The English continued to protest
their innocence, 'and prayed the Ministers that they might
all receive the sacrament as a seale of the forgivenesse of
their sinnes and withall thereby to confirme their last
profession of the innocencie'. This was too much for the
ministers and 'would by no means be granted'.

Coulson now begged the minister that he might ask
a question. '"You manifest unto us the danger of dissimu-
lation in this case," he said, "but tell us, if we suffer
guiltlesse, being otherwise also true believers in Jesus
Christ, what shall be our reward?" '

To this the minister had a ready answer: '"By how much
the cleerer you are, soe much the more glorious shall be
your resurrection."'The narrative continues:

With that word Coulson started up, embraced the
preacher and gave him his purse with such money as

*The Massacre of Amboyna deeply shocked the English nation.
The East India Company merchants were tortured with fire
and water before having their limbs blown off with gunpowder.
After enduring a week of brutality, they were executed by the
Dutch commander.*

hee had in it, saying, 'Domine, God bless you. Tell the Governor I freely forgive him; and I entreat you to exhort him to repent of this bloody tragedy wrought upon us poor innocent souls.'

Here all the rest of the Englishmen signified their assent to this speech.

Then spake John Fardo to the rest in the presence of the ministers as followeth; 'My countrymen and brethren that are heere with mee condemned to dye, I charge you all as you will answer it at God's Judgement Seat if any of you bee guilty of this matter, whereof we are condemned, discharge your consciences and confesse the truth for satisfaction of the world.' Hereupon Samuel Coulson spake with a loud voyce, saying: 'According to my innocency in this treason so, Lord, pardon all my sinnes and if I be guiltie thereof, more or lesse, let me never be partaker of Thy heavenly joys.' At which words every one of the rest cryed out, 'Amen for me, amen for me, good Lord!' This done, each of them knowing whom he had accused, went one to another begging forgiveness for their false accusation, being rung from them by the pains or feare of torture. And they all freely forgave one another: for none had bene so falsely accused but he himself had accused another as falsely.

The Dutch ministers found themselves deeply moved by the spectacle of these condemned men professing their innocence and one of them offered to bring them a barrel of wine in order that they might 'drive away their sorrow'. But the men steadfastly declined the offer, not wishing to spend their final hours in a state of drunkenness. Instead they asked the ministers for ink and sat quietly writing

their final protestations of innocence. One of these, bearing Samuel Coulson's signature, is inscribed into his copy
of the Psalms of David which eventually found its way
back to Europe. Written on 5 March 1623, 'aboard the
Rotterdam lying in irons', it begins:

> Understand that I, Samuel Coulson, late factor of
> Hitto, was apprehended for suspicion of conspiracy;
> and for anything I know must die for it: wherefore
> having no meanes to make my innocency knowne,
> have writ in this book, hoping some good
> Englishman will see it. I do here sweare upon my
> salvation, as I do hope by His death and passion to
> have redemption for my sinnes, that I am cleere of all
> such conspiracy: neither do I know any Englishman
> guilty thereof, nor other creature in the world. As this
> is true, God bless me – Samuel Coulson.

William Griggs also managed to scribble a few lines on
that final night: 'We, through torment, were constrained to
speake that which we never meant, nor once imagined; the
which we take upon our deaths and salvation, that tortured
as with that extreme torment of fire and water, that flesh
and blood could not endure … And so farewell; written in
the dark.'

How Towerson passed his final night is unknown for he
was still held in isolation and unable to communicate with
his compatriots. Everything he wrote was confiscated and
destroyed except for a couple of lines which he scrawled
onto a bill of debt against the Company. This passed
undetected until it fell into the hands of an English agent
in the Banda Islands: 'Firmed by the firme of me, Gabriel
Towerson, now appointed to die, guiltless of anything that

can be justly laid to my charge. God forgive them their guilt and receive me to His mercy. Amen.'

That his suffering was at least as great as the rest of the men is clear from an account by Beomont, one of the released, who visited him on the morning of his execution and 'found him sitting in a chamber all alone in a most miserable condition, the wounds of his torture bound up'. He clutched Beomont's hand weakly and prayed him that if he ever reached England he should seek out his brother Billingsley and certify him of his innocence 'which,' he said, 'you yourself know well enough'.

As day broke the men were reminded of their impending execution by the beat of drums and tramp of soldiers echoing through the town. This was to summon spectators wishing to view the bloodshed about to take place. Executions in Amboyna were colourful events; flags and bunting were strung out, bands played, and large crowds 'flocked together to behold this triumph of the Dutch over the English'. The prisoners, meanwhile, were assembled in the great hall for the last time. At the door stood 'the quit and pardoned', those lucky two who had been released on the orders of the governor. To these men the condemned now made their last farewells and solemnly charged them 'to bear witnesse to their friends in England ... that they died not traitors, but so many innocents merely murdered by the Hollanders, whome they prayed God to forgive their blood-thirstinesse and to have mercy upon their own soules'.

As they spent their last minutes in the hall the Japanese prisoners were ushered in and lined up against the opposite wall. This spectacle angered both parties for each believed the other group to be the cause of their present plight. ' "Oh you Englishmen," said one of the Japanese in a voice of despair, "where did wee ever in our lives eat with you, talk with you, or (to our remembrance) see you?" The Englishmen replied: "Why then have you accused us?" ' It was only at this point that all realised the scale of the Dutch deception and 'the poore men, perceiving they were made believe each had accused others before they had so done, indeed, showed them their tortured bodies and said, "If a stone were thus burnt, would it not change his nature? How much more we that are flesh and blood?" '

The men then embraced each other before being ushered into a courtyard where their sentence was read out by an official standing in a gallery. Here they were reunited with Towerson whose wounds and sores had become so festered that he could scarcely walk. Then, accompanied by five companies of soldiers, they were led in procession to their place of execution, a long and melancholy cortège that wound through crowds of cheering onlookers before arriving at the execution ground.

As they stood facing their executioner Samuel Coulson drew from his pocket a short prayer which ended in a defiant declaration of his innocence. This being done, he threw the paper into the wind and watched as it fluttered high into the air before being caught by a soldier and taken straight to the governor.

One by one the men stepped forward to the block. Before the executioner proceeded with his bloody work, each man affirmed in a clear voice that he was innocent of all the crimes of which he was accused. 'And so, one by one, with great cheerfulness, they suffered the fatal stroke.'

Only Towerson was singled out for special treatment. As the leader of the little English contingent he was accorded the special honour of having a small piece of black velvet tied to the block prior to his being beheaded. In a bill of charges later received by the English East India Company, the cost of this cloth was added to the list on the grounds that it was so bloodstained as to be unusable.

If van Speult had any qualms about his rough justice, he was about to receive an admonishment from on high. 'At the instant of the execution there arose a great darknesse with a sudden and violent gust of winde and tempest; whereby two of the Dutch shippes riding in the harbour were driven from their anchors.' Worse was to come; within two weeks of the execution 'there happened a great sickness on the island such as was there never seen or heard of, so that the people cried out that it was a plague upon them for the innocent blood of the English.' When the sickness finally subsided, more than a quarter of the island's population had lost their lives. The surviving Englishmen took comfort in these events, remembering Emanuel Thomson's dying words that 'he did not doubt but God would show some sign of their innocencie.'

The small English community in Batavia knew nothing of these events until they met with two pallid Englishmen disembarking from a vessel in the harbour. When asked to explain their miserable state these men poured out the story of the Amboyna massacre. The English were shocked by what they heard and sent an immediate protest to the new Dutch Governor-General, Pieter de Carpentier, remonstrating against van Speult's 'presumptuous proceedings' in 'imprisoning, torturing and bloodily executing his majesty's subjects' and 'confiscating their goods in direct violation of the Treaty, whereby the King was disgraced and dishonoured and the English nation scandalized'.

Carpentier treated the protests with cool detachment, but the letters he sent back to Holland reveal that he realised the matter was of the utmost gravity. Although believing that Towerson and his fellow men had indeed been engaged in conspiracy, he condemned in the strongest words the methods used by the fiscal. 'He called himself a lawyer and had been taken into the Company's service as such,' he wrote, but he 'should have shown better judgement in the affair'. He continued: 'We think the rigour of justice should have been mitigated somewhat with Dutch clemency (with consideration to a nation who is our neighbour), especially if such could be done without prejudice to the state and the dignity of justice, as we think could have been done here.'

When news of the massacre reached London there was uproar. King James at first refused to believe it, claiming it was too foul. But when he heard the story from the mouths of the survivors he was deeply shocked and although not accustomed to show emotion was said to have shed tears over the fate of Towerson and his companions. The Lords of the Privy Council also wept when they were told of the tortures, while the merchants of the East India Company were stunned to silence. Stranger was the reaction of the English public who indulged in what was little short of a national outpouring of grief. Up and down the country pamphlets and broadsheets were published with graphic details of the tortures and in towns and villages men eagerly discussed the gruesome business. A mob gathered around the Dutch Chapel in Lothbury and jeered at the congregation as they entered the church. 'Hypocrites, murderers,' they shouted, 'Amboyna will cost you paradise.' More than fifty years later the poet John Dryden used the massacre to whip up anti-Dutch feeling, publishing his tragedy *Amboyna, or The Cruelties of the Dutch to the English Merchants*.

All through the winter indignation grew, and the directors of the East India Company did not fight shy of stoking the public outrage. They commissioned artist

Richard Greenbury to produce a huge oil painting depicting the agonies of Towerson and companions, with van Speult and the fiscal gloating over their bloody victory. Greenbury apparently excelled himself, painting a gruesome picture in which he 'lively, largely and artificially' depicted the tortures. The work was to be exhibited in the Company headquarters 'as a perpetual memorial of Dutch cruelty and treachery' and the public were invited to come to view it. So effective was the painting in inciting hatred against the Dutch that the directors were ordered by the government not to display it until after the Shrove Tuesday holiday for fear of a general uprising against the large population of Hollanders living in London.

Greenbury himself was delighted with the reaction and demanded £100 from the directors. In this he was to be disappointed for they told him that 'one proffered to cut it out in brass for £30, which was a great deal more labour and workmanship than to draw it on cloth.' In the end Greenbury settled for £40.

With anti-Dutch protests growing in London there was a feeling that something had to be done. 'For my part,' wrote one notable to Sir Dudley Carleton, the English ambassador at The Hague, 'if there were no wiser than I, we should stay or arrest the first Indian ship that comes in our way and hang up upon Dover cliffs as many as we should find faulty or actors in this business and then dispute the matter afterwards: for there is no other course to be had with such manner of men, as neither regard law nor justice, nor any other respect or equity or humanity, but only make gain their God.'

The States General were extremely concerned at the aftermath of the Amboyna Massacre and unsatisfied with an official report compiled by the directors of the Dutch East India Company. Far from denying that van Speult used torture it actually justified his methods, arguing that 'the torture of the water is much more civill and less dangerous than other tortures for the paine of water doth but cause and produce an oppression and anxiety of breath and respiration.' The report was riddled with inconsistencies and offered no real evidence against the English. After deliberating over its contents the States General recalled van Speult to Holland to answer for his brutality, but he died before he reached Amsterdam. Others made it back to Holland but the special court that convened to investigate their conduct deliberated for months before declaring it could find no reason to punish them for something they did in the belief that they were acting in the best interests of their country.

The directors of the English East India Company protested, informing the King that they would be forced to abandon trade with the Spice Islands unless 'the Dutch make real restitution for damages, execute justice upon those who had in so great fury and tyranny tortured and slain the English, and give security for the future'. The King acted upon their advice, appointing a committee comprising the country's most distinguished servants to examine all the evidence that had arrived in England. This committee concluded that the massacre had less to do with any conspiracy than with a Dutch plan to permanently evict the English from the Spice Islands. They recommended to the Lord High Admiral that a fleet should be sent to patrol the entrance to the English Channel, lay hold of any outward or homebound Dutch East India ships and keep them in England until suitable compensation was forthcoming. What form that compensation should take was never in doubt. There was only one possible way for the Dutch to atone for the Amboyna Massacre, and that was to hand back the tiny island of Run.

CHAPTER TWELVE

STRIKING
A DEAL

SOME FIFTEEN YEARS AFTER the Massacre of Amboyna, a renegade Dutchman arrived in London bearing some disquieting news. He informed the directors of the East India Company that he had recently visited Run and was surprised to discover that every nutmeg tree on the island had been chopped down. Where once there had been a verdant forest covering Run's mountainous backbone, there was now nothing but exposed soil.

The news was yet another blow to England's increasingly forlorn hopes of recovering a foothold in the region. It required only a cursory glance at an atlas for London's merchants to see the tragic story writ large. The Banda Islands were now totally under Dutch control: studded with castles and defended by permanent garrisons, they were probably lost forever. Amboyna, too, was indisputably in Dutch hands. They had chosen it as their regional centre of operations and its jagged coastline was protected by a string of imposing forts. It was much the same story in the northerly islands of Ternate and Tidore which had slowly but surely fallen under the Dutch sphere of influence.

To the dwindling band of Englishmen who lingered in Coen's new capital, Batavia, there were more tangible reasons for pessimism. Every month saw the arrival of more factors from abandoned outposts; haggard, destitute men who had struggled to keep trading until insolvency or the machinations of the Dutch forced them to flee. Even such far-flung settlements as Siam, Patani on the Malay Peninsula, and Firando in Japan – of which there had been such high hopes – had come to nothing. One by one their traders had been forced to abandon them, leaving decaying warehouses and tarnished reputations. The only places that managed to continue a trade of sorts were those scattered along the coastline of India, but even these would soon be brought to their knees by a devastating and wholly unexpected famine.

The horrific news of events in Amboyna sent a wave of panic through the small English community still living in Batavia. Despised by both the Dutch and the natives, they lived in the town on sufferance of Pieter de Carpentier, the new governor-general, who showed little concern or interest in their welfare. He dismissed their protestations about the massacre at Amboyna, unsettling the English who felt themselves to be in the most vulnerable of positions, surrounded by enemies and with no obvious means of escape. If Carpentier chose to emulate the butchers of Amboyna, they would be unable to resist.

A meeting of the factors ended in decision: scouts were to put to sea at once in order to search for a suitable island upon which the English could build a new headquarters, and the Company's president was to write to London to beg the directors to 'liberate us from the intolerable yoke of the Dutch nation'. Although his letter evoked no response, the scouts soon returned with good news. After sailing around the southern coastline of Sumatra they chanced upon the low-lying island of Lagundi which, they confidently declared, was perfectly suited to their needs.

Why they alighted on this blighted spot remains unclear for it had an extremely unhealthy climate and no source of fresh water. But in October 1624, the remaining Englishmen in Batavia heaved a heavy sigh of relief and fled 'this perfidious people', sailing directly to Lagundi. The flag was raised, the supplies landed, and Lagundi was renamed Prince Charles Island.

Hardly had they made the island their home than their luck once again deserted them. Many of the men succumbed to tropical fevers and dysentery and the wretched remnants spent as much time digging graves as they did on constructing their warehouse. After only a few months a meeting was convened and the survivors elected to return to Batavia, a decision that was fraught with difficulty. Too few to man a ship, the men were forced to beg a Dutch captain to carry them back to the port. They were welcomed with rude cheers and 'a merciless whipping in the public market place'.

The news from London during this troubled period gave few grounds for optimism. Although King James was determined to have his revenge for the heinous crimes perpetrated at Amboyna, more than three years were to pass before a fleet of India-bound Dutch vessels was seized in the English Channel and towed into Portsmouth. By then, King James was dead and it was left to his successor, King Charles I, to pursue the claim for reparations. The directors at last saw a real chance of obtaining redress, but no sooner had they compiled a report of their grievances than they learned that the King had inexplicably released the vessels. He justified his extraordinary behaviour by explaining that the Dutch had promised to send a negotiating team to England, but few believed such an explanation and rumours of backhanders to the King only fuelled the belief that a secret deal had been struck. One report claimed the King had been handed £30,000 by the Dutch captain; another said he had been given three tons of gold. The Dutch themselves stoked the fire by bragging they had bought the King's jewels back from his pawnbroker.

The Company was about to enter its darkest hour. The number of ships sailing to the East dropped by almost two thirds and, with trade at a virtual standstill, its stock slumped by more than 20 per cent. In the good years subscribers had freely stumped up more than £200,000 per annum; now the Company beadle was lucky to collect a quarter of that figure. More worrying was the news that the debts were spiralling out of control: when the auditors checked their accounts in the spring of 1629 they were horrified to learn that they were more than £300,000 in the red.

A series of meetings was called to discuss the parlous state of the Company's finances and it was reluctantly decided that the overheads and expenses should be slashed. The eighteen London employees were the first to feel the squeeze. A list was prepared of their salaries and expenses, together with suggestions of how money could be saved. A few were to be fired, ineffectual workers were to have their pay docked, and others would be retained on much-reduced salaries. First on the list was Mr Tyne, the book-keeper, whose salary was cut from £100 to his 'former proportion' of £80. The apologetic directors explained that with so few ships returning from the Indies he no longer had much book-keeping to do. Mr Handson, the auditor, was the next victim but when he learned that the axe was about to fall he chose to depart with honour, graciously standing down from his position and thereby saving the Company £100 a year. Mr Ducy, a timber measurer, was no less fortunate: his annual £50 salary was cancelled and he was, in future, to be paid by the day. Others found they were surplus to requirements: Richard Mountney was informed that his salary had been 'recalled' as his services were no longer required.

Such petty measures were cosmetic and useless in halting the Company's decline. Further cuts in salaries were followed by the abandonment of shipbuilding activities and, in 1643, the forced sale of the Deptford shipyard. 'We could wish,' wrote the directors to their long-suffering factors, 'that we could vindicate the reputation of our nation in these partes [the East], and do ourselves right … [but] of all these wee must brave the burden and with patience sitt still, until wee may find these frowning times more auspicious to us and our affayres.'

Throughout these 'frowning times' the directors clung to the hope that Run would one day be restored. In both 1632 and 1633 they sent letters to their Bantam merchants ordering them to reoccupy the island and, in the following year, they actually despatched a vessel to the Banda Islands but the untimely arrival of the monsoon forced it to return to Bantam. In 1636 a spirited English merchant sailed single handedly to Neira to demand the return of Run. He was welcomed by the gleeful Dutch commander who told him that if he rowed across to survey the island he would be a little less hasty in demanding its return. The Dutch, increasingly concerned by the continued English interest in the island, had taken 'all courses to make the iland little or nothing worth'. One onlooker watched with astonishment the Hollanders 'demolish and deface the buildings [and] transplant the nutmeg trees, plucking them up by the roots and carrying them into their owne ilands of Neira and of Poloway [Ai] … and at last finde a meanes to dispeople the iland and to leave it so as the English might make no use of it'.

The Dutchman who brought this news to England had been dismissed from the Dutch Company and was determined to have his revenge. He offered to pursue the King's claim for damages in return for a small fee and, to this end, was despatched to Holland to work in tandem with England's ambassador. The men were armed with reams of evidence about Dutch brutality, including a lengthy report investigating 'the barbarous behaviour of the Governor of Banda in burning and torturing the inhabitants, robbing them of gold, silver, jewels, and goods and destroying the nutmeg trees and other spices'. They also had documents listing the 150 Englishmen who had been murdered over the past two decades and a further list of 800 who had been sold into slavery.

The ensuing negotiations fill page after page of East India Company records – a litany of complaints, grievances and hard bargaining. The English team were given considerable flexibility when it came to discussing reparations but the bottom line was that Run should be replanted with nutmeg trees and restored to England. In addition, the directors demanded a one-off payment of £200,000 for losses suffered, both human and financial. This sum dropped steadily over the months that followed but still the Dutch refused to pay a single guilder.

By unhappy coincidence it was during these long years of negotiations that the Banda Islands entered their most productive period, producing hitherto undreamed of quantities of nutmeg and mace. In the five years between 1633 and 1638, for which records are still extant, the combined weight of nutmeg and mace exported to Holland exceeded four million pounds. That, of course, was only the official quantity. Many Dutch settlers on the islands were amassing private fortunes by clandestinely selling nutmeg to native merchants and traders. Although this practice was strictly prohibited by the Dutch authorities, the ragged coastline of the Banda Islands proved impossible to police and the settlers had few difficulties in finding buyers for their spice.

The success of the nutmeg plantations was due, in no small part, to Coen's strategy of ridding the islands of their native inhabitants and replacing them with Dutchmen. Before leaving the East Indies, he had announced that the Dutch Company was inviting applications for grants of land in the Banda archipelago. In return for defence against foreign attack and slaves to work the plantations, applicants had to agree to settle permanently and produce spices only for the company. Many 'free burghers' living in Batavia – men who had completed their contracts but remained in the East – proved only too willing to take up Coen's offer and applications were soon flooding in. The Banda Islands were parcelled into small estates, sixty-eight men were chosen to farm them, and the surviving Bandanese were compelled to teach them how to cultivate the nutmeg tree.

Success and riches went to the heads of most settlers who, having procured the necessary slaves to work their land, sank into a life of dissolute drunkenness. Coen himself complained that most of the settlers were 'wholly unsuitable for the planting of colonies [and] some are worse than animals'. In this he was correct: they were generally lazy and unruly and needed harsh measures to keep them in check. A journal kept by one Company employee records that in the space of one five-year period he witnessed the following punishments: two persons burned alive, one broken on the wheel, nine hanged, nine decapitated, three garrotted, and one 'arquebussed' – a punishment which entailed being shot to pieces by the matchlock arquebus gun favoured by the Dutch.

The Dutch grasp over the Banda archipelago was now so complete that the English directors began to despair of ever recovering Run, especially when the outbreak of the English Civil War put paid to any immediate hopes of despatching a fleet to the East. 'Wee are fearfull how far wee shall be able to performe in this troublesome tymes,' they wrote, 'when all trade and commerce in this kingdome is fallen to the ground through our owne unhappie divisions at home.' Intermittent fighting, a breakdown of communications, heavy taxation and increased risks at sea caused a complete loss of trade and the directors bemoaned that 'as the badnesse of trade and scarsity of monyes are here, so is all Europe in little better condition, but in a turmoyle.'

By the winter of 1656 the East India Company was on its knees. For more than four decades its merchants had struggled to compete with the Dutch, despatching increasingly decrepit ships to the Spice Islands and clinging to the last threads of their trade. Now, even that had come to nothing: the grand fleets that had once sailed majestically down the Thames were little more than a distant memory. The Deptford shipyard had been sold, the warehouses lay empty and the employees were on the breadline, only drawing money on the rare occasions when a ship limped back from the Indies.

Overseas the Company's remaining assets were of little worth. The factors still living in Bantam had almost ceased trading and their sole success during this grim period – the acquisition of a modest cargo of pepper – was immediately scuppered when the Dutch captured the ship and gleefully towed her to Batavia. On India's north-west coastline the trading post at Surat had, for a while, reaped considerable profits for the Company. But it had been hit hard by pirates and its fortunes were dealt an even harsher blow when the great famine of 1630 wiped out the town's population. 'The land was allmost voyde of inhabitants,' wrote one of the factors living in Surat, 'the most part fledd, the rest dedd.' His vivid account of the crisis left the London directors in no doubt that it would be many years before their Surat trade would recover. 'Noe less lamentable was it to see the poor people scrapeing the dunghills for food, yea in the very excrement of beastes ... our noses were never free of the stinck of corpses [for] they dragg them out by the heels stark naked of all ages and sexes, till they are out of the gates, and there they are left so that the way is half barred up.' Surat had become a ghost town and when the factors at last strayed out of their compound 'we hardly could see any living persons where heretofore was thousands ... women were seen to roast their children [and] men travelling in the waie were laid hold of to be eaten.'

The other factories in India had also been brought to their knees by famine. For a brief moment the Company's fledgling settlement in Madras had offered a ray of hope: no sooner had the battlements of Fort St George risen above the shoreline than native artisans flocked here in their hundreds, lured by the promise of calico weaving and chintz painting. After fourteen years of relative prosperity the famine virtually eliminated the local population and decimated the small English garrison. Just ten soldiers and two factors were left alive, and even these proved too expensive for the Company to maintain. The directors publicly declared that three ships would shortly be sent to the East in order to wind up their affairs.

The crunch came on 14 January 1657. The governor of the East India Company, William Cockayne, summoned a general court of all the adventurers who still had money invested in the Company. To a grim-faced audience he explained that the coffers were empty and that there was no hope of a revival in fortunes. Every avenue had been explored, every hope extinguished. The Lord Protector, Oliver Cromwell, had been petitioned for help but had repeatedly refused to come to the Company's aid, pleading too many 'great affaires'. As Cockayne spelled out the enormity of the crisis it slowly dawned on the merchants that this really was the end. The Company was no longer viable, the balance sheet did not add up. As the sun set on that chill winter's evening the adventurers threw in the towel and declared for liquidation.

'It is resolved to appoint a sale of the island [Run], customs, houses and other rights in the Indies.' So read the minutes of that historic final meeting. The suggested value was a mere £14,000 – the low price explained by the fact that most of these were paper assets – for which the buyer would receive the titles to Run, the factories in Bantam, Surat and Madras, and a remote customs post in Persia. Their business at an end, the merchants ordered a beadle to post bills in the Exchange advertising the forthcoming sale.

As the door closed on that sombre evening there was a deep sense of shock among the merchant adventurers. This, then, was the end; the dying hours of a Company that had blazed such a glorious path to the East. In the early years there had been so much hope. The pioneering expeditions of Sir James Lancaster; the indomitable Middleton trio; the doughty William Hawkins – all had risked their lives in sailing to the Indies and some had returned with undreamed of quantities of spice. Once, the Thamesside wharves had been filled with the scent of nutmeg and the estuary cluttered with ships from the Indies. The King himself had sent expeditions on their way and cheering crowds had welcomed them home.

Now, more than half a century later, it was time to count the price of failure. Numerous ships had been sunk in the great spice race and hundreds, possibly thousands, of men had lost their lives. For nothing had the victims of Amboyna met their gruesome ends; in vain had Nathaniel Courthope laid down his life in the heroic defence of Run. That very island, lost after such a struggle, was now up for sale with an asking price lower than the cost of a small ship. It was an end of which no one could be proud.

This should have been the conclusion to the story; the final death throes of a Company and a dream. But unbeknown to the merchant adventurers of London, no one would be given the opportunity to make an offer for their few remaining assets in the East. For scarcely had news of the sale been announced than they found themselves summoned to a meeting with Cromwell's Council of State – a meeting to discuss the future of the East India Company.

Oliver Cromwell and his Council of State were genuinely alarmed by the news from the Exchange. For too long they had refused to listen to the arguments put forth by the Company – that trade with the East Indies was doomed to fail unless organised as a regulated, joint-stock system, a system that allowed no room for privateers to spoil the trade. Now, learning of the Company's plight, the Council of State invited the merchants to put their side of the argument, then withdrew to consider their verdict.

The Council reconvened the following morning and,

without hesitation, pronounced itself swayed by the arguments. Twelve days later Cromwell agreed, thereby snatching the Company from the jaws of death. A new charter was drawn up, sanctioned by Parliament, and passed the Great Seal on 19 October 1657. With the stroke of a pen, the East India Company found itself reborn as a modern, permanent and united joint-stock corporation. The very same day a meeting was called by the jubilant directors and a new subscription posted in the Exchange. London's merchants responded with unbounded enthusiasm and within a matter of months a staggering £786,000 had been raised. Trade with the East could begin once again.

But it was not to the Spice Islands that the merchants despatched their ships. Throughout the lean and desperate years it was the Indian subcontinent that had kept the East India Company afloat, surviving off a modest trade between Surat and Persia and a much smaller trade between India and London. Although the Company continued to import 'long pepper, white pepper, white powdered sugar, preserved nutmegs and ginger myrabolums [a plum-like fruit], bezoar stones [and] drugs of all sorts', spices had ceased to be its mainstay. They had been replaced by silks and saltpetre, the latter an essential ingredient in gunpowder which was freely available in India.

As the factories in the Spice Islands fell into decay, new ones sprang up on the Indian coastline and when Surat officially replaced Bantam as the eastern headquarters of the East India Company it was clear to all that its horizons had changed forever. 'Behold then,' wrote Sir Thomas Mun in 1667, 'the true form and worth of foreign trade, which is the great revenue of the King, the honour of the

Kingdom; the noble profession of the merchant; the school of our arts; the supply of our wants; the employment of our poor; the improvement of our lands; the nursery of our mariners; the walls of our Kingdom; the means of our treasure; the sinews of our wars; the terror of our enemies.'

His triumphalism was a far cry from the laments of old and it would grow ever louder as the Company's fortunes grew. Under King Charles II's benevolent rule the directors were granted even more extensive rights: to acquire territory, declare war, command troops, and exercise civil and criminal jurisdiction. When the directors passed a 1689 resolution about local government in India, it was clear that the Company was irrevocably changing. Arguing that good government would lead to increased profits they concluded, ''tis that must make us a nation in India.' With these words the story of the East India Company had, in effect, become the story of British India.

The Company's turn-around in fortunes was an astonishing and wholly unexpected event, yet there was to be an even more extraordinary twist in the tale. In the yellowing archives of the East India Company are a handful of documents that lie unnoticed and unread; documents which reveal that Run — defended with such courage by Nathaniel Courthope — was to yield a far greater dividend than anyone could ever have imagined.

London merchants had never abandoned their dream of recovering Run, their 'ancient and rightfull inheritance'. and held regular meetings to discuss how this could be achieved. But it was not until the affairs of the Company were in the process of being wound down that they saw a glimmer of hope on the horizon.

In April 1654, the Anglo-Dutch war was terminated by a peace treaty, the Treaty of Westminster, in which it was decreed that all claims for damages – claims that stretched back decades – should at long last be settled. Each side was given three months to prepare its case. The English not surprisingly called for the immediate restoration of Run, but upped the stakes considerably by also demanding the island of Great Banda. In addition, they filed a staggering £2,695,990 claim for lost revenue as well as decades of accumulated interest. If they thought this would place them in a strong bargaining position they were in for a rude shock. The Dutch argued that their trade had been seriously damaged by the English and responded with a counter-claim of almost three million pounds.

The commissioners charged with dealing with the claims wisely chose to ignore them and instead spent their time sifting through the evidence. Their findings were straightforward and favoured the English: Run was to be immediately restored and £85,000 was to be paid in damages, plus a further £4,000 to the families of the victims of Amboyna. To the surprise of everyone both sides agreed the deal and the Treaty of Westminster was duly signed. Almost fifty years of hatred, bloodshed and mutual animosity were, on paper at least, 'obliterated and bury'd in oblivion.'

In London, news of the treaty was greeted with weary enthusiasm by the cash-strapped directors of the East India Company. The parlous state of their finances, together with continuing legal wrangles with the Dutch, delayed any hope of immediate action and it was not until Cromwell had unexpectedly rescued the Company – more than three years after the treaty was signed – that London's merchants were able to consider sending an expedition to Run.

The receipt of a letter from Jeremy Sambrooke, a servant of the Company, gave them cause for optimism. Sambrooke had recently sailed to Run and assured his superiors that once the English were 'setled upon Pollaroone they will find the Indians [and] inhabitants of the adjacent islands ready to come and inhabite, plant and trade with them'. He added that the natives were 'soe well affected to this nation that assuredly they will deal for the clothing etc. and returne spices untill this island shal be reestablished to its former condition, as in former times of peace'. Sambrooke also reported that the island's nutmeg groves were once again flourishing and that the Company could look forward to an annual yield of more than a third of a million pounds in weight of the spice. When they learned this, the directors immediately established a special Committee for Pulo Run which, at its inaugural meeting, 'resolved to send sixty men of several conditions to remain on the said island, they to be either English, Scotch, or Irish'. These men were to include 'seven house carpenters, seven bricklayers and masons, six gardeners, four smiths and armourers, four coopers, and two plumbers', as well as 'twenty youths from fourteen years upwards, and ten young husbandmen'. Run was to be England's glorious colony in the East. In the winter of 1658, Captain John Dutton was selected to be the first governor of Run, a job which was to earn him a generous £200 a year salary, a further £100 in expenses, and the right to travel with his beloved wife. His orders were to take possession of the island and 'with drum and trumpett proclaime the same,' and he was asked, en route, to stop at the Atlantic island of St Helena and claim it for the Company as well. Unfortunately it took so long to select the settlers for Run that by the time Dutton put to sea, England and Holland were once again on the brink of war. Concerned for the safety of his ship he decided to remain on St Helena until he received further orders. And so, in May 1659, this strategically placed island received its first inhabitants and a small settlement, Jamestown, was built on its northern coastline.

A whole year was to pass before the East India Company considered it safe enough to despatch another fleet to Run. This time they prepared four supply ships under the command of John Hunter and selected a further thirteen colonists for the island, all of whom were to be paid a salary of £12 a year except for the appropriately named George Smallwood who, 'by reason of smallnesse of stature,' was to receive only £10.

The aim of the voyage was clear: 'The King [has] given authority, under the great seal of England, to the Governor and Company or to such as they may appoint, to receive, possess, plant, and fortify the Island of Roone.' The island was to be permanently settled and it was the duty of the colonists 'to keep possession of the said island'.

The ships sailed first to St Helena where they picked up an impatient Captain and Mrs Dutton, then headed directly for Batavia where the couple requested an audience with the Dutch governor-general. The governor-general was initially most welcoming, volunteering the information that his superiors in Amsterdam 'doe order, command and advise' him to hand over the island in accordance with the Treaty of Westminster. But there was a small matter of bureaucracy to be settled before he could sanction their voyage. He required a letter from 'His majestie of Great Britain', written in the King's fair hand, stating that Dutton was a bona fide employee of the East India Company. This request caught the captain by surprise: he was not in possession of such a letter and when he explained this to the governor-general he was met with an icy stare. The governor-general began to rail at the

Englishman, saying he was most displeased to hear that the King was once again creating troubles for the Dutch and 'doth renew and ripp open severall ould sores and debates formerly enacted which have bine long buried'. In short, he intended to refuse the English the necessary permission to sail to Run.

Dutton was astonished by this change of heart and vowed to sail to the Banda Islands without further ado. He hoped to be able to induce the local governor to let him settle the island and, if not, entertained the possibility of taking the place by force. But in this too he was to be disappointed. His arrival at Neira was greeted with anger by the Dutch governor who gave an 'obstinate denial to surrender the island' and added that any attempt on Run would be met with gunshot and cannon fire.

Dutton was not surprised; he had long suspected that the English were being duped and that the Dutch Company 'never really intended to deliver the island which, after many years' detention by them, has been the most profitable blood in the veins of their trade'. His two options were to return to Batavia to plead with the Dutch authorities or to storm the island. Although the records of his mission have been lost, he appears to have chosen the latter option until discovering that his subordinate, John Hunter, adamantly refused to take part in such a plan. Having lost the confidence of his crew there was little Dutton could do but write to the directors in London informing them of the sorry state of affairs. His letter elicited from the directors a stern reprimand for Hunter, finding that his cowardly behaviour compared unfavourably with Courthope's heroic defence of the island some forty years previously. 'Wee cannot but conclude,' they wrote, 'that if our Agent [Hunter] had byn

posessed with the head and heart of a man, hee would ...
have done something worthie the name of an Englishman,
and not have retorned back soe dishonourably, to our
greate losse in perticulaer and to the generall shame of the
nation.' Despairing of ever recovering their beloved island,
the directors once again resorted to adding up their losses
that stemmed from the debacle which they now computed
to be 'above four millions'.

After all the fuss and bluster it is ironic that when Run
did at long last slip back into English hands, it passed
unnoticed in both London and Amsterdam. On 23 March
1665, two English vessels pulled into the island's little
harbour, made contact with the handful of Dutch traders,
and demanded Run's surrender. An agreement was struck,
the Dutch packed up their belongings, and after an interval
of two days they sailed to Neira and left the English to
unload their supplies. 'Concerning all this,' records a memo,
'the Company have no certain knowledge because their
letters were lost in the Royal Oak.'

Run's liberation was to prove short-lived. No sooner
had word of a new outbreak of hostilities between England
and Holland reached the East Indies than the Dutch
promptly despatched a vessel to Run and recaptured the
island. To dissuade the English from ever again attempting
a landing, 'great waste and spoilation [was] committed on
the island'. The nutmeg groves were once again chopped
down and the vegetation burned to its roots. Run had
become a barren and inhospitable rock.

Although the high-handed tactics of the Dutch failed to
stir the temperate King Charles II, they incensed his
brother, the impetuous James, Duke of York. He was stung
into action by the news trickling back from the East Indies
and, as head of the powerful Royal African Company, was

determined to avenge the wrongs. 'The trade of the world is too little for us two,' he declared imperiously, 'therefore one must lie down.' Already in 1663, James had commissioned four vessels to sail down the African coastline and seize the Dutch trading post of Cape Corso on the Gold Coast. Flushed with success, he now ordered his vessels to cross the Atlantic and seize the Dutch-held territory of New Netherland. This brazen act of aggression was justified as being in response to the 'inhuman proceedings' at Amboyna four decades previously. ''Tis high time to put them out of a capacitie of doeing the same mischeife here,' declared the royal commission.

In choosing to attack Manhattan, James had picked an easy target. The island's principal defence, Fort Amsterdam, was a decrepit bulwark whose walls were in an advanced state of decay. The barracks and church were built of wood and vulnerable to fire while the outer walls were lined with wooden houses. The town's governor, Peter Stuyvesant, was also hampered by a lack of weapons. The fort's twenty-four guns were rusting and useless and the available powder was old and damp. 'If I begin [to shoot] in the forenoon,' said the chief gunner, ''twill all be consumed by the afternoon.'

The English had the added advantage of their fleet looking considerably more impressive than it was. As Stuyvesant surveyed the Hudson from Fort Amsterdam he could see four ships carrying a total of a hundred guns. But only one, the *Guinea*, was a ship of war. The others were rotting trading vessels that had been hastily converted before sailing from Portsmouth. The number of men on board had also been grossly exaggerated. Stuyvesant had been told that the ships were carrying a crew of eight hundred. In fact, there were less than half that number.

The governor was nevertheless undeterred and vowed to

go down fighting. But the confidence of his men had been drained by stories of the war-like English soldiers and none in New Amsterdam had a stomach for the fight. When the English offered an honourable surrender, Stuyvesant was reluctantly forced to agree. On Monday, 8 September 1664, he signed away the Dutch rights to Manhattan and, two hours later, his small band of troops left their fort 'with their arms, drums beating, and colours flying'.

When he heard the news of the town's capitulation, King Charles II was delighted. 'You will have heard of our taking New Amsterdam,' he wrote to his sister in France. ''Tis a place of great importance ... we have got the better of it and 'tis now called New York.' The Dutch did not share the king's enthusiasm and protested in the strongest terms, arguing that the English had seized the island without 'even a shadow of right in the world.' King Charles shrugged off the protests; after all, the Dutch had behaved with equal aggression when they had seized Run, an island to which they had even less claim than Manhattan.

With no resolution in sight, the two countries once again tumbled into war, fighting it out on the high seas for more than two years with neither side gaining the upper hand. The English had small consolation when they captured two richly laden East India ships – lucrative prizes which were filled with nutmeg, mace and other precious commodities. So valuable was their cargo that Samuel Pepys made a special journey down the Thames Estuary to view the prize. 'The greatest wealth lie in confusion that a man can see in the world,' he wrote. 'Pepper scattered through every chink, you trod upon it; and in cloves and nutmegs I walked above the knees; whole rooms full. And silk in bales, and boxes of copper plate, one of which I saw opened ... as noble a sight as ever I saw in my life.'

Striking a Deal

With the war dragging on inconclusively it was agreed, in March 1667, that both sides should meet at Breda to discuss their grievances. The English demands were predictable: compensation for Dutch outrages and the immediate return of Run. The Dutch grievances were equally well rehearsed: compensation for English piracy and the return of New Amsterdam. Although the English negotiating team were given considerable flexibility in their handling of the talks, on the question of Run they were allowed no leeway. They were to 'represent to the ambassadors that the detaining of Pulo Run is one of the greatest foundations of the vast profits and strength of the Dutch in the Indies, but extremely prejudicial to the English nation.' To this they were met with a familiar cry: 'New Netherland must be restored'. As the talks faltered and broke down, the peace commissioners stepped in and proposed the only remaining solution: that in return for the Dutch keeping Run, the English should be allowed to retain Manhattan.

Still the English hesitated, fearful of signing away their richest asset. They deliberated for days but were unable to reach a decision and wrote to London asking for advice. On the morning of 18 April 1667 there arrived a letter with one simple instruction: 'we acquiesce.' A deal had at last been struck.

The resultant treaty, the Treaty of Breda, was a work of exquisite diplomacy, tactfully naming neither of the islands that had caused so much bloodshed. But the exchange, which included the whole of the New Netherlands, was there for all to see, enshrined in article three. 'Both parties shall keep and possess hereafter, with plenary right of sovereignty, propriety, and possession, all such lands, islands, cities, forts, places, and colonies ... [as] they have by force of arms, or any other way whatsoever, gotten and detained from the other party.'

As the ink dried on the treaty, few can have realised that they were signing one of the most significant documents in history. In exchanging a tiny island in the East Indies for a much larger one on America's eastern seaboard, England and Holland had sealed the destiny of New York. Until 1667, Manhattan had been a small trading centre with a population of less than one thousand. Now, the island was set to enter a new and ever more prosperous period in its history – a period that would see it rise and rise until the name New York was fabled around the globe. By the time of the War of Independence, the city had become the largest city in North America and was the natural choice to be the country's new capital.

That a deal should have been struck between England and Holland was due, in no small part, to the courage of a simple trader, Nathaniel Courthope, whose defiance and heroism forty-seven years earlier had sparked an unstoppable train of events. His bravado in defending Run, his stand against an army hundreds of times more powerful than his own, and his devotion to his country's flag became the rallying cry for the East India Company. Yet Courthope's motivation was simple: patriotism, duty, and an unswerving belief that what he was doing was right. He always knew that he would die for his ideals; indeed he looked 'daily and hourly' for his final end. When given a final opportunity to surrender the sovereignty of Run he had countered with an emphatic refusal: 'I could not,' he replied, 'unlesse I should turne traitor unto my King and Countrey.' For Courthope, a trader, there were some things too precious to be bought and sold.

Almost four centuries after his death, Courthope finds

himself on the margins of history, forgotten by English and Americans alike. No statue of him graces the streets of Manhattan; no plaque commemorates his achievements in Westminster Abbey. Yet the stand he made on Run was to reshape history on the other side of the world, and although his death robbed England of her nutmeg, it gave her the biggest of apples.

EPILOGUE

A T AROUND MIDNIGHT ON 9 August 1810, a small party of Englishmen could be seen loading weapons into a tiny boat moored off Great Banda. They carried no torches or lanterns and were working in total silence for their mission was one of great secrecy. Led by an irrepressibly energetic commander by the name of Captain Cole, their task was to storm the Dutch castle on Neira and force the governor to surrender. They were then to take control of the rest of the archipelago.

The Dutch knew nothing of the English presence in the Banda Islands for Captain Cole had kept his men out of sight until long after dark. Suspecting neither treachery nor attack, the garrison of Fort Belgica were all asleep and even the night watches, bored with pacing the battlements, had retired inside. Undetected by anyone, Cole and his men drew up their boat on Neira's rocky foreshore, seized the battery and redoubt without a fight, and began scaling the stone-lined walls of Fort Belgica. By the time the Dutch alarm had been sounded, the English were in virtual control of the fort and there was only the briefest of skirmishes before the Dutch troops surrendered. Cole then directed the bastion's formidable firepower onto Fort Nassau, the island's other castle, and blasted shot after shot at its battlements until they crumbled to dust. Here, too, the Dutch capitulated and

Nutmegs being harvested in traditional manner. The English sounded the death-knell for the Bandanese economy in the 19th century when they uprooted hundreds of nutmeg seedlings and transported them to Ceylon, Pinang and Singapore.

without the loss of a single man, Cole found himself in effective control of the Banda Islands.

The English commander justified his action on the grounds that Napoleon might use the 'spiceries' as the base for a campaign against India. Such a threat was always remote, but Cole's forces remained in the Bandas until 1817 when they abruptly pulled out, explaining to a bewildered population that a Holland deprived of the Indies would make for a very weak ally in Europe.

Although Cole's action serves as little more than a footnote in the history of the Bandas, it did have one significant and devastating effect on their future. Before they left, the English uprooted hundreds of nutmeg seedlings along with several tons of the unique soil and transplanted them to Ceylon, Pinang, Bencoolen and Singapore. Within a few decades, these thriving new plantations were far outstripping the production on the Bandas.

The decline of the archipelago had, in fact, set in many years earlier. Although the islands had for a time reaped fabulous dividends, the Dutch settlers proved hopelessly indolent and corrupt and allowed their poorly managed estates to go to ruin. Even more damaging was the volcano, Gunung Api, which was entering one of the most violent and unpredictable phases in its history with no fewer than five major eruptions during the seventeenth century, all followed by devastating earthquakes and tidal waves. In 1629, Neira town was virtually swept out to sea; whilst the winter of 1691 ushered in five years of misery as the volcano belched sulphur and lava in the direction of the governor's residence. Nature was scarcely less destructive in the eighteenth century. In 1778, the twin forces of an eruption and earthquake, followed by a hurricane and an immense tidal wave, all but wrecked the Banda Islands' nutmeg groves. One out of every two trees was felled and production of nutmeg plummeted to a fraction of its former levels.

Although descendants of the early Dutch settlers doggedly clung to their land, the overseas English plantations had sounded the death knell for the Banda Islands. As demand for nutmeg in Europe steadily fell, even the great Dutch East India Company found itself lurching from one financial crisis to another and when auditors examined the accounts in the 1790s they found the Company to be a staggering twelve million guilders in the red. Soon afterwards, the monopoly was lost and the Company slipped quietly into the history books.

Despite the decline, few of the older residents were inclined to return to Holland – a country that most had never even visited – preferring instead to enjoy the substantial inherited fortunes that many still possessed. The end of the nineteenth century saw the islands enter a twilight golden age as vast sums of money were squandered on grandiose waterfront mansions, all of them filled with the choicest antiques and crystals, marble and glass. Each evening the burghers of Banda would dress in their finery and stroll up and down the promenade to the rousing music of a military brass band, and when the Dutch governor-general arrived in the winter of 1860 he was welcomed with such extravagance and excess that he could almost have been fooled into believing that the islands were as rich as they had ever been. His triumphant procession through Neira town was led by a troupe of musicians, dancers and players, all dressed in costume, and the main (and only) street was gaily decked with flags, flowers and bunting.

No less diverting than His Excellency's official visit was the regular arrival of one or another of the local steam packets, bringing naturalists and wealthy Europeans in search of the exotic and unusual. All were delighted with what they found in this tropical archipelago, as testified in their numerous journals and diaries. 'A sail of two nights and a day [from Amboyna],' wrote the naturalist Henry Forbes, 'brought us to Banda. Coming on deck, before breakfast, we found ourselves slowly steaming in through a narrow winding entrance between thickly foliaged cliffs ... it was the most lovely spot we had yet visited. Fronting us as the steamer warped itself to the jetty lay the town as a cluster of white houses ... [and] from an elevated plateau, a battlement fort overlooked us, the scarlet of its Dutch ensign floating in the wind.'

Although the frivolity and heady excess of fin-de-siècle Banda provided the illusion of prosperity, many of the younger generation soon tired of the stagnant social life and lack of prospects and bought themselves one-way tickets to Holland, leaving the islands to their fate. With Dutch expenditure on the Bandas far outweighing revenue, they became an increasingly costly drain on resources and it was not long before the governor himself was withdrawn and the archipelago returned to an obscure provincial backwater seldom visited by Dutch officials. There were a few brief moments that reminded the world of the existence of these islands. In the 1930s, two prominent anti-colonialists, Mohammed Hatti, later vice-president of Indonesia, and Sutan Sjahrir, who served as prime minister, spent six years in exile on Neira Island; whilst in 1944 the Japanese bombed and then occupied the archipelago. Although they found the islands of little interest except as a rendezvous for shipping, their

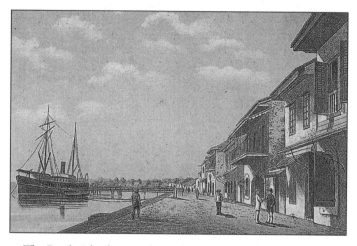

The Banda Islands entered a twilight golden age in the 1890s as residents squandered inherited fortunes. But younger inhabitants tired of the stagnant social life and lack of prospects and bought one-way tickets to Holland.

occupation did have one malign consequence: with few supplies reaching the islands, the locals were forced to cut down many of their remaining nutmeg trees and turn the land over to vegetable cultivation.

The end of the war brought tragedy to the Bandas. An American bomber raiding Japanese bases in the region appeared in the skies above Neira in the spring of 1945 intent on destroying the shipping anchored in the harbour. But one stray bomb scored a direct hit on the town of Neira, exploding directly above a wedding party and killing more than a hundred guests.

Today, the Banda Islands have once again retreated into obscurity – an archipelago so small and insignificant that it rarely features on a map of the region. Scarcely more accessible than in the days of Nathaniel Courthope, it requires patience and a good deal of luck to reach the islands. In the summer of 1997, the antiquated fourteen-seat Cessna plane that used to fly between Amboyna and Neira was flipped over by the monsoon winds and dashed to pieces on the airstrip. Now, the only way to reach the Bandas is on the KM *Rinjani* ferry, an eight-hour journey through the choppy waters which separate Neira from Amboyna.

Neira remains the 'capital' of the Banda Islands, home to a couple of stores, a fish market, two streets and two cars. A wander through the town reveals a Dutch church (the hands of its clock stuck at 5.03, the exact time of the Japanese invasion), a handful of crumbling villas and the former Dutch governor's residence which today lies empty and abandoned, its baroque chandeliers slowly shedding their crystal-glass finery. The only other 'sight' is the pentangle-shaped Fort Belgica which occupies a commanding position on a bluff of rock above the port – impregnable to all but volcanic boulders and Captain Cole's intrepid troops. The castle has recently received a much-needed face-lift but the restorers have been over-zealous in their work, rendering walls and installing doors. The ghosts that were until recently said to trudge its ramparts have been forced to flee to other castles in the archipelago – rambling, ivy-clad places where one can still scoop musket-shot from the sand-filled dungeons.

Unlike the central group of Bandas – connected to each other by prahus or native canoes – the outlying island of Run can only be reached by twin-engined powerboat. Even so, the journey is a treacherous one, especially when the monsoon whips up a storm and sends mountainous waves roaring through the ten-mile channel that separates Neira and Run. As our boat smashes its way through these waters in defiance of nature, we slowly catch a fragrance in the wind – the sweet, odoriferous scent of nutmeg blossom.

We land on the island's northern shoreline – the point at which Nathaniel Courthope landed 381 years previously – which is sheltered from the monsoon by the island's precipitous cliffs. A couple of fishermen glance at this newly arrived stranger while their womenfolk wander off to fetch us some coconut milk, but otherwise nothing stirs. The island's small wooden settlement is a soporific place; a village of swept alleys, tidy gardens and shaded verandas lined with flowerpots.

No one here knows anything of the extraordinary history of their island, even though they are forever turning up coins and musket-shot in their vegetable plots. Nor are they aware that their home – just two miles long and half a mile wide – was once considered a fair exchange for a very different island – Manhattan – on the far side of the globe.

Yet they are unmoved when told of the cruel blow that fortune has dealt them, happy to see out their days on this unknown and unspoiled atoll. For although their flickering televisions allow them a glimpse of America through reruns of *Cagney and Lacey* and *Starsky and Hutch*, they will tell you that the view from their windows is infinitely more magnificent than Manhattan's glittering skyline.

For there on the cliffs, high above the translucent sea, the willowy nutmeg tree is once again setting its roots, bursting into flower each spring and filling the air with a heady, languorous scent.

BIBLIOGRAPHY

N*athaniel's Nutmeg* has been drawn largely from original journals, diaries and letters. A brief glance at this bibliography will reveal the author's indebtedness to Samuel Purchas who collected the writings of East India Company adventurers and transcribed them into his monumental *Purchas His Pilgrimes*. The 1625 edition is now extremely rare and even the twenty-volume 1905 reprint is only to be found in specialist libraries.

The Hakluyt Society is the other source for original writings but most of these volumes are also long out of print. They can be found in the British Library's Oriental and India Office Collections, along with many original manuscripts.

Those wishing to delve further into the letters written by overseas factors, or to read the official Company documents, will need to turn to the East India Company archives and Colonial State Papers – a task not for the lighthearted since they run to forty-five volumes. The relevant editions are listed below.

The two standard works on the Dutch East India Company are K. J. Johan de Jonge's thirteen-volume *De Opkomst*, a collection of journals written in old Dutch; and François Valentijn's *Oud en Nieuw Oost-Indien*. Full details are to be found below.

Nathaniel's Nutmeg

Contemporary journals and diaries

Borough, Stephen, in Hakluyt's *The Principall Navigations*, 1599.

Chancellor, Richard, in Hakluyt's *The Principall Navigations*, 1599.

Courthope, Nathaniel, in *Purchas His Pilgrimes* (vol. 1).

Davis, J., *Voyages and Works of*, Hakluyt Society, 1880.

Dermer, Thomas, in *Purchas His Pilgrimes*; see also I. N. Phelps Stokes, *The Iconography of Manhattan Island*, 1922.

Downton, Nicholas, *Voyage to the East Indies*, ed. Sir William Foster, Hakluyt Society, 1939; see also *Purchas His Pilgrimes* (vol. 1).

Drake, Sir Francis, *The World Encompassed by Drake*, Hakluyt Society, 1854; see also *New Light on Drake*, ed. Z. Nuttall, Hakluyt Society, 1914.

Finch, William, in *Purchas His Pilgrimes* (vol. 1).

Fitch, Ralph, in *Purchas His Pilgrimes* (vol. 2).

Fitz-Herbert, Sir Humphrey, in *Purchas His Pilgrimes* (vol. 1).

Floris, P. W., *His Voyage to the East Indies in the Globe*, ed. W. H. Moreland, Hakluyt Society, 1934; see also *Purchas His Pilgrimes* (vol. 1).

Hakluyt, R., *The Principall Navigations*, 1599.

Hawkins, William, in *The Hawkins Voyages During the Reigns of Henry VIII, Queen Elizabeth, and James I*, ed. C. Markham, Hakluyt Society, 1878. (This is the journal kept by the William Hawkins who sailed with Edward Fenton.)

Hawkins, William, in *Purchas His Pilgrimes* (vol. 1). (This is the William Hawkins who lived in India.)

Hayes, Robert, in *Purchas His Pilgrimes* (vol. 1).

Hudson, Henry, *Henry Hudson the Navigator*, Hakluyt Society, 1860. See also *Purchas His Pilgrimes* (vol. 3).

Jourdain, John, *The Journal of*, ed. W. Foster, Hakluyt Society, 1905.

Keeling, William, in *Purchas His Pilgrimes* (vol. 1).

Lancaster, Sir James, *Voyages of Lancaster to the East Indies*, Hakluyt Society, 1877.

Michelborne, Sir Edward, in *Purchas His Pilgrimes* (vol. 1).

Middleton, David, In *Purchas His Pilgrimes*, (vol. 1).

Middleton, Sir Henry, *Voyage to Bantam and the Maluco Islands*, Hakluyt Society, 1855; *Voyage to the Moluccas, 1604–6*, ed. Sir William Foster, Hakluyt Society, 1943.

Roe, Sir Thomas, *Embassy to the Great Moghul* (2 vols), Hakluyt Society, 1899.

Saris, John, *Voyage to Japan, 1613*, Hakluyt Society, 1900; see also *Purchas His Pilgrimes* (vol. 1).

Willoughby, Sir Hugh, in Hakluyt's *The Principall Navigations*, 1599.

Bibliography

Letters and state papers

Calendar of State Papers: Colonial (vols 1–9), ed. W. Noel Sainsbury, 1860–93.

Chalmers, George, *A Collection of Treaties between Great Britain and Other Powers*, 1770.

Collections of the New York Historical Society (vol. 1), 1841.

East India Company, *Calendar of the Court Minutes of, 1640–79* (11 vols), ed. Ethel B. Sainsbury, 1907–38.

East India Company, *The Dawn of British Trade to the East Indies ...*, *1599–1603*, ed. Henry Stevens and George Birdwood, 1886.

East India Company, *The English Factories in India, 1618–1669* (13 vols), ed. William Foster, 1906–27.

East India Company, *Letters Received from its Servants in the East* (6 vols), ed. F. C. Danvers and William Foster, 1896–1902.

East India Company, *Register of Letters etc. of the Governor and Company of Merchants of London trading into the East Indies, 1600–1619*, ed. George Birdwood and William Foster, 1892.

East India Company, *Selected Seventeenth Century Works*, 1968.

East India Company, *A True Relation of the Unjust, Cruel and Barbarous Proceedings against the English at Amboyna, 1624. The Answer unto the Dutch Pamphlet made in Defence of the Unjust and Barbarous Proceeding against the English at Amboyna, 1624. A Remonstrance of the Directors of the Netherlands and the Reply of the English East India Company, 1624.*

A General Collection of Treatys, etc. (4 vols), 1732.

Reference works

Borde, A., *Fyrst Boke of Introduction to Knowledge*. Early English Texts Society edition of 1870 (ed. F. J. Furnivall) contains Borde's *Dyetary of Helth*.

Chaudhuri, K. N., *The English East India Company 1600–40*, 1965.

Crawfurd, John, *A Descriptive Dictionary of the Indian Islands and Adjacent Countries*, 1856.

Danvers, F., *Dutch Activities in the East*, 1945.

Dodwell, H. H. (ed.), *Cambridge History of India*, vol. 4, 1929.

Elyot, Sir Thomas, *The Castel of Helth*, 1541.

Flick, Alexander (ed.), *History of the State of New York* (10 vols), 1933.

Foster, W., *England's Quest of Eastern Trade*, 1933.

Foster, W., *John Company*, 1926.

Gerard, J., *Gerard's Herbal*, 1636.

Hanna, Willard A., *Indonesian Banda*, 1978.

Hart, Henry, *Sea Road to the Indies*, 1950.

Jonge, Johan K. J. de., *De Opkomst van het Nederlandsch Gezag in Oost Indie* (13 vols), 1862–88.

Keay, J., *The Honourable Company*, 1991.

Khan, Shafaat Ahmad, *The East India Trade in the Seventeenth Century*, 1923.

Loon, Hendrik van, *Dutch Navigators*, 1916.

Masselman, George, *The Cradle of Colonialism*, 1963.

Murphy, Henry C., *Henry Hudson in Holland*, 1909.

Parry, J. W., *The Story of Spices and Spices Described*, 1969.

Penrose, Boies, *Travel and Discovery in the Renaissance*, 1952.

Phelps Stokes, I. N., *The Iconography of Manhattan Island*, 1922.

Pinkerton, J., *A General Collection of the Best and Most Interesting Voyages*, 1812.

Powys, Llewelyn, *Henry Hudson*, 1927.

Rink, Oliver, *Holland on the Hudson: An Economic and Social History*, 1986.

Rosengarten, F., *The Book of Spices*, 1969.

St John, Horace, *The Indian Archipelago* (2 vols), 1853.

Valentijn, François, *Oud en Nieuw Oost-Indien* (5 vols in 8 bindings), 1724–6.

Van der Zee, Henri and Barbara, *A Sweet and Alien Land: The Story of Dutch New York*, 1978.

Van Rensselaer, Schuyler, *History of the City of New York in the Seventeenth Century*, 1909.

Venner, Tobias, *Via Recta ad Vitam Longam*, 1637.

Vlekke, Bernard, *The Story of the Dutch East Indies*, 1946.

Willson, Beckles, *Ledger and Sword*, 1903.

Wilson, F. P., *The Plague in Shakespeare's London*, 1927.

Wright, Arnold, *Early English Adventurers in the East*, 1917.

INDEX

Index

Index